Bint Al-Huda Collection

All Novels and Short Stories

by

Aminah Haider Al-Sadr
[Bint Al-Huda]

Translated by

M.N. Sultan

Book Title: Bint Al-Huda Collection - All Novels and Short Stories

Author: Aminah Haider Al-Sadr [Bint Al-Huda]

Translation: M. N. Sultan

Compilation, Editing and Graphics: Abu Yahya al-Hussaini

Publisher: Jerrmein Abu Shahba

Year: 2019

ISBN: 978-1-7330284-5-5

CONTENTS

TRANSLATOR'S NOTE

Ideological conflicts caused by the world's dominating cultures have produced negative effects on the Muslim community. The alien Western ideals flooding the Islamic world have tried to uproot Islamic concepts and beliefs. This methodical foreign invasion has greatly damaged the successive Muslim generations. The slogans of freedom, equality and justice have swept the Islamic world and distorted the Islamic culture. As a result, the Muslim Ummah is suffering today from cultural chaos and deviation, which is damaging the core of the community.

Deliberate falsehoods have been perpetrated by the enemies of Islam to degrade the sublime religion of Islam. Due to such conspiracies, Muslim women and men have forgotten their religious beliefs, duty and commitments. Hence it is necessary to take serious steps to save the society from falling into the abyss of disbelief, which could not only crush the whole community but could also destroy the religious belief still surviving.

Such a situation has compelled the Muslim intellectuals to know their duty in saving the society. It is a very difficult task to bring the deviated generation to the right path of Allah's religion. Hence our aim is to assist such achievements and to help Islamic concepts and values to spread throughout the world, guiding the youth to the right direction. Such a motive is behind translation and publication of Bint ul-Huda's books. The famous Iraqi woman writer presents Islamic ideals in her stories within a framework of interesting and modern circumstances. Through her characters she exposes the contradictory behavior of some Muslims. Her stories are guiding lights for the young generation currently misled by the brightness of pseudo-civilization. Bint ul-Huda, through her heroes' logical conversations, attempts to reach young men and women and awaken their awareness. She deals with topics of particular interest to Muslim women, presenting various models, which, though imaginary, have their counterparts in present-day life. In these stories Goodness and Virtue are engaged in an everlasting struggle against Evil and Vice. We hope such efforts produce the effective result that the martyred writer, Bint ul-Huda, has aimed at.

In conclusion, we must inform our readers that we have used more familiar Islamic names instead of the Arabic names in the original stories. Moreover, a free translation of such stories is a necessity due to the different features of both Arabic and English literature.

M.N. Sultan

A SHORT BIOGRAPHY OF AUTHOR

Amina Haider Al-Sadr was a famous Muslim author popularly known as Bint Al-Huda. She played a significant role in creating Islamic awareness among the Muslim women of Iraq. Bint al-Huda was born in the holy city of Kadhmain, Baghdad on February 23, 1937. Her father, a renowned religious leader, died when she was two years old. She enjoyed the loving care of her mother and two kind brothers, Sayyid Ismael and Ayatollah Muhammad Baqir Al-Sadr. Bint Al-Huda did not attend any government school, but was well educated at the hands of her two scholar brothers, especially Ayatollah Muhammad Baqir Al-Sadr, who recognized her bright talent. As a teenager, Bint Al-Huda was a voracious reader who always spent her pocket money on useful books and increasing her knowledge.

The first half of this century indicated that Western cultural values dominated the Arab and Muslim countries of the world. Secular systems spread deviation and corruption and branded Islam as reactionary and as a hindrance to progress.

At the age of 20, Bint Al-Huda began writing articles in *Al-Adhwa* magazine published by the religious scholars in the holy city of Najaf, Iraq in 1959. Her articles drew the attention of intellectuals in Najaf and became torches which illuminated the darkness for women. Her writings awakened a society which, like many societies in other Muslim countries, was being deviated under the pretexts of freedom and equality. Possessing keen insight, she felt the great damage that was being inflicted upon Islam through the deliberate corruption of women. Her simply-written stories tackled these wrong traditions and presented truly Islamic concepts concerning woman and her specific role in a healthy society.

It is a great pity and a serious setback that the Muslim women of the world lost this great woman writer so early. A major crime of the Iraqi Ba'thist regime was the tortured murder of this noble lady and her brother and religious scholar, Ayatollah Muhammad Baqir Al-Sadr (May Allah bless them both).

The tyrannical, anti-Islamic regime of Saddam was well aware of their brave struggle for the sake of Islam and decided to finish them off. They were arrested in April, 1980, and killed in cold blood three days later on 9th April. The Saddam regime never returned her body, but her secret burial site is said to be in famous Wadi Al-Salam graveyard, Najaf. To date, her grave remains unknown.

FOREWARD BY THE AUTHOR

Dear readers,

I am not a professional storywriter. What I present herein are but a few of the many portraits of life in which Good confronts Evil and spiritual faith and belief confront an imperialist, dominating culture.

The apex of my hope is to produce a faithful image of the ideological call for virtue to prevail over vice.

Muslim men and women live contradictory existences of contemporary life as presented in the following fiction. I have tried to pave the way for the revival of one of the propagative apparatus, the story, which influences our lives at this juncture in Islamic history.

Bint Al-Huda

Novel 1

An Encounter At The Hospital

PART 1: THE MEETING

Dr. Miyad was half asleep when the telephone rang. She struggled between sleep's powerful domination and her duty to answer the phone. It rang insistently until she finally answered it, as she knew she must. It was after mid night.

An urgent case on the hospital's seventh floor made her quickly put on her Islamic modest dress and soon she was hurrying towards the patient's room. A nurse near the door told her that an elderly woman in the room was seriously ill.

Dr. Miyad quickly entered and saw a young woman, modestly dressed, standing next to the old woman's bed. The young woman said anxiously, "Oh doctor, this is my grandmother. She was complaining of severe pain and she's unconscious."

The doctor carefully examined the elderly woman, who began to moan, and the young woman paced the nearby corridor. Her grandmother had had a serious heart attack and needed to be hospitalized for a number of days. After giving the patient the needed medicine, Dr. Miyad approached the young woman, whose eyes were filled with tears. The doctor felt that she had to comfort her and give her hope. She smiled, saying, "I'm sure she will soon be well I have done all that is necessary."

"I am very grateful, doctor."

"Don't thank me. It's my duty to help all my patients." She noticed that the woman's face was pale, so she took her hand, which was cold to the touch, and told her kindly, "You are tired. Why don't you sleep for a while?"

"Yes, I am tired, but I can't leave my grandmother alone."

"Don't you have a sister or anyone else to help you?"

"No," the young woman replied sadly. "She is not only my grandmother, but is a mother to me as well."

The doctor felt sorry for her and comforted her, saying, ' 'I'll look after her for you so that you can rest."

"Oh no, you need rest. You work so hard."

"I 'm used to it, and I don't feel tired. I've slept for a few hours and that is enough for me. Now it is your turn to rest, but first I'll get a book to read. I'll be right back."

The young woman thought the doctor was a wonderful woman and felt she could depend on her.

Dr. Miyad soon returned with a book in her hand and said, "Now you can sleep, I 'll sit here and read. By the way, I'm Dr. Miyad."

"I'm Warqa, I'm pleased to meet you."

Warqa stretched out on the sofa and soon fell asleep. When she awoke she found that she had slept for over an hour. The doctor was still reading near the sick woman, who slept well with the help of an oxygen mask. Warqa got up and approached Dr. Miyad. She asked about her grandmother's health. The doctor put aside her book and said, "She's all right. Now I shall sleep for a while after doing my morning prayer. I'll see you later today, God willing."

"I don't know how to thank you," said Warqa. "You have been very kind and helpful. I am all alone."

"You're not alone; Almighty Allah is with you. You seem to be a committed believer, and faith can help you throughout life."

Warqa thanked the doctor again and walked with her to the door. When she came back into the room, she saw the book, which the doctor had just left, and the title attracted her attention. It was entitled, **Medicine: A Sanctuary for Faith**. She wondered, "What does it mean? What relation is there between the two? Isn't medicine a science which cures bodies or diseases, and religion worship of Allah in order to escape from Hell? How can medicine be a sanctuary of faith?"

Curiosity prompted her to pick up the book. First she examined the cover, which showed a drawing of a human brain and the Qur'anic verse:

This is Allah's creation, but show Me what those beside Him have created. (Luqman: 11)

Warqa read a few lines from the book and thought deeply for some time, and then she read more until she got up to perform her morning prayer.

A nurse entered the room in the morning to give Warqa's grandmother a dose of medicine. A specialist and another female doctor also came in later.

The doctor's hair was uncovered and her high heels clicked as she walked. She turned to give Warqa some instructions and Warqa noticed that her face was heavily made up. Warqa saw a big difference between this doctor and Dr. Miyad, whose appearance was natural, and she was eager to see Dr. Miyad again. She needed her encouraging words wanted to ask her a few questions about her book. She wondered why Dr. Miyad had not returned. Warqa's grandmother was feeling better, and Warqa was glad to see her getting well.

"I 'm so happy that you are well again," said Warqa. "You don't know how worried I was yesterday."

Her grandmother replied, "I'm sorry to see you worry; especially since you are alone."

"This time I wasn't alone. Dr. Miyad was here. She is a wonderful woman and she insisted that I sleep while she sat near you for over an hour."

"Praise be to God for sending you such a person at this time."

Warqa pleaded with her grandmother to sleep and not to talk or otherwise tire herself. She continued to read and she occasionally glanced at the door. At noon, she became quite anxious to see Dr. Miyad and thought to herself, 'Why am I so anxious to see her? I've known her for only a few hours. She is just a doctor performing her duty. Maybe she won't even come again.' Some inner voice told her: 'You have a right to feel this way. This doctor is filled with compassion and sympathy. She is not only a doctor, but is also a good person without whose help you would have suffered more hardships.'

Warqa was deep in thought when she heard a knock on the door. She hurried to the door. It was Dr. Miyad. They shook hands warmly, and the doctor said, "I heard from a colleague that your grandmother was better. I was busy all morning in the delivery room, so I must apologize for not coming sooner. "

"Oh, there's no need to apologize; you were not obliged to come. However, I did want to see you."

The doctor looked concerned and examined her patient. "Has she complained of any pain?" she asked.

"No, she is much better, thank God. As a matter of fact, I was in need of you. Won't you please sit down?"

"I will stay for a while. You look tired; you need to sleep," said Dr. Miyad.

"Oh, I don't need sleep, but, rather, a thorough waking up. I would like to ask you about some of the things I have read in this book," Warqa told her. She sat near the doctor, who said, "Oh, I see I have left my book here. You must have enjoyed reading it."

"Yes, it really made me think deeply."

"How?"

"Well", Warqa explained, "I never thought there was any relationship between medicine and faith. I know medicine deals with human bodies, while faith is only worship."

Dr. Miyad said, "But science leads to faith. The more knowledge one has, the more one believes in the Creator. "

"How is that so?" asked Warqa.

"If someone ignores something, he cannot appreciate its value. For instance, if you take a look at this electric heater, you don't think about the great effort and care it took its maker to make it. You won't think about the numerous experiments that preceded this final product. Yet, anyone with a little knowledge can talk about its complex technical design."

Warqa tried to suppress a smile. Dr. Miyad was silent for a moment and then said, "Are you a student?"

"Yes, I'm in my final year at the university." She did not mention what her major was. Dr. Miyad told her, "You're studying at the Engineering College, aren't you?"

Warqa was surprised, and said, "Yes, but how did you know?"

"Because of your small smile on hearing me mention the electric heater. I guessed that you are familiar with the subject. It wasn't a good example but you didn't object, out of courtesy."

"It is a good example," Warqa said. "Please go on."

"So you see, even a minimum of knowledge about something doubles its value. Science, with all its branches, brings scientists nearer to Almighty Allah. Medicine is the most important and accurate science. To a scientist who is not a fanatic, science is a road which clearly leads to faith."

"My religious knowledge is very limited," said Warqa.

"It is only traditional commitment, such as fasting, praying and observing Islamic modest dress. Sometimes I feel embarrassed about my lack of religious information. Would you be kind enough to explain some matters to me?"

"I'm ready to answer all your questions. Consider me as your sister, since we share the same beliefs. Now, what do you want to ask me?"

"Why has a drawing of a brain been chosen for the cover of the book?"

"You know that the brain is the most important part of the human body. It is the organ, which controls the entire body, including the nerves and the cells. Every cell obeys the brain which, though small, contains thousands of millions of nerve cells."

"How amazing!" exclaimed Warqa.

Dr. Miyad continued, "You know that every cell has its own function but, at the same time, it cooperates with other cells. If some cells are damaged, the result will be bad."

"I never imagined that the brain was such a delicate structure."

Dr. Miyad noted, "A scientist lectured about the brain in 1957 and said that if all the world's telephones, telegraphs, radar systems and televisions were made into a small, complicated device, it would not be as complex as the brain."

"How wonderful for one to have such a marvelous apparatus in one's head! But what a pity it is that we know so little about our bodies."

"It may take a long time to discuss the human body. You know that the nervous system has a two-fold function: voluntary and involuntary. The nervous system controls the body's muscles, the hands, the feet, the tongue, etc.

Of course, some organs function automatically, such as the lungs, the heart, the stomach and so on. Here, the Wisdom of our Creator becomes manifest. If they functioned at the will of a creature, it would be impossible for him to motivate and monitor the processes of these organs all the time, even during sleep, thus they would cease to function.

"The same can be said of the organs which function voluntarily. If they functioned automatically, a human being would go on, for example, talking and talking all his life."

Warqa was very interested in the discussion and listened attentively. The doctor suggested that she read the whole book and told her that she would learn much about the body's secrets. In fact, Warqa wasn't very enthusiastic about reading, but Dr. Miyad said, "Hearing isn't enough. One should depend on one's brain to comprehend matters. If one listens more than one reads, then one will depend on others for knowledge."

Warqa's grandmother awoke, and both women approached her. Dr. Miyad asked her how she felt. She smiled and thanked the doctor for her help, saying, "I prayed for you. You have been kind to Warqa. I shall always remember that."

Dr. Miyad said, "Oh, I've done nothing. I pray that you will have a long life."

"What is your name, my dear?" she asked.

"Miyad."

"That's a nice name. What's your family name?" asked the grandmother.

The doctor didn't reply but said; "I'll see you every day until you fully recover, which will be soon. God Willing, with Warqa's help." Dr. Miyad left and Warqa kept the book to read.

PART 2: A SICK FRIEND

The two young women's friendship grew stronger as time passed, and Warqa continued to ask the doctor about ideological questions. Then all of a sudden, the doctor stopped visiting her elderly patient. After three days, Warqa asked another doctor about Dr. Miyad. She told her that Dr. Miyad was ill. Warqa asked if she was at home, but the doctor told her that Dr. Miyad was in that same hospital. Warqa learned from a nurse that her friend was in room number seven.

"Is her illness serious?" Warqa asked.

"She has influenza," the nurse replied. "The doctor advised her to remain in bed for a few days."

Warqa made arrangements for the nurse to stay in her grandmother's room after 12 o'clock noon so that she could visit Dr. Miyad. Warqa thanked the nurse and went to room seven. When she knocked, she was surprised to see a young man open the door. She asked hesitantly,

"How is Dr. Miyad?"

The young man said, "Come in, she's awake."

Warqa entered the room, anxious to see her friend, who smiled and said, "I 'm all right. How is your grandmother?"

"She's fine. She sends her regards and wishes you a speedy recovery."

As she sat down near the bed, Warqa noticed that Dr. Miyad's face and neck were flushed. It was the first time she had seen the doctor without her headscarf on. Warqa wanted to stay, but she thought about her grandmother and soon arose.

Dr. Miyad sensed her uneasiness, saying, "You mustn't leave your grandmother alone for long."

"But I don't want to leave you alone either."

"I'm not alone. My brother is here. When you leave, please tell him to come in."

"Where will I find him?" asked Warqa.

"He'll be in the reading room. His name is Sinad. He was the man who opened the door for you."

Warqa said, "Oh I thought he was a stranger, a doctor."

Dr. Miyad said, "He is a doctor, but he's also my brother. Otherwise, I wouldn't have allowed him to see me without my scarf on."

"I never thought of that."

"He left the room so that you would be at ease," Dr. Miyad remarked.

Warqa wished her friend good health and said goodbye. She saw Dr. Miyad's brother near the room and didn't speak to him, since he had seen her leave.

She hurried to her grandmother, who was still sleeping. When she awoke she asked Warqa about the doctor and Warqa said that she was very ill.

"Is she alone?" asked Warqa's grandmother.

"No. Her brother is with her, although he left the room when I entered."

"He seems polite," her grandmother remarked.

PART 3: FURTHER QUESTIONS

The following morning, Warqa visited Dr. Miyad and saw that she was feeling better. The doctor appreciated Warqa's visits. When Warqa expressed concern about her friend's health, Dr. Miyad said that she seemed upset.

"Oh that's to be expected."

"You are right. A lot of processes take place in the body when it is in such a state."

"What processes?"

"There is a network of nerves in the body. It carries impulses between the brain and all of the different parts of the body. Hence, sensations like cold, heat and pain are received through the nerves. There are millions of nerve cells carrying out this job."

"How do they function?" asked Warqa. "The brain is the centre of the nervous system. It controls all of the muscles and organs. Thus, when we touch something hot, the hand is withdrawn very quickly. We may not think much about such actions, but what the Creator has planned is really a source of wonder."

Dr. Miyad continued to speak. Warqa enjoyed listening to her simple explanations and wished she could stay longer, but she didn't want to tire the doctor.

Warqa said, "Your words are so interesting and I am in need of religious knowledge, especially about the Great Creator, since I lack such information. I can't answer the questions of skeptical people. At first, I planned to attend medical college, but my exam results weren't good enough."

"My religious knowledge has nothing to do with college," Dr. Miyad told her. "In fact, I knew many things before I went to the university."

"That's wonderful! You knew about your religion early on."

"Yes, from early childhood my brother encouraged me to read. He helped me to understand many difficult matters."

"Which of your brothers helped you?"

"I only have one brother. He always took care of me when I was sick. He's everything to me."

"May Allah protect you both," Warqa said.

Dr. Miyad added, "He has not gone to his clinic because of me. He stays near me when I'm sick."

"I thought he worked here."

"No, he has his own clinic."

Warqa looked at her watch. She felt that she had stayed long enough and that her grandmother might be in need of her. She got up, saying, "I 'm sorry to leave you again. I must take care of my grandmother."

"Don't worry, my dear; my brother will soon come."

"Then I'll see you tomorrow," said Warqa.

"Please do come."

"I may trouble you with my questions."

"Not at all. I'll be happy to see you whenever you come."

When Warqa visited her friend the next day, she asked about her health and when she would begin work again.

"I feel fine, except for some pain near my spleen. I'm waiting for my laboratory results."

Warqa said, "I hope nothing is wrong with your spleen, although I think this organ is not very important."

Dr. Miyad smiled and said, "On the contrary, it is very important. Every organ God has created has its own importance.

"The spleen is similar to a movable graveyard, really. It receives the dead red blood cells, which usually die after two months. It is interesting to see the iron particles carry the dead cells for burial and return to produce new ones."

"Do the iron particles produce red cells?"

"No," said Dr. Miyad, "but it is helpful in their manufacture. The main process involved in making the red and even the white blood cells takes place in the bone marrow. So you can see what a wonderful factory there is inside the human body. Each organ has its own special function."

"Please continue," urged Warqa.

"The cardiac system exchanges the gases through the circulation of blood. Oxygen is carried to the tissues by the blood and, on the way back to the heart, remnants of burnt out tissues are transported in place of the oxygen."

"You mean that the blood's circulation helps the digestive system?"

"Yes, that's what I mean," replied Dr. Miyad.

"The respiratory system helps as well. We breathe as long as we are alive, yet we never think about the Creator's design of our breathing apparatus. The necessary gas, oxygen, is provided and carbon dioxide is removed. Hence, our blood is purified and whatever substance is useless is discarded. It is the delicate design of Allah. Consider the digestive system. We eat and drink whatever we like, but we forget that Merciful Allah has given us the organs, which make use of starches, proteins, fats, minerals, water and vitamins. These organs remove the unwanted waste products from the body."

Warqa then asked, "What about the liver?"

"The liver is a large reddish-brown organ which secretes bile and purifies the blood. It is similar to a defense front." Dr. Miyad hesitated, giving Warqa time to think. Then she asked how her grandmother was. Warqa replied that she was much better and that that was why she was able to leave her for a while. Her grandmother wanted Warqa to go back and attend her college lectures from the coming week, but Warqa had not yet made up her mind about it.

Dr. Miyad said, "You have been absent from your studies for a long time. You should return to them. I'll be near her while you are away."

"Poor grandma," said Warqa. "She has tried hard to give me a comfortable life. She loves me very much, but I feel so lonely, since I am her only granddaughter. Her son, my father died when I was one year old, and my mother died shortly after my birth."

"Neither of us has a sister, let's be sisters to each other."

Warqa's face brightened as she asked, "Will you have me as your sister?"

"With great pleasure," the doctor replied.

"That's settled then. I wanted you to read this book." She held out a book entitled '**Perfection in Islam**' towards Warqa, who took it and said good-bye.

Two days later, Dr. Miyad had recovered and was once again on duty, and she made a point to visit Warqa's grandmother every day while Warqa was at college. Warqa read the religious book and asked her friend for another volume. She really wanted to understand what she had read, and spent many hours at the hospital, reading and discussing various questions with Dr. Miyad. Warqa was greatly influenced by the doctor and longed to be with her always. One day she asked the doctor, "Is it true that the body's cells change?"

"Yes. Everything: the cells, the blood, the fat, the proteins, even the nerve cells are changed. Basically, the complete body structure is renewed and replaced every ten years."

Warqa commented, "Even the nerve cells. Does that mean a person could forget his previous knowledge and memories? "

"This is one of the mysteries of creation, and because of this we can understand that memory is not matter, and that it cannot be explained. It is a spiritual phenomenon with no physical characteristics. If it was matter attached to the nerve cell, then one would forget everything with the passage of time. One would have to re-learn everything again and again, even one's name and one's father's name. The average human being gathers nearly half a million pictures in his memory each day. Thus, tens of billions of images are stored in his memory during his lifetime, in addition to the other information received through the other senses."

Warqa was listening attentively and said: "What an enormous number! It's difficult to believe."

"It is an enormous amount. Some scientists say the memory can hold enough information to fill nine million volumes. Consider how great is the wisdom of the Creator."

Then Warqa asked, "With such facts, can't we prove the existence of Almighty Allah to unbelievers?"

"It can be," said Dr. Miyad. "But some may even deny the existence of the universe. They deny such a reality and think that everything is an illusion."

"Who are these people?"

"They are those who deny the Creator, the universe and themselves. They doubt the existence of everything and try to persuade others to consider everything as merely a dream or as their imagination. In any case, we can refute their claims by ascertaining whether or not they are sure of such claims."

"Of course, they are sure," Warqa, commented.

"If they are sure, then they profess certainty in some matters, which is in contrast to their claims of doubt. This then devalues their doctrine of belief."

"That's quite true," said Warqa. "Please continue."

Dr. Miyad said, "We can ask them whether they consider our profession of faith to be in opposition to theirs or not. If they agree that there is a contradiction, then they must also agree that these opposites cannot meet. This is a fact, which cannot be doubted, and, therefore, it follows that certain statements cannot be denied. If they say that there is no such impossibility, the two parties may both be right. Then those who believe in the Creator can also be right."

"That's logical," said Warqa.

"There are other proofs which we can discuss later, when we meet again, God willing."

Warqa said, "I know you are very busy but I am really looking forward to our next chat."

"Which will be on the day after tomorrow," said the doctor. "Meanwhile you can read this book."

Warqa took the book and left. She read the book carefully and thought seriously about it. At their next meeting, Warqa was ready to listen to her friend. She welcomed her warmly and they sat close together to continue their discussion.

Dr. Miyad began, "Those who doubt the existence of everything should be asked to prove their doubt. If they cannot, then their claims are groundless."

"But suppose they can," said Warqa.

"If they say they can, then they should be asked if there is a relationship between the proof and its outcome. If there is no relationship, then it is of no value. But if they claim there is, then they must believe in a cause that brought about such a result. Thus, there is a law of cause and effect."

Warqa noted, "They may reject such a law."

"They must have evidence to do so," said Dr. Miyad.

"Otherwise, their claim is groundless. If they can produce, evidence, then they are confessing to the law of cause and effect. "

"I should take notes," said Warqa.

"That's a good idea," agreed Dr. Miyad. "You won't forget various points"

PART 4: A PROPOSAL

Warqa stopped writing and looked at her friend, waiting for more information. However, Dr. Miyad said,

"Now it is your turn to help me."

"I am ready. How?" asked Warqa.

"It is about my brother, Sinad. I am thinking about a wife for him."

"How can I assist you in this matter?"

"Well," said Dr. Miyad, "you know that my brother is very dear to me. He is a good believer and is well mannered. He is loving, compassionate and calm. I want to help him find a good wife, and I have recently found someone."

"Thank God for that," said Warqa.

Dr. Miyad continued, "However, I would like to know whether both sides would be happy with such an agreement. I want to persuade the girl; can you help?"

"How?"

Dr. Miyad explained, "You persuade her to marry him. She can trust me with regard to his righteousness."

"But who is she?" asked Warqa. "Where can I find her?"

"Can't you guess?" asked the doctor with a smile.

"She is very close to you."

Warqa blushed, cast her glance down and remained silent.

Dr. Miyad continued, "You have guessed. Why don't you answer? Haven't we already agreed to be as sisters? Don't you trust me? Believe me, I care a lot about your future, just as I care for my brother's. I have thought carefully about the matter and I am sure that it is right for both of you. You can ask whoever you like about his character."

Warqa said shyly, "I am sure of your good intentions; I am just taken by surprise, as I never thought about this before. I must speak with my grandmother."

"The important thing is that you are convinced," Dr. Miyad stressed.

Warqa wanted to say, "Yes!", but she thought it would be better to think the matter over. "Please give me some time to think about this," she said.

"Of course, you have the right to think and then decide. But when can I have the answer?"

"Within a few days," said Warqa.

"All right, my dear. I hope your decision is for your own good."

Warqa smiled and said, "I have never thought about my own affairs. My grandmother has made me depend on her for everything."

Dr. Miyad told her, "You should think for yourself with regard to your future."

"Yes, I will make my own decision. In any case, knowledge is gained through experience."

"That is not always the right criteria," said Dr. Miyad.

"Why not?"

"This is what the experimentalists claim. They don't believe in any fact without experimenting, even though they ignore the fact that their doctrine indicates the possibility of believing in matters without the least experiment."

Surprised, Warqa said, "Please explain more. We have a female lecturer at our school who always insists on this subject."

"I will tell you tomorrow," Dr. Miyad replied.

"Now it is time for me to check on my patients, so I will see you later."

PART 5: AN OBSTACLE

Warqa sat thinking of her friend's proposal. She asked herself happily, 'should I agree, and become her brother's wife? Will he help me to understand Islam and lead me to the right path? How lucky I am!' She almost scolded herself for not agreeing immediately, as no obstacle stood in the way. She spent some time daydreaming and then her grandmother awoke. Warqa assisted her and then she sat down, anxious to tell her the happy news. She began by saying, "Dr. Miyad has been here; she just left."

"Oh," said her grandmother indifferently.

"She had something special to ask me."

"What was that?" asked her grandmother.

"A marriage proposal..."

Warqa's grandmother looked annoyed and said, "What does it have to do with you?"

"It concerns her brother."

"What relationship is there between you and her brother?" said her grandmother angrily.

Amazed at her anger, Warqa said, "She wants me to marry him."

"What was your answer?"

Warqa was confused by her attitude and told her, "I postponed the answer until I could consult you."

Her grandmother turned her face away and said, "No. This marriage must not take place."

"But why not, grandma?"

Her grandmother did not answer her, so Warqa insisted, "Why shouldn't it - please tell me why you disapprove, because I am convinced that I should accept this proposal." Still her grandmother didn't speak.

"Why don't you talk to me? Perhaps you are mistaken," said Warqa

"I am not mistaken," said her grandmother. "I know what I am saying and you must give up this idea. It will not happen, so do not mention it again."

Warqa was silent for a moment and then said, "Don't I have the right to know why? It is not easy for me to decide without knowing the reason for your refusal."

"Of course, you have the right to know. Are you ready to hear?"

Warqa nodded, and her grandmother said, "However, after hearing what I have to say, you must end your relationship with Dr. Miyad."

Warqa was shocked at the idea and said, "But why? She is my best friend!"

"Then don't insist upon knowing the reason."

After a moment Warqa agreed, "All right. I am ready to hear what you have to say." "When you were a child, your father died, as you know. But you never learned how he died. He had a good friend, and they decided to go into business together. They opened a workshop making unbreakable plates. He was happy and optimistic about the business, but did not have the necessary funds. Because of his experience, your father's friend was to provide the technical skill. In order to raise the money for the project, your father had to sell half of the fertile land that he owned.

"However, the half was less than that officially approved for selling. So the landlord, Mr. Hamid, bought that half on the condition that the whole area be registered in his name. He was to give us half of the produce of the land, while your father retained the right to buy it back when the debt was repaid. The land could not be sold to anyone else, because it was in Mr. Hamid's name."

"The money was not sufficient for the workshop and your father mortgaged his house on the condition that Mr. Hamid would get half of the land's produce. Your father and his friend became the night watchmen for the factory. One morning, I went to the factory, where I saw a crowd of people at the entrance and a police car was parked there also. I entered the building and to my surprise and horror, your father lay on the floor, dying. I rushed to his side. His partner was crying crocodile tears. I bent over your father to talk to him, but he did not speak. He was taken to the hospital and on the way he opened his eyes, looked at me and said the name of his murderer: Abdul Majid Muhammad Rajie, Dr. Miyad's father."

Shocked and dismayed, Warqa cried out, "Oh no, it could not be her father!"

"Yes, her father, I was one of the witnesses in court, but one witness was not enough proof. He proved to the court that he was not at the factory at any time that day that the murder occurred. He lied and, heated often. The crime was recorded as a robbery." "Was anything stolen?"

"Yes, of course," her grandmother replied. "Money and important documents were taken from a safe. So we lost the land and the right to buy it back, as well as the ownership of the house. Mr. Hamid managed to produce papers proving his ownership of the property, but we could not get it back. With regard to the house,

Mr. Hamid has been patient and understanding all these years. He has an aim, but only God knows what it is.

"I knew that Abdul Majid had twins, a boy and a girl. That is why I asked the doctor what her father's name was. She ignored my question. I asked a nurse what Dr. Miyad's father's name was and she told me. Now, are you ready to marry the son of the man who murdered your father?"

Warqa bitterly replied, "I won't marry him, but I will remain friends with Dr. Miyad," she cried quietly and thought about her friend. She spent a very sad day thinking about all she had heard. She said to herself, 'what is their guilt in their father's crime? If their father was a criminal, why should they pay for his misdeed? What can I say to Dr. Miyad? How can I explain my refusal of her brother's proposal? Should I tell her the truth? Perhaps they know nothing about this matter; how can I explain it to them? "She remembered that she was to meet Dr. Miyad the following day. She felt that if she lost the doctor's friendship, it would be a great loss. Warqa spent a sleepless night. The next morning she visited her grandmother, who was planning to leave the hospital the same day, without the doctor's permission. Warqa could not make her change her mind. She searched for Dr. Miyad, but to no avail. Dr. Miyad was on 24-hour leave. Warqa could not leave without saying good-bye to her dear friend, so she decided to write a letter to her to express her gratitude. She wrote:

Dear Dr. Miyad,

I don't know what to tell you. I am facing a dilemma and I can find no solution. My grandmother insists on leaving today, so there is no chance to see you. It is as if Almighty Allah has deprived me of His paradise. I am very sad and broken-hearted about my sudden departure. May Allah help me.

Please don't be angry about my behavior. I have been forced to act thusly. As for your brother, I hope he will find someone better be his wife. I have no particular reason for refusing him. It is just Allah's will.

If you still think of me as a sister, please write to me.

Your sincere sister

Warqa

Warqa gave the letter to a nurse and begged her to give it to Dr. Miyad, than she left the hospital with her grandmother.

The days dragged on. Since her grandmother was not completely well. Warqa had to look after her in addition to attending to her college studies. She was sad and anxious to hear from Dr. Miyad. Her grandmother sometimes saw tears in Warqa's eyes, but she never asked about them. A week passed, and a letter arrived from the doctor which said:

Dear Warqa,

Assalamu alaikum

I was very stunned by your letter. Now that the shock is over, I am writing to you. It was hard for me to see you leave without a good-bye. I cannot give up your friendship so easily. You are like a sweet- smelling flower that should fill the spring air with its beautiful scent. If such a flower lacks the hand, which waters it and the shade, which keeps away the sun's rays, it may not blossom and may fade away before it fulfills its role in life.

I feel a spiritual pull towards someone who needs my help. It is my duty to respond, and I am ready to help. You have indeed become a sister to me, and you have brought me happiness. I wanted you to become my brother's wife, but suddenly, without any warning, you disappeared and left only a few written lines. The shock was too great to tolerate, so it took me some time to answer your letter.

I thought the matter over and found I must strengthen our friendship. You should know that I am still your loving sister. I won't ask for an explanation for fear it may hurt you. You are so dear to me. Please keep writing to me at the hospital address.

May Allah keep you well and safe

Miyad

Warqa felt a little happier after reading the letter. She decided not to tell her grandmother about the letter. That night, she wrote to her friend:

Dear Miyad,

God only knows how I long to see you and how sorry I am about this situation. I have indeed been thirsty and in need of water. I found a spring to give me water and it was you. Then time's cruel hand denied me water. I am again suffering from terrible loneliness, though I have always needed someone who would value my feelings; someone I can talk openly to and confide in, who can lead me on the right path and allow me to rest under his shade. When I first saw you, I thought of you as the real sister of my dreams. I loved you and felt at ease with you. I really appreciated your friendship. Then life changed the game and I was deprived of you. I am again sad and lonely. Life is unkind to me - it takes whatever is dear to me and this war has no truce.

I suffered so until I received your letter this morning. It gave me hope again. You drew me towards yourself and then to my Creator, hence it is difficult to keep away from you. I rejoiced at your letter and learnt another lesson of sacrifice and unselfishness, a practical stance, which pays no heed to personal gain. I thank God first and then you, dear sister. I am still ready to meet with you at anytime and anywhere that you suggest.

Your sister forever

Warqa

PART 6: ANOTHER MEETING

Warqa posted the letter the following day and waited for Miyad to fix a date for their next meeting. A letter soon arrived and Warqa planned to meet her friend at the hospital the next day. Warqa told her grandmother she would be late in coming home and she went to the hospital directly from college. She waited a moment to calm down and then knocked on the doctor's door. Dr. Miyad met her with a bright face, and Warqa felt like crying. The doctor said, "Welcome, dear. I have missed you very much, as if I had lived with you all my life."

"I have also suffered a lot. God knows how worried I was that you might be angry at me."

"Why should I?" asked Dr. Miyad. "You are free to make your own choice. Perhaps you think that my brother is not good enough for you."

"Please don't say that. What happened was not my own decision. I was satisfied with what you told me about him."

"What then?"

"It was my grandmother," Warqa confessed.

"Has she given a reason?"

Warqa became confused and remained silent, but the doctor repeated her question and Warqa told her, "There is a reason."

"A good enough reason for your refusal?"

"Yes."

"Then I won't insist on discussing it further. Let us keep our friendship," said Dr. Miyad.

"Yes, please. I feel quite at ease with you. I was very upset these past few days. I have many girlfriends, but you are the most trustworthy one. I have had difficult times, but never one such as giving up your friendship."

"Forget it, and be sure of our friendship," said Dr. Miyad reassuringly.

"Now we must continue our discussion," said Warqa. "You promised to explain the relationship between empiricists and science."

"What do you know about empiricists?" asked the doctor.

"They rely on observation and experiments, not on theory. They deny the role of brain and rational reasoning. Every issue should be proved through experimenting." "Right," said Dr. Miyad. "So we shall refer to this fact in our arguments. If a piece of iron is kept near fire, it expands, so the general rule is that fire causes the expansion of metals. This is accepted through observation of iron, but the general rule is a mental calculation. The brain produces such knowledge."

"It is quite interesting," noted Warqa. Dr. Miyad continued, "There is something else; the thesis and anti-thesis doctrine. Opponents never agree. This is a basic fact in mathematics and without it this science would be nullified."

"What do you mean?"

"I mean that we cannot say that the water in this glass, for example, is both hot and cold. It is either hot or cold. We cannot say that the sun is both bright and dark at the same time, or that something is long and short."

"What does this have to do with mathematics?"

"For instance, we say that one plus one equals two; a basic fact in this science. We cannot say one plus one equals three, it is in contradiction with the symbol meaning equal to. It is a well-known fact. So the empiricist either believes it or doesn't. If he does, is it from experimenting?"

"So it is impossible to bring opposites together."

"Yes," said Dr. Miyad. "Such a result is the outcome of rational reasoning, which needs no experiment. Warqa then said, "It may be the result of long experience. Opposites in the universe cannot be found together."

"Such a thing may indicate the non-existence of opposites being together, not the probability of such an occurrence. Such a thing can never be the result of experimentation."

"What if they believe in its possibility?" asked Warqa.

"Then they might abolish the most important science: mathematics."

Dr. Miyad was silent for several minutes to give Warqa time to think about the discussion. Warqa was interested in the subject and had listened attentively. She said, "I was in need of such information and I still need more."

"When will you come again then?" asked Dr. Miyad. "I will come as soon as I get the chance. Now I should go home, my grandmother might be worried.

Warqa visited Dr. Miyad from time to time. One day she arrived home late and found that her grandmother was angry and demanded to know where she had been. Warqa guessed that her grandmother knew of her visits to Dr. Miyad and waited for her to say so. "Why are you asking me, grandma?" she inquired.

"Have you come directly from the college?"

Warqa did not lie, but simply replied, "No."

"From the hospital," said Warqa.

"I know that you see Dr. Miyad often," said her grandmother angrily. "Admit it. I thought you were wise enough not to meet with the daughter of your father's murderer."

Warqa said quietly, "How did you guess?"

"I asked your friends."

"What's wrong with that? I refused the proposal of her brother, but I won't give up her friendship. I need a sister, and there is nothing wrong in that."

"You are not interested in the girl but in her brother, who is an attractive gentleman," her grandmother remarked.

"That is not fair!" cried Warqa. "I have only seen him twice, quite by chance. I beg you to stop imagining things. "

The next day Miyad waited for Warqa to come, and when she saw her, she noticed how pale Warqa looked. "What is wrong?" she asked.

"Nothing. I was up late last night. Please continue with your talk."

"You are in a hurry, it seems. Has anything happened? "

"No, nothing," Warqa replied.

Dr. Miyad began, "The empiricists don't even believe in authenticated matters." "What are authenticated matters?" asked Warqa.

"Matters, which are true beyond a doubt. In fact, any authentic fact needs a preceding fact and so on, until we come to a starting point. Otherwise, we can't receive any kind of knowledge."

"How is that?"

"Suppose you want to become acquainted with a particular girl and you want to know about her conduct. Where would you get such information?

"I'd ask her friends," said Warqa.

"You may contact a friend of hers indirectly, through someone else. It is logical that your enquiry might end with someone you know. This is the starting point."

"Quite right," Warqa admitted.

"This is the case with authenticated matters. There should be a starting point well- known, with the least experimenting."

Warqa then asked, "Can you give me an example?"

"For instance, if we say that a part of a book is smaller than the whole, someone might say: 'How do you know?' This is quite simple. Since we refer to a part, surely there must be a whole."

"If simple facts need no experiments, since the brain comprehends then," Warqa asked, "then why can't a person learn these facts at an early age? Why can't they be retained until old age?"

Dr. Miyad explained, "There are two types of mental faculties: reasoning comprehension and imaginary comprehension. We can perceive such things as water, flowers, gold and so on, through our senses."

"And we can imagine unreal objects, such as a sea of milk or a mountain of mercury," added Warqa. "Here comes the perceived information through the power of the senses. But, again, we depend on previously received information. We cannot say, for example, there is a date palm without imagining the date tree first. It depends on imaginative perception. That is why a child cannot comprehend authentic information; he cannot imagine the actual thing."

"It is so interesting to listen to you, but I am afraid I cannot stay any longer," said Warqa.

"We can continue tomorrow," the doctor said.

Warqa said good-bye and left. When she reached home, her grandmother was quite upset. Warqa kissed her and said, "Please don't be angry at my seeing Dr. Miyad. I will obey all your other wishes." Then her grandmother asked, "You will obey me in other matters?"

"Yes, except with regard to Dr. Miyad."

"Will you swear to that?" asked her grandmother.

Warqa was about to swear that she would when something stopped her. "I won't swear, but I do promise. That is sufficient."

"You will keep your word of honour, won't you?" asked her grandmother.

"I will do that," said Warqa. Her grandmother's face brightened and she kissed her granddaughter with an easy mind. She told herself, 'She has promised to obey me. I am sure she will accept her cousin's proposal. Poor man, I was the cause of the delay until now. I was waiting for Warqa to finish her studies, but he has again expressed his wish to marry her. He is rich and educated, even though he is not religious. She can guide him to the right path. When she marries, she will have no time to see Dr. Miyad."

The next afternoon, Warqa attended some lectures and went to see Dr. Miyad again. The doctor was waiting for her at the hospital door and she greeted her, saying, "We shall go home together. I have some work to do."

"Whose home?"

"My home, of course," said Dr. Miyad.

"Will anyone else be there?" asked Warqa.

"No one, be sure of that. We will leave before sunset."

"As you like," Warqa agreed.

"It is not far; we can walk."

They soon reached the doctor's home and she unlocked the door. It was a small home with a tidy little garden. The house furniture was simple but in good taste. Warqa asked, "Who cleans your home for you?" "I come here twice a week," said the doctor. I usually clean it myself and arrange it for my brother."

"Does he live alone?" Warqa asked.

"Yes, I am his only sister. We are alone in the world." Warqa felt sorry for them. She knew that the doctor was lonely but tried to conceal it.

Warqa was deep in thought when the doctor said, "What is the matter? Won't you give me a hand?"

Warqa was happy to help her friend. When they finished their work, they sat in the shade of a tree. Warqa was looking at a small orange tree in front of her and Dr. Miyad said, "I planted that tree and I am very happy that it is bearing fruit."

"It is nice to see plants grow, flourish and bear fruit," Warqa commented.

"But how sad it is to see such trees uprooted by a wicked hand or a strong storm."

"Oh yes," agreed Warqa. "But I want to ask a question. Is it you or the seed that caused the plant to grow?"

Dr. Miyad answered, "Neither I nor the seed. Almighty Allah has done it. We are only means created by Him. He created the whole universe, and caused all things to come into existence."

"How wise our Creator is. I don't know how some people can deny His existence and relate existence to causes other than Him, such as materialists who claim that the unceasing motion of matter has made all creatures."

"Such people, if they think rationally, will confess that Allah has designed all life. Sometimes they agree with us on the rudiments of a subject, but they differ at the outcome," said Dr. Miyad.

"In what ways do they agree?"

"They, too, agree that we have not come from nothing; that there is an everlasting One Who created life. One Who is the Owner of the things that He bestows upon us. What we have cannot have come from nothing. These are matters they agree with us upon. What do we believers say?"

Warqa said, "We say Allah is the Creator."

"The materialists claim that the everlasting motion of matter is the cause of life. One could ask them: When did it start to create countless living creatures? If it is everlasting, how, then, can it have a beginning?"

"They cannot answer that," said Warqa.

Dr. Miyad continued, "Science says that the earth separated from the sun billions of years ago, and that it took one billion years for the earth's surface to cool."

"That means that life on this earth had a beginning," noted Warqa.

"Yes. Such scientific facts are undisputable. Thus, if motion is everlasting, then creation must be everlasting."

"Otherwise, scientists could not have calculated the age of this planet," Warqa added. "This fact cannot be denied. But if the materialists confess that motion is not everlasting, it must be something separate from and, hence, added to matter. Then we can ask: Who has created motion? How could it create when it itself was created? How can they claim motion is the source of creation?"

Warqa asked, "Suppose they say that motion is everlasting and that matter designated the time of creation."

"This is unacceptable," said Dr. Miyad, "for creation is a process, the result of great Wisdom; substance is not."

"How can a person prove that matter lacks intelligence?"

"Science has proved that it is comprised of electrical charges," said the doctor. "Hence it cannot think or comprehend. According to our belief, it is under some influence, which causes its motion and existence."

Warqa suggested, "They might say that the beginning of creation was postponed in order to prepare the rudiments, like a traveller who begins his journey four hours later than he intended. Maybe the matter needed time in order to create life."

"What prevented it from starting earlier?" asked Dr. Miyad.

"Well, like the traveller who was delayed because he needed time to prepare for the journey, so life came into existence after billions of years," said Warqa.

Dr. Miyad replied, "The answer suits the traveller, but not in the case of the universe, because it is claimed that time exists through everlasting motion. Such answers could be true if the universe actually did begin in a manner similar to that of the traveler, which would mean that motion is accidental and that time is limited; an excuse for a late start."

"Thank you for this explanation. By the way, sometimes I hate time, because it moves so quickly, as in the case of our meetings," laughed Warqa.

"I hope you won't be late," said Dr. Miyad. "Let us leave now. We will come here again sometimes, just for a change."

PART 7: CONFLICT

When Warqa arrived at home, her grandmother met her at the door and said, "We have visitors. Go upstairs and get ready, then come down right away."

"Who are the visitors?"

"Mr. Mahir, a cousin of your parents."

"What does that have to do with me?" Warqa asked.

"He is your cousin too."

"It makes no difference to me," said Warqa. "He is a stranger and I don't want to sit and talk with him for no reason."

"Who said there is no reason? He is a wonderful man-educated, understanding and rich," said Warqa's grandmother.

"That is enough for you to welcome him!" said Warqa.

Her grandmother took hold of her and said, "I won't let you go until you promise to come down. You promised to obey me. Come on now and say 'salam'."

"That is all," said Warqa. She walked into the living room and saw Mr. Mahir and his mother sitting near each other, facing the door. She murmured a few words of welcome as her cousin stood up and asked her to take a seat. Her grandmother said approvingly, "Come here and sit by your cousin."

Warqa did not move, but said politely, "I am sorry," I have a lot of homework to do. Excuse me, good-bye." With that, she left the room, and her grandmother became vexed and the guests confused.

Warqa ran quickly up the stairs to her room and burst into tears. She did not know how to get out of this difficult situation. She would not accept Mr. Mahir as a husband since he had loose morals and was not a committed Muslim. It was impossible for her to accept him. She decided to fight the battle, no matter how difficult it might be. An hour later, her grandmother came up to her room. She spoke gently to her, saying, "You have not behaved well today. It wasn't right to treat your cousin that way; you were hard on him, while he loves and respects you. He only wanted to introduce himself to you."

Warqa told her, "I don't like him. He is not a committed Muslim."

"You are mistaken," said her grandmother. "He is a gentleman and is rich and successful. He has no relatives except his mother. Just imagine, he has three private cars!" "That is exactly why I think he is worthless! What needs would anyone have for three cars?!"

Her grandmother ignored Warqa and continued, "A few months ago, he asked for your hand in marriage. I suggested to him to wait until you finished your studies. Now that you are taking your final exams, he has renewed his request. He is ready to offer a very high dowry, in addition to a special car of your own."

"Are you serious?" asked Warqa. "Did you think I might agree to marry him? His wealth and his cars won't tempt me at all to sacrifice my religion."

"What does religion have to do with it?"

"You know he is not a committed person. He does not even pray."

"It isn't for you to judge him. He, too, has a God who will call him to account."

"I won't marry such a person-be sure of that," insisted Warqa.

Her grandmother persisted, "He is much respected. I know he is not a committed person, but he can't harm you. Think it over a while so you won't regret refusing him." "I'll never regret it," stressed Warqa.

"If you don't get the man of your dreams, Warqa, what will you do?"

"Then I won't marry. Anyway, it is quite possible to marry the man I wish."

"You are still a child. You should not reject your cousin's offer from sheer nonsense." Warqa smiled bitterly and said, "Why do you think it is nonsense? I refused Sinad because you said his father killed my father. Yet he has done no harm to my father. Mr. Mahir has committed a crime against his Creator; he is an infidel who disobeys and disrespects Allah. He mocks the Hereafter. My religion is the dearest thing I have, even dearer than my father. How could I live with someone who is my enemy?" Her grandmother was quite annoyed by this time as she said, "You still speak well of Sinad? I know you have rejected Mahir because of him!"

Warqa replied, "I speak well of him because he deserves it. But to say that I have refused Mahir because of him is not true. To me, that is finished. He may be planning to marry someone else for all I know."

"He is good and praiseworthy although he is the son of your father's murderer? Mahir is your cousin and so you should consider the matter seriously. You will do your father, as well as me, a great injustice if you refuse him."

Warqa did not sleep well that night. The next day, she visited Dr. Miyad and she forgot about her troubles for a while. She did not tell her friend about Mahir, but listened carefully to the useful discussion. She asked, "Will you please continue where we left off last time?"

Dr. Miyad said, "You don't seem to be happy today. I am afraid you won't enjoy the subject."

"I will enjoy it," insisted Warqa. "I intend to forget my problems by listening to you. The best times for me are when I am learning something new."

"Let us argue with them then," said Dr. Miyad.

"With whom?"

"With the materialists who claim that life was created through the motion of matter, which is everlasting. We can ask them to explain the different stages of that matter and the different outcomes, while matter has only one simple stage."

"What do you mean?"

"I mean that through chemical processes and a combination of gases, new substances may result. Through radiation, a compound substance may produce a new one. Hence, we have a chain of elements and minerals that stops at a certain stage."

"Why does it stop?" asked Warqa.

"Well, this is the question we must answer. They claim that development is the result of a conflict between the original direction and its opposite, or through unification. For instance, through just such a process, hydrogen combines with other gases to produce various compounds.

"But the amazing thing is why doesn't all the hydrogen combine and disappear in the process? Here we come to know that there is an Everlasting, Wise Power that designed everything. Science has proved that electricity is merely negative and positive charges, therefore, it is not an intelligent source of power. It can't have created such a mighty universe as this."

Warqa's silence prompted the doctor to ask her if anything was wrong

"Nothing at all," replied Warqa.

"I hope you will always be strong," Dr. Miyad said.

"With the help of Allah, I will. I feel better when I talk with you. It makes me strong."

"But you are pale," said the doctor. 'I'll give you some pills. Dissolve one in a cup of water and drink it once a day."

"Oh, I should remember that you are a physician. I think of you as a psychiatrist," Warqa said.

"I am prouder of this than of being a doctor."

"It is time to leave," said Warqa. "I can't come tomorrow, I have lessons in the afternoon, so I will see you the day after tomorrow, God willing."

"You will find me waiting for you."

Warqa's grandmother did not discuss the subject of marriage that day. Warqa was low-spirited and tired, so she went to bed early. The next morning she got ready and left for college. At the bus stop, an expensive car stopped near her and Mr. Mahir got out of the car and came up to her. "Good morning, Warqa," he said. "It is good to see you. Can I give you a lift?"

"No thank you, Mr. Mahir," Warqa declined.

"Come on, get in. Are you waiting for anyone?"

"I am waiting for the bus," Warqa said.

"How strange!" Mr. Mahir remarked. "You are waiting for a bus and refuse a ride in a car?"

His words increased her contempt for him, and Warqa turned her head away, saying, "Please don't trouble yourself. I won't get in your car."

"There is no trouble in giving you a life," he persisted. "It would be a pleasure for me. Consider the car as being yours and get in."

At that moment the bus arrived and Warqa boarded it. She left Mahir bewildered by her behaviour.

When Warqa saw Dr. Miyad the following day, she felt uncomfortable and was in poor spirits. She found her friend busy cleaning the house and she tried to help the doctor, but Dr. Miyad noticed her discomfort and begged Warqa to rest on a seat in the garden, where she sat looking dejected and depressed.

"What is the matter with you?" Dr. Miyad asked.

"I am upset," Warqa replied.

"That is obvious. But you should not take anything too seriously -be strong."

"I am strong. But some disappointments make me tired. A cousin of my parents has recently asked me to marry him and my grandmother approves of him, since she says he is rich, young and educated."

"Is he a good Muslim," asked Dr. Miyad.

"No, he is not. That is why I am upset. I have refused him, but my grandmother never stops bringing up the issue. He is trying to impose himself on me, and I feel as if I am at battle."

"With whom?"

"With my grandmother and her displeasure."

"I feared it was a war within yourself," said Dr. Miyad.

"No, the matter is quite clear to me," Warqa said.

"I hope so. It is better to face such a situation now then to have to tolerate it permanently," Dr. Miyad noted.

"Do you mean as a result of marrying an unbeliever?"

"Yes, of course. Such a marriage could affect both your life now and in the Hereafter."

"I only wish I could make my grandmother see my point of view."

Dr. Miyad said, "She would not accept it. She believes in her own view. You should try gently to make her give up the idea."

"But she is so determined! Warqa replied. "She won't give up, but I will continue to resist."

"Why does she insist so? How will she benefit from such a marriage?" asked Dr. Miyad.

Warqa did not answer her. She thought her grand- mother's reason was to keep her away from her friend, Miyad, but she could not mention it. To change the subject, Warqa said, "Yes, there is a reason for everything. That is why those who deny the existence of the Creator claim that matter created itself."

Dr. Miyad said, "Yet they sometimes agree eventually with those who believe in Almighty Allah."

"How is that?"

"Both parties believe that the universe has been created, which means that there is some influential power behind it. They also agree that the universe is a reality, which is in contrast with what idealists believe-that is a dream or an illusion.

"They both also believe that human life depend on this Power which caused life to exist; however, both sides differ with regard to the nature of this Power."

"Do materialists admit such a belief in their literature?" asked Warqa.

"Yes," said the doctor. "In some of their books on religion they say: 'In fact, we must confess that we know nothing about the origin of the universe'."

"Is this common knowledge among them?"

"Yes. The materialists claim that matter and its motion are behind creation, while we believe that Almighty Allah is," said Dr. Miyad.

"Matter can't last forever, since it can change," said Warqa. "The eternal, the everlasting does not change."

"That is right. Mutable things must have a beginning and an end," said Dr. Miyad. Warqa continued, "Physics has proved that the atom is made up of an electron and a proton, and that it can be split to produce energy. Hence, matter is not everlasting, it is a compound."

"For argument's sake," said Dr. Miyad, "we can ask the materialists how the first compound came into existence. Was it everlasting originally, or did its components come first?"

"One might say that its components came first," suggested Warqa.

"In that case, there must have been a reason which caused its existence."

Warqa then said, "Suppose one says that the parts and the whole existed simultaneously?"

"Then we must ask if these parts can be separated either by transformation or development, such as the chemical processes which break water down into oxygen and hydrogen. It is quite possible for a compound to dissolve and vanish, so it can't be everlasting. The everlasting cannot be affected. Whatsoever depends upon a cause may disappear, as in the case of the atom," concluded Dr. Miyad.

"Science has also recently proved that there is a continuous change in heat energy, which proves that the universe is not everlasting," said Warqa.

Dr. Miyad commented, "Yes. This change in temperature proves such facts. Had the temperature remained the same, the whole universe would have suffered the same degree of heat for ages. Life would thus have been impossible."

Warqa then said, "Through various calculations, science has proved that the universe is expanding and that it is not everlasting. Otherwise, the planets would have been separated by unlimited spaces." Dr. Miyad ended the conversation by adding, "The universe has been created by an everlasting Power, Almighty Allah."

Warqa glanced at her watch and said, "I am sorry I have to leave now. I won't see you for a week. I will be preparing for the final exams."

"I wish you success. I will be waiting for you the following week, God willing." That week Warqa was quite busy with her studies. She thought only of her finals and she even forgot all about Mr. Mahir. She passed her exams successfully and at the end of the week she went to see Dr. Miyad, but could not find her, so she left a note saying that she would see her the next afternoon. Warqa returned home to find her grandmother happy that she had finished her studies. She kissed Warqa warmly and said, "I am still alive to see you become an engineer."

"I have not got the results yet," Warqa said with a smile.

"I am sure you will succeed."

"Warqa went up to her room and found a large crystal vase filled with beautiful flowers on her table. Next to the vase was a small white box and a note on which was written: ' To Warqa, with much love...Mahir.'

Warqa knew that the gift was serious. She went downstairs and asked her grandmother, "Who brought this bouquet of flowers for me?"

"Mr. Mahir's chauffeur. He said Mr. Mahir and his mother will visit us this evening."

"Where is his house?" Warqa asked.

"Why? I don't know where his new house is. Why do you ask?"

"So I can return his flowers," stated Warqa.

Her grandmother was shocked and said, "You want to return the flowers?! Are you crazy? Haven't you seen the precious diamond ring in the box?"

"No, I have not looked at it, and I don't want to," Warqa said.

"You must be mad. If you were sane, you wouldn't do such a thing. He is your cousin and your fiancé."

"What? What have you said? Who is my fiancé?" demanded Warqa.

"Mahir!" said her grandmother.

"Since when? I never agreed to marry him."

Her grandmother said, "You should think carefully before you reject him. He is an excellent person and would be very good for you."

"I have made up my mind not to marry him."

"What is wrong with him?" her grandmother asked angrily.

"He is not a committed person," Warqa said.

"You can guide him to the right path."

"What if he never listens?"

"Then you can mind your own business and leave him. You don't have to share his grave, you know. You will enjoy his great wealth and he alone will suffer in Hell," her grandmother told her.

"Then this would not be a marriage, just a business deal for exploitation-no more, no less," Warqa objected.

"What about his gift?"

"All his gifts, cars, property and other wealth count for nothing, since he lacks religious belief. Give him back his gift and tell him to look for someone else to marry."

"I won't do that," replied Warqa's grandmother, "You can do it yourself if you wish to."

That evening Mahir came alone. Warqa's grandmother welcomed him and tried to speak with him alone before Warqa came in the room. She began by saying, "Thank you so much for the gift you gave Warqa, Mr. Mahir."

"Oh, it is nothing. Warqa is worth much more. I hope the ring fits."

"She is still young," Warqa's grandmother said with a sigh. "She needs to be brought round gradually."

"How is that?"

"She has refused to try on the ring. She says she is tired from the exams."

"She must rest," Mahir agreed. "I only want her agreement. I have chosen a very expensive set of diamonds to match her beauty. I have come to fix a date for the engagement."

Confused, Warqa's grandmother said, "I will get in touch with you later. I shall persuade her to agree."

"I am very surprised. Why does she need to be persuaded? It is a good match. It seems she is childish," Mahir said.

"She is young, but she is also wise and prudent, thank God. She may have a different point of view, but I will make her change her mind."

Suddenly Warqa opened the door and entered the room with the small white box in her hand. Her grandmother was upset and expected a confrontation. Warqa greeted her cousin and sat down in a chair by the door. Mahir stood up to welcome her.

Warqa spoke first, "Thank you for the flowers. They were a nice present from a cousin, but I can't accept this one." She held out the box.

Mahir was stunned and was at a loss for words.

Finally he said, "What do you mean?"

"I mean that we are cousins, nothing else. That is enough."

"But can't I seek a closer relation?" Mahir asked.

"No!"

"Can you tell me why? Have I done anything wrong?"

"Of course not. But it is for our own good."

"How do you know it is good for me?" he then asked.

"Because I cannot be a real wife for you. There is a barrier that cannot be ignored, so let us just remain cousins."

"If you think my wealth is a barrier, be sure that it is not important to me that you are not rich. When you become my wife all my wealth will be yours."

His words annoyed Warqa, but she tried to stay calm. She explained, "You don't understand me. I was not referring to wealth."

"Then is it our social standing? We are both engineers."

"Please let me finish," Warqa said sharply.

"I am sorry, please go on," said Mahir.

"What I mean is that the religious situation is what makes the real difference." She sat silently for a moment. Mahir coughed to hide his confusion. Warqa's grandmother used the opportunity to say, "This is unimportant. He won't make you change your commitment, will you Mr. Mahir?"

Seeing a way out, he quickly said, "Of course, I won't prevent her from performing her religious duties. If this is her reason, there is no question of it."

Warqa smiled bitterly and said, "In short, I would like you to answer a question: How do you view marriage?"

Mahir had not expected such a question and he hesitated and then said, "A happy life together."

"You have not really given your opinion. To you, it is just an end in itself."

He laughed meaninglessly and asked, "How do you view it, then?"

"It is for you to answer!"

Warqa's grandmother interrupted, "Stop this talk. He is your cousin, and that is enough."

Warqa turned to her, saying, "At least you should understand me, even if he won't. Married life is not a business agreement or a social ritual. It is a mutual life course and a uniting of two spirits and their beliefs. Such unity cannot take place if the points of view of both sides are quite opposed. If we differ ideologically, we can't agree emotionally. This is a serious reason for marriages, which fail. I don't wish to suffer in such a marriage."

Her grandmother persisted," You can each have your own way of life."

Warqa said impatiently "That would be a schizophrenic situation. There would be mental disorders in such a life."

"After marriage you may come to understand each other," her grandmother pleaded.

"I don't think so," said Warqa. "That would require a compromise on both sides, and I am not ready to do so. My religion is very important to me, and it should control my future."

Mahir commented, "I don't know what religion has got to do with your future. You are an engineer with or without it. I have my career, though I am not a committed person."

"You misunderstand me again. By the future, I mean the afterlife in the Hereafter. You have no thought of that life, while I am quite concerned about it; more than about my future career, which, however long it may be, will still be a limited one. The other life is everlasting."

Mahir looked pale, as if her words had affected him.

In an attempt to end the dispute, Warqa's grandmother turned to her and said, "Go to your room now. We have plenty of time to settle the matter." Warqa didn't leave the room and her grandmother insisted, "Get up and go. No more childish talk."

Mahir laughed and said, "She is excused. She has had an unusually complicated life. I hope to give her a long and happy life of openness and freedom. Surely she is under the influence of a bad male or female acquaintance."

Warqa's grandmother understood what he was implying and said angrily, "You should not say such things. Warqa is a good, honest girl and is well-behaved. Warqa, go up to your room."

Warqa was vexed but said nothing. She went upstairs and sat on the edge of her bed, waiting for Mahir to leave.

Her grandmother tried to apologize for Warqa's behaviour, which made Mahir determined to win this stubborn girl who refused all of his wealth. He tried to appear patient and kind, saying, "Don't apologize, I have my own ways of getting her to agree. You can phone me if there is any progress."

He said good-bye and left; his mind made up that he would either get her or ruin her life by tarnishing her reputation so that no one would marry her.

PART 8: A CONSPIRACY

Warqa felt better, since she thought she had put an end to the matter. She felt she had won that round of battle and she was in good spirits the next morning.

Her mood surprised her grandmother, who had expected her to be angry about the previous day's discussion. Warqa was anxious to see Dr. Miyad and tell her the details, but the doctor was busy with an urgent case and Warqa returned home. Her grandmother met her at the door and whispered," Go to your room and keep quiet."

Surprised, Warqa said, "What is the matter?"

"Sh! go up there quickly and don't come down until I call you."

Warqa went upstairs. She was disturbed, since she did not know what was upsetting her grandmother. She looked at her watch, which seemed to be standing still.

After an hour had passed, Warqa heard the front door close and her grandmother called her. Warqa went quickly downstairs and found her grandmother sad and pale.

Warqa was terrified. "What is wrong, grandma? By God, tell me what has happened!"

"Do you know who was just here?'

"It was Mr. Hamid, the man who took away our land."

"What did he want?"

"He wants his right to the mortgaged house. We have no papers to prove we repaid the money, since all the papers were stolen, as I told you. He said he had been waiting until you finished college. Now he wants his money, unless..." she left the sentence unfinished.

"Unless what?" asked Warqa.

"Unless you agree to marry his son. Then he would give us back the land and the house."

"What did you tell him?"

"Allah helped me give him the right answer. I told him that you are already engaged so that he would not think about it anymore."

"How could you do that?" asked Warqa. "He will find out it is not true."

Her grandmother told her, "Now you must agree to Mahir as soon as possible. In any case, Mahir is much better than the landlord's playboy son."

Warqa moaned as if in pain and did not speak. After a while she said, "I won't marry Mahir. Let Mr. Hamid take everything-I don't want the land or the house. I will sacrifice all for the sake of my religion."

Her grandmother burst into exaggerated cries of despair. She insulted Warqa, using every unkind word she knew. Warqa tried hard to calm her and then she went to her room and lay on her bed, miserable and exhausted.

The next morning, Warqa did not come downstairs as usual. Her grandmother thought she was still sleeping, so she waited for some time before going up to her room to awaken her. She went up to Warqa's bed and called her softly, but she was shocked when she touched Warqa's hand and found it was hot and she saw that Warqa was taking quick, shallow breaths. Warqa opened her eyes and looked at her grandmother, who asked her quickly, "What is wrong Warqa dear?"

"I don't know."

"Shall l call a doctor?"

"Yes please. I don't feel well." Her grandmother did not know who to call, and she phoned Mr. Mahir to ask him to bring a doctor. She reached him at his office and told him, "Oh Mr. Mahir, please come quickly and help Warqa. She is very sick."

"What is the matter with her?" he asked rather indifferently.

"She is sick and needs a doctor."

"Doctors are not in their clinics in the mornings."

"You can find one. Not all of them work in hospitals," Warqa's grandmother persisted.

"I am quite busy with some clients. Wait until the afternoon and if she is still sick, call me."

Distraught, Warqa's grandmother hung up the telephone. She tried some herbal remedies, but nothing helped Warqa. That afternoon, she telephoned Mahir again, but she was told that he had gone out of town on business and would not be back until the next day. She recited some Qur'anic verses and different prayers by Warqa's beside.

In the evening Warqa's condition worsened, and her grandmother was at a loss as to what to do. She called Mahir's office, but in vain. She did not try to call anyone else, but when she saw how sick her granddaughter was, she cursed herself and said, "I have killed my granddaughter with my own hands! I must do something to save her."

She dialed the number of the hospital and asked to speak with Dr. Miyad. The nurse who had answered the telephone told her that the doctor was asleep, but Warqa's grandmother insisted upon speaking to her. The nurse promised to give the doctor Warqa's phone number and she hung up. The telephone rang almost immediately, and Warqa's grandmother tearfully told the doctor about Warqa's condition, begging her to come quickly to save her.

Dr. Miyad noted her address and promised to come immediately.

After a short while the doorbell rang. Warqa's grandmother, forgetting all about her hatred, opened the door for Dr. Miyad and welcomed her. She showed the door to Warqa's room and Dr. Miyad expressed grave concern for Warqa's health. "I must have assistance," Dr. Miyad said.

"She is critically ill."

"Where can you find another doctor at this late hour?"

"My brother is in the car outside."

"Oh please ask him in. He may be able to save her," Warqa's grandmother urged.

Dr. Miyad asked her brother to come in. He examined Warqa and diagnosed her sickness. They agreed that she should be taken to the hospital, but Warqa's grandmother was terrified. "Is she that sick? Is she dying? Woe to me, I have killed her!"

The doctor said, "It is vitally important that she be taken to the hospital. Won't you agree?"

"Of course I will," said the grandmother quickly.

An ambulance was requested and it soon came. Dr. Miyad promised to take care of Warqa and so her grandmother remained at home. Dr. Miyad reassured her and said she would stay in touch by phone.

Warqa responded well to treatment but she was still unconscious. Dr. Miyad and her brother were by Warqa's bed when they heard her murmur: "It is not possible that their father is a murderer...Oh, Miyad can't be the daughter of a killer ...please, grandma, make that silly man Mahir go away... let them have the house...how can I refuse her brother, I only saw him twice...I don't want...

Dr. Miyad looked pale and turned to her brother, "You heard what she said, didn't you?"

"Yes. It seems she had a reason for her refusal."

"What shall we do now?" asked Miyad.

"Let her recover first and we can settle the matter later."

Two days later Warqa was much better and Miyad was in her room when she awoke and looked around in amazement. She saw her friend, but closed her eyes again in disbelief, thinking she was dreaming. Dr. Miyad took her hand and said, "How do you feel now, dear sister?"

Warqa opened her eyes and asked weakly, "Are you really Dr. Miyad, or am I dreaming?"

"Oh no, you are not dreaming. Thank God you are well again."

"Where is my grandmother?"

"She is at home. I told her I'd take her place and stay with you. I will send for her now to come see you."

"How was I brought here?" Warqa asked.

"You are tired now, so rest. I will tell you all about it tomorrow. I will go phone your grandmother now."

"Please don't leave me alone; I am afraid."

"You are getting well. Why are you scared?"

"I am not afraid of sickness," Warqa explained, "I am afraid of people."

"I won't be away for long, just a few minutes."

At that moment the door was opened by her grandmother, who rushed toward her.

Dr. Miyad said, "She is all right and has asked about you." The grandmother kissed her gently and Warqa asked, "How did you get here, grandma?"

"The doctor who was with Miyad the day you became ill brought me."

Dr. Miyad was proud of her brother and said, "My brother, Sinad, is wonderful, isn't he?"

Warqa didn't understand, so she closed her eyes and said nothing.

PART 9: THE TRUTH REVEALED

Warqa's grandmother sat near her and Dr. Miyad left the room. She was very happy to see Warqa improving. Warqa's grandmother was at a loss as to how she should feel about Dr. Miyad. She explained to Warqa how she had called Dr. Miyad for help after Mahir had shown no concern. She told her how the brother and sister had worked to save her. Warqa then said, "Now you can see the difference between their behaviour and Mr. Mahir's."

Her grandmother began to say, "In fact, they are good examples of unselfish, kind people. Mahir has shown his true face, but..."

Warqa guessed what she had been about to say, but turned to Almighty Allah for help.

The next morning Dr. Miyad came and was pleased to see Warqa was quite well. The doctor told Warqa's grandmother, "You can take a rest. I will sit by Warqa in the meantime." She agreed, and lay down on the sofa with her face to the wall.

Warqa thanked Dr. Miyad for all she had done and told her, "Twice you have done me a great favour. You helped me with my belief as well as with my health. I don't know how to thank you."

"This is the duty of every sister. Actually I am grateful to your grandmother for calling me."

"Oh sister, she is very happy with you," Warqa said, and then she closed her eyes and said nothing.

"You call me sister, but you don't know the details of my life," said Dr. Miyad.

"Is it a special life story then?"

"Yes. It begins years before my brother and I were born."

"Are you twins?"

"Yes, we are, but he was ahead of me in his studies because I was very ill for three years during my childhood. Did you notice the resemblance between him and me?"

"Well, I never thought much about it," said Warqa.

"I thought so," said Dr. Miyad. She continued, "The story is also about my real father, who died in a car accident a month before I was born. My brother and I were born orphans. But our father died two years ago."

Warqa's grandmother turned in order to listen better.

The doctor resumed her story, "My father, Abdul Razzaq, was a poor man, but a virtuous one. My mother married him after having refused to marry a wealthy cousin of hers who was a loose, deviated man. My mother was rich and beautiful. When my father died, she suffered a lot. The rich cousin and his mother were nearby to help, and a few months later his mother persuaded my mother to marry her son. At first she refused, but the young cousin promised to behave well and take care of her small family.

"He expressed his love and compassion until my mother finally married him. Then, when she discovered that he had attached our birth to his name, she became angry and went back to her father's old house. Her husband still did not leave her alone and he eventually took her back to his house. We grew up thinking he was our real father. We were always surprised by his cruelty towards us."

"He was unkind to you?" asked Warqa.

"Yes, he was. He never kept his word to my mother. He squandered all of his wealth and she suffered much. She died a few years ago. When we were old enough, she told us about our father, and even gave us proof of it."

"What kind of proof?"

"Some letters which he had written to her in which he wrote the reason why he gave us his name. She also told us of certain persons who knew the facts. We suffered from his bad reputation until he died two years ago. Then we found, in a private box, an official letter in which he confessed that we were not his own children. He had written the name of our real father. Perhaps he did not want us to inherit the wealth he had made by cheating and stealing. Anyway, his last will helped us to regain our real father's name. Now you know, dear Warqa, who our real father is."

"Oh yes! How happy I am to find you!" Warqa exclaimed joyfully.

"Almighty Allah has returned you to me", added Miyad and recited the Qur'anic verse:

Most surely He Who has made the Qur'an binding to you will bring you back to destination... (Al-Qasas: 85)

THE END

Novel 2

VIRTUE PREVAILS

CHAPTER 1

On the spacious balcony of a home in the capital of an Islamic country, two young women sat nearby talking. Sumayah, the resident of the house, looks younger than her twenty years. She listens to her visitor with a disapproving look on her face. Fitnah, Sumayah's cousin, has recently returned from a European country, where she and her husband had lived for several years. Having heard of Sumayah's impending marriage, Fitnah hastened to visit her, with evil intentions. She spoke about European life and the advantages of western civilization. She also relates off-color jokes, but Sumayah does not join in her laughter.

Sumayah, a polite young woman, was raised in a religious family. Her future husband, Ahmad, has completed his education and is now managing a successful business. Ahmad and Sumayah are officially engaged, and he visits her home often.

Although Sumayah does not agree with her cousin's way of thinking, she doesn't want to insult her guest, who is saying, "The best place for your honeymoon is Europe."

"Europe!" replied Sumayah, "We won't go to any European country. We may visit another Islamic country."

Fitnah laughed and said, "Perhaps you intend to spend your honeymoon performing your pilgrimage in Mecca!"

Sumayah ignored her sarcasm, "No, we have decided to perform our hajj at a later time."

"Why don't you suggest to Ahmad that you visit Paris or London? Can't he afford it?"

"Oh, he can afford it, but neither one of us like the idea of spending our honeymoon in Europe."

Fitnah asked, "Is he afraid to travel by air? Then he can travel by car or by ship. By the way, has he a car?"

"Yes, he has. And he has never been afraid of flying! In fact, he is a good Muslim and does not want to have his honeymoon in Europe."

Fitnah exclaimed, "Oh, this is terrible! Is he a reactionary?"

"Absolutely not. He is a very enlightened and educated person", Sumayah replied.

"Is he a very religious man?" Fitnah asked.

Sumayah smiled, "Thank God, he is!"

"Oh, what a pity! You do not know what it means for a modern girl to marry a religious man! You don't know of the limits, chains and strict instructions that he will impose upon you."

Sumayah replied, "I am quite sure that you exaggerate. I am a Muslim believer and I know Islam has its own morals and value system."

Fitnah continued, "These so-called morals are nothing other than chains and rules; an abyss in which you will be kept away from society. You are at the threshold of life; don't allow reactionary ideas to disturb your happy future!"

"You are mistaken. There is nothing reactionary in religion. Ahmad is sure to make me happy. He is everything to me and I love him very much."

Fitnah told her, "Yet, you won't be everything to him. You will be just like any other thing in his life."

"Oh, no, I am aware of my status in his heart."

"Well, as long as you are engaged, he will display all his love and passion. But when you live together, you will find out what a Muslim man is really like!"

Losing patience, Sumayah asked, "Am I not a Muslim also?"

"Yes, you are a Muslim girl, but not of Ahmad's type! My point of view is that the woman should have complete freedom to enjoy all of life's pleasures. Ahmad will only control yours, as if you were his slave."

"This is strange," Sumayah commented. "Why do you hate and misrepresent Islam, although you are a Muslim woman? Has Europe corrupted you?"

Fitnah answered, "Oh, no. My affection for you has prompted me to speak frankly. Though I was happy when I heard the news of your engagement, I also felt sorrow, since I wished a better future for you."

"How can you be so sure that I won't have a good life?" Sumayah asked.

Fitnah said, "If your husband is of those few who boast of Islam and its ethics, he will never make you happy."

"What do you mean by 'few'? Can't you see there are millions of believers everywhere?"

"I mean those who have only recently adopted hollow ideals, which they use to dominate woman and control her by imposing limits and barriers on her under the cover of Islam."

"But a Muslim man also has limits", Sumayah replied.

"Well, they are free to do what they like. Hasn't Ahmad been to Europe several times?"

"He is going to Paris soon, as a matter of fact, in order to forward his thesis for his doctorate and to sign some business contracts."

"Then he has the right to go, but you have not! Can't you see? He is free to go wherever he wishes. As for you, Islamic limits hold you back."

"I don't agree with you. Ahmad and I share the same ideas. I am satisfied with Islamic limits."

"I am afraid you will wake up suddenly one day and it will be too late!" Fitnah predicted gloomily.

"What do you mean?"

"I mean to say that marriage won't be successful unless it is founded on progressive norms. A modern girl won't have a good marriage unless she is released from family pressure and is free to choose the man she wants to marry."

Sumayah said, "Family ties, which you call pressure, are for the benefit of the whole family. In any case, I have been free to choose Ahmad."

Fitnah then said, "You will be faithful to him, I'm sure. But men are unlike women. They cheat their wives by various methods. They exploit women by referring to religious instructions, which imprison women in their homes."

"Why do you consider a woman's own home to be a prison?" Sumayah asked.

Fitnah replied, "A woman cannot keep her eyes on her man unless she accompanies him on his trips and parties! A woman who sits in her house and leaves her husband free to enjoy himself cannot have a happy life."

"Oh, you don't know what a wonderful man Ahmad is. I wish you knew him."

Fitnah remained silent for a moment and, trying to sound normal, said, "I have never seen him."

"When you meet him, you will change your ideas about Muslim believers."

Fitnah suddenly stood up and said, "I must leave now. I am going to a party tonight."

Sumayah was surprised by her cousin's abrupt departure. She walked with her to the door and then returned to her mother, who asked, "Why have you been sitting on the balcony all alone?"

"I was not alone," Sumayah told her, "Fitnah has just left."

"What has she told you? I am sure she speaks about nothing but Europe and western so-called civilization."

"You are quite right, mama!"

"Woe to her! Has not it been enough for her to spoil her own nature? Can she not stop herself from pouring her poisonous words into your ears? She is afraid of talking in my presence; that is why she preferred to sit on the balcony! She is Satan himself."

Sumayah said, "Oh, mama! She is your niece. You shouldn't talk about her like that!"

"I don't like her manners and her deviated behaviour." Sumayah's mother told her. "She has caused her mother's death. My sister never condoned her daughter's bad behavior. Now tell me, what did she say to you?"

"Mother dear, forget it. She never has ill intentions."

"I wish you knew her real character so that you would not be tempted to listen to her."

"Oh mama, take it easy. I never agree with her ideas, but I do not agree with you in calling her a Satan. She is my cousin."

Sumayah went to her own room, trying to forget Fitnah's words. She was sure of Ahmad's love and that he was an excellent person. She knew that her cousin was unhappy, and that all she had gotten out of life was an unemployed husband who was good for nothing. Due to a substantial inheritance, he is free to spend much on his pleasures without the least consideration of Allah's bounties in regard to gratitude and good works. Her cousin thinks of nothing but money. In fact, she lives for the sake of money. Sumayah decided to ask Ahmad about woman's status in Islam and his own viewpoint. She knew that he would no doubt explain everything to her and elaborate on the differences between the roles of men and women.

CHAPTER 2

Fitnah got into her car and drove away quickly, as if she wanted to escape. She arrived at her house, parked the car and walked directly to her room without greeting her husband, although she knew he was at home. She sat down on a chair and murmured, 'Woe to her! How stubborn she is. Was it not enough for him to treat me so cruelly that he has proposed to my cousin and renewed my pain? He thinks Sumayah matches his ideals and morals, while she is only making a show of being virtuous. Years ago, I tried to make him love me, but he never cared for me. He said I was a fool and a deviated person. He will soon know that Sumayah is no better than I am. I know how to draw her to this corrupted life of mine.

'I married this playboy in order to get his wealth and enjoy life. I must tolerate living with him for the sake of his riches. Oh, I will deprive Sumayah of Ahmad as he deprived me of himself. I won't allow him to fulfill his dream of marrying a committed Muslim girl. I'll show him this is impossible and that Sumayah is just like me. Now Ahmad is getting his doctorate while my husband, Hamid, has not even managed to get any degree. I'll never let Sumayah get such a husband as Ahmad. I know he is bright, clever and has strong belief, yet he is also stubborn, reactionary and full of vanity.'

At that moment, the door opened and Hamid entered. A smile was on his face as he said, "I thought you were sick. May I enter?"

Fitnah tried to appear normal as she told him; "I have a headache, that is why I did not join you in the living room."

Hamid said, "You look quite well! Does it make you sick to see me?"

"Oh, Hamid, do not make me nervous. I didn't know you were at home!" she lied.

"But didn't you see my car? You are absent-minded today."

Fitnah said, "I told you, I have a headache! Please leave me alone now. Do not make me angry."

"Alas I am nothing but one of your many lovers and." he began.

"Oh, stop it. I know what you are going to say, so don't repeat it."

Hamid said, "You don't want to hear it! You are lucky to have a husband like me, otherwise you are good for no one."

"What about you? "Fitnah asked. "Could any other woman tolerate life with you? You talk about me, but you forget all about yourself."

"Am I so bad?" Hamid asked her. Fitnah replied, "You should know. Had I not been a good wife, I would not have lived one day with you. There is nothing to benefit me in living with you!"

"Then why did you marry me? Why did you attract me to yourself?"

"Oh, what a rascal you are!" Fitnah exclaimed.

Hamid said, "Never mind! I know what attracted you to me! It is my wealth, which you adore. And you have beauty, which I love. I like to live free of limits and you do also, hence we match each other."

"Have you finished?" Fitnah sighed.

"No, I have not seen you for ages. At night you attend parties and during the day you visit friends and shops. You forget you have a house and a husband! Why don't we have a child?"

Fitnah became impatient and cried, "Please leave me alone. I am sick and tired. I must sleep!"

"Then you won't even have lunch with me?"

"No, go away", she said.

Hamid asked, "What if I go and never return to you?"

Fitnah was about to say: Go, I don't care, but she controlled her feelings. He is her golden goose! Can she give him up? She does not love him. She despises him and thinks of him as being a worthless creature, but for his wealth; even his indecency is nothing to her. In fact, she has encouraged him to adopt her loose way of living so that she can live free of restrictions.

His great wealth, luxurious house and magnificent car are too precious for her to risk losing. She smiled and said quietly "You know dear, life is dull without you, but I have this headache. Otherwise, I would have been happy to join you."

"I wish you were not so beautiful. Then you would see how I could treat you and make you feel less proud! Surely, you now think, 'I wish you were not so rich'. Had I been poor, I would not have been your prey!"

"Oh, Hamid, you do me an injustice by these words. I love no one but you."

"Thanks a lot. Yet you insist on turning me out."

"I always love to have you near me, but now I need to rest." "This is your usual way," Hamid said, leaving the room. "Sweet words but stingy deeds. I am leaving you, so be at ease."

He left the room, displeased. Fitnah imagined for a moment that she might lose him, but she dismissed such an idea, since she was sure of her own beauty. She said to herself, 'Oh, it is nothing important. As soon as I smile at him, he will come quickly. Now I must think about Ahmad, who never cared for my beauty and called me a foolish, deviated girl.'

She lay on her bed, thinking of only one thing: revenge on Ahmad and his belief, which blocked her way to his heart. No, she must engineer a revenge through her cousin. She is determined to do her best to spoil this marriage, and lay thinking of the best way to achieve her aim.

CHAPTER 3

Sumayah was anxious to meet Ahmad to ask him about women's status in Islam. He usually called on her every day on his way home from work. That afternoon, she welcomed him with a lovely smile. He felt that she had something to say, so he encouraged her to speak her mind. She asked him if he was ready to listen to her.

Ahmad told her, "By all means, I always like listening to you."

"I would like to know the difference in rights between a male and a female in Islam."

"There is no difference", Ahmad replied. "They have equal rights. They are both created of the same clay."

"Why, then, are limits imposed on women rather than on men?" Sumayah asked him.

"No limits are imposed on women except that which is necessary in regard to their nature and biological structure. Islam does not put woman under any kind of pressure."

Sumayah persisted, "Doesn't *hijab* hinder her from enjoying life as she likes? Is it due to my *hijab* that I cannot travel with you to Europe?"

"Oh no, *hijab* cannot prevent woman from doing anything. I would take you with me to Europe, if it were a healthy, decent society. I oppose Muslim girls' travel to Europe for fear that they may become deviated. If it were a useful journey, I would surely take you with me."

Sumayah asked, "Don't you think that seeing western civilization can be useful?"

Ahmad said, "This is exactly the point which is the source of much trouble. We Muslims should not think that civilization is a western phenomenon. In fact, if the matter is explored deeply, you will see that it is Islamic civilization that has brought to Europe its present scientific progress. European so-called civilization is nothing but an expression of the *jahilliya* (Pre-Islamic Age of Ignorance), with regard to European women."

Sumayah then asked, "Well, does not the European woman have her rights in full, the same as man?"

Ahmad disagreed, "Absolutely not. Through recent European laws, the European woman has gained only a part of woman's rights that are already granted by Islamic laws. The European woman has lost her feminism. She has become a mere commodity and is a tool manipulated by men. Islam has granted woman her independent identity. She is free to handle her own financial affairs and personal life. European women have been trapped by the false, bright colours of life exposed by the so-called liberation of woman. Freedom is just a cover with which man hides his own exploitation of woman at all levels. Believe me, my dear, if Europe was a good place, I would encourage you to go."

"I am quite aware of this. I only wanted sound evidence to answer anyone who doubts our Islamic morals and beliefs," Sumayah replied.

Ahmad said, "You won't find a better, happier life except in Islam and when Islamic instructions are respected and applied. I wish you really knew about the great misery that engulfs families deviated from Islamic norms. A marriage based on Islamic foundations will be quite successful. Our future life will certainly be happy."

Sumayah smiled and said, "I know you will do your best to ensure such a happy life. By the way, have you decided when you will begin your trip?"

Ahmad said, "I am on my way to settle that. It is a matter of a few days. Then we will be able to plan living, together in our own home when I return."

At this point, he said good-bye to Sumayah and left for his home. He promised to return later for further discussion.

Sumayah was sure of her Islamic belief; she just wanted to know the best, answers to all the questions raised by her cousin and others.

On his way home, Ahmad thought about his fiancée. He was sad that some deviated girls were trying to confuse her thinking. He decided to explain any matters that were unclear for her. Above all, he wanted her to be in thorough harmony with him in his beliefs and ideals. What caused him to seek her hand in marriage was her good conduct and strong personality. Ahmad recalled an old incident when an unreligious girl used many tricks to try to tempt him and trap him. He wondered what had become of her. He couldn't even remember her name. He is quite happy with the choice he made in his future wife.

CHAPTER 4

A week passed by and Sumayah was about to forget everything her cousin Fitnah had said. She was quite happy and a bit anxious about her fiancé's trip. One day, as Sumayah stood waiting for a bus, to go to her tailor, her cousin pulled up, stopped her car and offered her a ride. She got in and sat next to her cousin, who usually drove her own car.

Fitnah said, "I thought you said Ahmad has a car!"

"Yes, he has," Sumayah replied, "He is out of town on some business."

"One day I will come to know him, though I do somehow fear him," Fitnah said.

"You are mistaken. He is a kind and polite person."

"But you say he is strict."

Sumayah protested, "No, I never said that. He is very reasonable."

Fitnah told her cousin, "Perhaps to you he seems to be like that. He has managed to make you agree with all of his ideas."

"I do not agree with you! He never imposes his beliefs on me, but I do share these beliefs with him."

"Then you are truly happy?"

"We are", Sumayah stated.

Fitnah drove in silence for a moment and then said, "By the way, are you ever going to learn how to drive?" "No, it's not necessary. Ahmad can take me anywhere I wish to go."

"Of course!" Fitnah exclaimed. "He won't allow you to drive a car. This is a good way for him to know where you go. As for you, you cannot follow him, since you are a Muslim believer."

Sumayah asked, "Why should I follow him? Do you think I should sit next to him at his office? I'm not suspicious!"

"What about his parties and trips?"

"Women have their own parties and meetings."

Sumayah answered. "In any case, Ahmad does not attend parties of both sexes or night clubs."

Fitnah said, "You are being misled. All men are of one of two categories: some are nice and peaceful. They share all social activities with their wives. On the other hand, some are strict and prone to exploit their simple-minded wives and keep them at home."

Sumayah disagreed, "Well, I think a good man is a man who shares his ideals and beliefs with his wife."

"What a strange idea!" her cousin retorted.

"It is not. I have always believed this."

Fitnah continued, "Well, this was your idea when you were a child. Now that you are at the threshold of adulthood, you should have new ideas."

"No, I do not agree with your viewpoint."

"I am quite surprised at your behavior. I do not know how to keep you from destroying your future with such reactionary beliefs. You are an educated girl, yet you stick to these limits on the pretext of being a Muslim. We are all Muslims. Do you think these millions are wrong and only Ahmad is right? Think of yourself. By giving in to Ahmad, you are going to lose much."

Sumayah told her, "My submission is to Allah only. I have my own belief and I am quite happy with Ahmad and my future."

Fitnah asked her cousin, "Can you really be satisfied with this isolated, worthless life?"

Sumayah replied, "It is neither isolated nor worthless! It is what I long for and it is filled with pleasures!"

Fitnah argued, "You still don't know what real pleasure is. You are unaware of life, although you are over twenty years old. Ahmad has managed to mislead you."

"I am quite aware of life and of my right course in it. Anyway, I have never been interested in this corrupted social life of yours. My own girlfriends are all committed Muslims. I am neither ignorant, nor in need of your advice."

"Oh, I am very sorry. I didn't mean to anger you. I do not know why you are upset."

"I am not angry. But I do not like your words!"

Fitnah pretended to feel hurt, "I have alienated you. I feel like I am your older sister, and I am very concerned about your future. I am sure if I introduce you to my friends you will like them all and have great times. Now I have lost all hope. I have spoken frankly to you, and I apologize for this frankness."

Sumayah didn't want her cousin to be hurt, so she said, "That's okay. Please stop. The tailor's shop is right here."

"Sumayah, do you want me to wait for you?"

"No, thank you. I can manage by myself", she replied.

"How can I let you return by bus? I'll pick you here in an hour", Fitnah told her.

Sumayah didn't answer her. She just got out of the car, thanked her cousin for the ride and waved good-bye.

Sumayah left the shop when her work was finished, without waiting for her cousin.

That afternoon, Fitnah visited her to apologize for being unable to take her back.

Sumayah told her that she didn't wait for her. Then Fitnah told her cousin about the party of the previous night and how the singers sang until daybreak. She spoke about films and western film stars, and mentioned the hunting parties that she often attended with her friends. She did not forget to also talk about swimming and the beautiful swimming pools she frequented. Finally Sumayah asked, "What about your husband? Why don't you mention him? Has he no place in your heart?"

Fitnah was vexed, but tried to sound calm. She thought the question was a challenge. Her husband's personality is the Achille's heel of her life. She forced a smile and said, "I am an independent wife. My life is not mixed up with his. I accompany him only to special parties. We both believe in our rights to live free."

"How strange it sounds to me!" Sumayah remarked. "You always say that a woman should follow her husband anywhere he goes. Now you say you are free and have the right to do as you like."

Fitnah told her, "You misunderstand me. I mean to say that I accompany him on some occasions, but I do not allow him to follow me anywhere I go. I am sure of myself, but I doubt my husband. A smart woman should never believe her husband and should never allow him to play his own way."

"Do you love your husband?"

Fitnah hesitated and said, "Of course I do. He is a wonderful man. I will introduce him to you. We may visit you soon." Sumayah shook her head, "I am sorry, but I won't meet him unless Ahmad is present."

"Oh, Ahmad again! I see he is an obstacle in your way."

Sumayah said, "Please be careful. He is to be my husband and I love him. I won't allow you to undermine his character."

58

"Had I been here before your engagement, I would have prevented it" Fitnah declared.

Surprised, Sumayah said, "You don't have the right to deprive me of a happy life!"

Fitnah told her, "You are being silly. How could you agree to such an engagement without knowing him first?"

"It makes no difference; I came to know him soon after our engagement. I am neither silly nor was he imposed on me. I have free will and I am sure I won't regret my choice in the future. You believe a couple should enjoy close friendship before engagement. Yet a boy or a girl can deceive each other. Things usually are uncovered in the long run during marriage."

"You are wrong. Society does not consider matters as you do. You are the only one with such old-fashioned ideas," Fitnah said.

"By society, you mean your own friends. As for me, I do not believe you. There are many like me."

"I have not seen any of them", her cousin retorted.

Sumayah continued, "Of course you cannot see things my way. Your way of living has blinded you and you won't believe what you see or hear! Just like those who live in utter darkness."

Fitnah said sarcastically, "Go on! I enjoy your fanatic ideas. You lack nothing but a sanctuary, where you can pray and recite sermons day and night!" "You are wrong. It makes no difference to me, whatever you say!"

"What a pity! you just repeat the words of ancient times. How quickly you have lost your liveliness. I feel sorry for you. How often I have told Hamid that you are a very beautiful girl. He is eager to meet you. Alas! You speak of nothing but advice and wise sayings."

Sumayah disagreed, "I speak of life without its false, decorative mask."

Fitnah then said, "Ahmad is clever to have taught you all this."

"Don't talk about him like that. I wish you knew him so you could know his real nature."

At these words, Fitnah became pale and said weakly, "Of course, one day I will meet him, but not now."

"Why not? I am sure that upon seeing him you will change your mind and you will admire him very much."

"I do not like men of his type, whoever it might be."

Sumayah pointed to a photograph on a table and said, "Here is his picture."

Fitnah did not want to look, for fear that her feelings would betray her. She no longer loved him. Her love had changed into hatred and devilish intention. She avoided looking at the picture.

"Please look at him. Can such a man deserve your unjust attacks?"

Fitnah had no other choice but to look at the photograph. She turned her head quickly, saying, "Perhaps I have seen him once or twice at night clubs."

Sumayah angrily said, "I do not believe you, Fitnah. I love and respect Ahmad. I am proud of him."

"Being a wife myself, I do appreciate a happy marriage. I hope you will have everlasting happiness." After an awkward moment of silence, Fitnah left and Sumayah joined her parents in having dinner. She felt uneasy and longed for Ahmad's imminent return. She wished Fitnah was not her cousin, in which case she would treat her quite differently. She wished she could reform her cousin, but she was at a loss as to how to do so.

CHAPTER 5

Fitnah felt quite worn out as she entered her room and thought over what had passed between her and her cousin. She was afraid that Sumayah noticed her hesitation and saw the confusion on her face when she glanced at Ahmad's picture. She stretched out on her bed and released the reins of her thoughts. She realized the risk of visiting Sumayah's house. What if Ahmad had seen her there? Her designs would have been in vain.

Fitnah decided it was best to remain on friendly terms with Sumayah in order to carry out her revenge. Her aim was to spoil her cousin's future. Fitnah was well aware of her own corrupted conduct, therefore, she wanted to drag Sumayah into the same swamp. That night, she slept fitfully.

The next morning, Fitnah bathed, dressed and called Nadia, her maid. Nadia, a young, pretty girl in her twenties, entered her mistress's room and greeted her.

Fitnah cast a long look at her, then asked: "Has anyone phoned me?"

Nadia replied, "The master is at home. He answers all calls."

Then Fitnah asked, "What about yesterday afternoon when I was out?"

"He was at home at that time as well."

"Was he at home last night?" Her maid answered, "Yes. He did not leave his room."

"Is he sick?" Fitnah inquired.

Nadia told her, "I don't know."

"Has anyone visited him?"

"Not that I know of. In any case, I am not a spy, paid to keep an eye on him!"

"Have I asked you to do such a thing? Get out, you impudent girl!"

Nadia turned to leave the room, but Fitnah told her to stop.

"Look, Nadia", she said, "I don't like your make-up and how your hair is done. One would think you are on your way out to a party. Wear a simple hair-style and do not use heavy make-up."

"But why, my lady? Am I not free to dress, as I like?"

Fitnah replied, "Well, have you ever seen anyone with such make-up and hair at such an early hour of the day?"

Nadia answered, "You, my lady, usually do such a thing."

"I am a married woman and society expects me to dress so. In any case, what business is it of yours? You are only a servant, and I can dismiss you any time I please."

Nadia replied, "Can you really?"

"Yes, I can!"

"Why don't you do it now?"

Fitnah looked sharply at her, "You make me angry. That's enough nonsense and impoliteness. Go, I cannot tolerate seeing you!"

"It makes no difference to me," Nadia shrugged, leaving the room.

Fitnah was quite upset. She controlled the urge to slap Nadia in the face. She knew Nadia was quite aware of all her secrets, so she thought it best to control her feelings.

Fitnah told herself, 'What a poisonous serpent she is! She blackmails me with what she knows about me. I am a coward! Why should I fear her? What can she say?

Men and women have the same rights. Why should I fear a scandal? Everyone around me lives scandalous lives. Yet I do fear one thing, my husband, Hamid, who is unaware of the extent of my mischief. He is the only source I have of wealth and riches...Money dominates everything and can overcome all obstacles. Hence, I must tolerate Nadia's devilish challenge. I know what her looks mean. Hamid stays at home for her own sake! I should have fired her long ago, before it became too late. Anyway, she is my maid and it is my own mistake. Now I will go to Hamid's room.'

Fitnah put on an expensive silk robe and entered her husband's room without knocking on the door, in order to catch him by surprise. She found him relaxing in a comfortable chair. Soft music was playing.

"Oh, what a surprise to see you! I thought you were ill", Fitnah exclaimed.

Smiling, Hamid asked, "What makes you think so? I am quite well."

"But you have not left the house for two days. This is not like you."

"How can you say that? You are always the first to leave and the last to come home," Hamid told his wife.

Fitnah then asked, "Is it possible that you spend all the time in the house?"

Hamid replied, "Well, nights are enough for me!"

"Oh, Hamid, you irritate me by your indifference!"

"Do I? Anyway, lately I have found that I prefer to stay at home."

"How do you spend your time?"

"Reading books and listening to the news."

Fitnah laughed, "That is wonderful! Since when do you read books and listen to the news?"

"Oh, you do me a great wrong. Am I so stupid and uninformed?"

"Now, be frank and tell me why you are really staying at home more often than usual."

"I told you, I have always done that."

"But why?"

Hamid said, "I have some important matters to take care of here."

Fitnah said, "Now, speak out; do not make me nervous. What are these important matters?"

Hamid asked, "Why should you be upset about them?"

Fitnah replied, "Of course, I know what you are talking about, but I want you be honest with me."

"Have you been frank with me? "Hamid asked his wife. "When I recently asked you to come on a trip with me, did you give a good reason for declining to accompany me?" Fitnah paced back and forth, "So, you are trying to get back at me."

"Does your behavior call for revenge? You know me quite well, I am free to have my own way. Keep in mind, this is my house!"

Getting to the point, Fitnah said, "But Nadia is my own maid!"

"Yet I pay her salary and I am her master."

"Well, I can send her away whenever I like", she told him.

Hamid stated, "You won't do it!"

"What do you mean?"

Hamid, "I mean, we should not quarrel. Let us have a truce!"

"Why are you bargaining?" Fitnah asked.

"Call it whatever you like."

Fitnah said, "Oh, you get on my nerves!"

"What about mine? Am I made of stone? Have I no feelings?"

"Your nerves are made of iron," Fitnah told him.

"But you can crush iron"

"Really, am I such a strong person? Then we are equal."

Hamid disagreed, "Oh, no, you are ahead of me."

"I am proud of that!" Fitnah smiled.

Hamid said, "Then enjoy your pride. Now what good fortune has sent you to my room? I don't believe love has brought you here. You have not entered my room for ages. Surely you are in need of money."

"You don't want to see me!" Fitnah pouted.

"Oh, no, I always long for a visit from you. Be sure of that. My love for you has taught me patience. To speak honestly, I am quite miserable with your love. But there is no way out; I do love you."

Fitnah tried to respond to his words although she despised him and felt no love for him. She wanted to dominate him for the sake of his wealth. She even felt no humiliation knowing that her maid was her husband's mistress. The false civilization she lived in had stripped her of all dignity and female pride. All she cared for was money, so she smiled and spoke passionately to her husband.

Fitnah moved close to her husband and whispered, "Oh, Hamid, you have no idea how much I love you. But believe me, it is life's concerns that keep me away from you." Her sweet words made Hamid forget her indecent conduct, his girlfriends and his mistress, Nadia.

"I am your slave. I can't live without you", Hamid assured her.

Fitnah found it hard to exchange words of love with him, but for the sake of money she carried on the role of a loving wife.

CHAPTER 6

Upon Ahmad's return from his business trip, he hastened to his fiancée's home.

"How happy I am with you", he told Sumayah.

Sumayah replied, "I fear something may spoil our happiness. I wish it could last forever. Ahmad assured her, "Real happiness can overcome anything. Neither the passage of time nor any incident can harm true love. The angelic brightness of your face overwhelms me. Love that changes like the weather is not real love. It is only an illusion, which vanishes in the end.

Happiness that stems from materialistic pleasures is sure to disappear. It is just a dream, after which one awakes to reality".

"Be sure, my dear, that our marriage will be wonderful. Our souls are mingled and our hearts are close. Our ideas and beliefs are in harmony. Nothing can spoil our relationship."

After Ahmad left her, Sumayah felt comforted by his words and dreamt of a joyful future.

Meanwhile, Fitnah's house was ablaze with colored lights. She had invited a special group of close friends to celebrate her husband's birthday. She dressed carefully, in the latest fashion, and precious stones encircled her neck and wrists. Fitnah looked quite beautiful as she smiled and welcomed her guests, who arrived one after the other.

Salah, a young photographer, was one of her guests and was in love with her. Fitnah had given up all other lovers for his sake. He tried to keep as near as possible to her throughout the evening, however, among the guests there was a new face who was attracted to the beautiful hostess, but was too embarrassed to begin a conversation with her. A friend of Fitnah joked, "Imagine Fitnah, my friend was reluctant to come to your party." Fitnah asked, "Really? Why?"

The friend said, "He feared you might ignore him!" Fitnah, in order to arouse her lover's jealousy, said flirtingly, "Oh, how could I ignore such a well-known engineer?"

Sami, the new friend, expressed words of thanks and Fitnah found it easy to make him attracted to her. She decided to use him as a threat if her lover, Salah, even threatened to leave her. She continued to chat with the young man until she was certain of his interest in her. Then she left Sami and went in search of Salah, who had left the group.

Fitnah knew he was annoyed by her conduct. She looked everywhere, and finally discovered him in the arms of one of her close friends in a secluded corner of the garden. She was quite upset at having lost him so quickly. She came near the couple and exclaimed,

"How wonderful! You have left the party to hide here and enjoy yourselves."

Salah was taken by surprise and the girl was very embarrassed.

Fitnah remarked, "I knew that you were occasionally unfaithful to me, but not to such a degree in my own home!"

"Fitnah please..." Salah began to say.

"Stop your nonsense, you, who change your partners like you change clothes."

Salah said, "But, it is you who..."

"I know what you want to say, so don't bother to explain yourself," Fitnah told him angrily. "It is my own mistake. I trusted you. Now I see you are no better than any other playboy."

Salah pleaded, "Oh, Fitnah, you never thought about my feelings. You lavished all your attention on that engineer."

Fitnah said, "What has that to do with you? Have you ever tried to behave, at least in my house? Go, you mean nothing to me!"

"Please, be fair to me, let me..." She turned away before he could finish his sentence. Salah was very unhappy, although his companion tried to cheer him up. He rejoined the party and begged for Fitnah's forgiveness.

In fact, Fitnah had planned to enjoy the evening with her lover, but she found that her husband was missing.

She went to his room and saw him sprawled on his bed, quite drunk. Her maid was sitting near the bed.

Fitnah asked, "Why has he come here?" Nadia told her, "I brought him."

"How could you have dragged him along?"

Nadia replied, "He was not drunk at that time."

Fitnah exclaimed, "You gave him too much to drink. How dare you? You tricky..."

Nadia interrupted, "Please, my lady, I am not a tricky person. I am the same as you are, not less, not more. At least I am satisfied with one, while you..."

Fitnah began, "Shut your mouth you stupid little..."

"I am not as stupid as you think I am," Nadia defiantly said, standing up.

Fearing that her guests would notice her absence, Fitnah ordered Nadia to wake up Hamid, since it was a matter of politeness to say good-bye to his guests. Feeling hatred and disgrace, she joined the others: Her lover tried to speak to her, but she gave him no chance.

Hamid was too intoxicated to wake up, so the guests left with only Fitnah to bid them good night. Salah alone remained. He knelt in front of Fitnah and swore that he didn't care for anyone but her. He was clever enough to articulate words of love and she finally forgave him. After he left, she went to her husband's room to find him in a deep sleep, so she went to her own room.

Fitnah could not sleep, and thought of Ahmad, and how she would get her revenge. She again thought of how to drag her cousin into her corrupt way of life. She felt sure that many men would be attracted to Sumayah's beauty and reasoned that no woman can resist temptation. She finally fell asleep, and awoke to see the sun high in the sky. She did not call her maid to assist her in having a bath. Fitnah bathed, dressed and tried to leave her home without attracting the attention of Nadia, but the maid surprised her by saying, "What? Are you leaving without breakfast?"

Fitnah did not answer, while Nadia continued, "Why haven't you called me to assist you this morning? Are you still angry with me?"

Fitnah replied, "Oh, no, I am not."

Nadia then said, "Have you seen my master?"

"No, how is he?"

"He is not feeling well, and plans to stay at home," her maid replied.

Fitnah felt a surge of jealousy, but managed to control herself. "Take care of him," she told Nadia. "I have an important appointment and I must leave now."

Fitnah hurried out and drew a deep breath, as if she had escaped from a prison. Her house was like a hateful cage of trouble and pain.

CHAPTER 7

Three weeks later, speaking over the telephone, Fitnah told her cousin, "I have missed you, Sumayah. Are we not cousins? Why haven't you called?"

Sumayah replied, "I am sorry. I have been busy with my fiancé, who is about to leave. In any case, I hope you are well."

"Oh, I'm sorry to hear that. I'll try to visit you soon. Why not now?" Fitnah asked.

Sumayah replied, "Oh, no. I cannot."

"Then I will come to see you this afternoon."

When Fitnah arrived, Sumayah greeted her warmly and apologized for not visiting her. Fitnah began talking about her life, "I have mentioned you to my husband, He is anxious to meet you. I also told him about Ahmad. He could not believe his ears. He wondered if such men still existed in this modern age. I also told him you are happy with your future husband."

Sumayah remained silent. She felt that it was better not to discuss personal matters with her cousin.

"Does Ahmad allow you to attend parties?" her cousin asked.

"Yes, of course. But only decent ones."

"Then will you come to my birthday party next month?" Sumayah replied, "Yes, with pleasure."

"You will see scores of men round you." Sumayah became angry, "Oh, then I won't come. I had forgotten that you invite both sexes. You want to make a show of me. How dare you say such a thing?"

"I never meant that, I just want you to stop sanctuary. I feel sorry for you and I want you to have a good time!"

"I am quite happy, so don't take the trouble", Sumayah answered.

Fitnah remarked, "Strange! Are you really happy to remain within these four walls?"

Sumayah told her cousin, "I am happy whether I go out or stay home."

Fitnah argued, "Your freedom is limited. What is this scarf around your head and neck? What is this black loose coat that hides your beautiful figure? You look like a shapeless sack. It is a crime that you wear old women's clothes. Why should Ahmad wear the latest fashion while you are deprived of that pleasure? It is a real injustice and a crime that a modern girl like you should obey a man; any man. What kind of a religion is it that makes a woman subservient to a man?"

Sumayah disagreed, "Islam does not make a man exploit a woman. This is a groundless claim. Muslim women, in fact, have privileges that no other women in other religions have. Muslim women's rights are protected in Islam."

"What are these privileges? Are they nothing more than cooking, cleaning and serving a husband and kids?" Fitnah asked.

"Islam does not impose these forms of work on a woman, but Islamic concepts do illustrate the benefits and blessings of caring for her husband and children. She has the choice of doing these services. She is never forced to do them. As for *hijab*, it is a decent dress that can protect a woman from devilish desires. I am proud to observe my *hijab* and I will always stick to it. Anyway you should admit that I am much happier than you are,"

Sumayah concluded.

"Well, I don't mean you only. Perhaps Ahmad has made you close your eyes to reality. I am against any ideas which are reactionary and which control the future of young girls. It is like destroying their best years of life."

"What you brand reactionary is a concept concerning social reform, with which women acquire a respectable status. In fact, nakedness is actually a reactionary idea, since it moves woman backward, back to the Age of Ignorance."

Fitnah replied, "You are misled. You have merely learnt a few words and phrases from Ahmad. If you think carefully, you will realize the truth. This is a modern age and modern society is all around us."

Sumayah protested, "I don't agree with you at all. I have great faith in Islam. I don't repeat Ahmad's words, but Islamic norms and ethics."

Fitnah realized it was useless to continue. She talked of other things and soon left her cousin. Sumayah decided to tell her fiancé about their disagreement.

CHAPTER 8

The next day, Sumayah told Ahmad about her relatives and mentioned Fitnah, saying, "She is my cousin. She is very beautiful; but I don't like her life- style."

Ahmad was surprised, since he knew that his fiancée's relatives were believers with good reputations. Sumayah explained, "She grew up an orphan. Her father died when she was a child and my aunt spoiled her. She is carefree and careless. Fitnah married at a young age and went to Europe with her husband. They stayed there for three years and then returned home. Her husband failed to get his degree, but he is quite rich and can afford a luxurious life. My cousin has been misled by Western values and European civilization."

"Who is her husband?" Ahmad asked.

Sumayah replied, "I don't know him, but they say he is very rich."

"Wealth, ignorance and idleness are all dangerous factors, which can destroy a person" Ahmad said. Sumayah agreed, and added, "Beauty too. My cousin is very beautiful. I will show you her picture. "Sumayah brought out her photo album and selected one of the pictures. "This is Fitnah before she traveled to Europe." Sumayah did not look at Ahmad's face, so she did not notice his surprise and dismay as he recognized the playgirl who, years ago, had tried to trap him. He wondered how such a girl could be in contact with, much less related to, his fiancée. He reflected that Fitnah probably remembered her failure and might harbour feelings of resentment. Ahmad was about to warn Sumayah to avoid her, but he hesitated, since Fitnah was now a married woman and was possibly leading a decent life. He did not comment on the picture, and gave it back to Sumayah, who said, "See how attractive she is? I wish she had better morals."

Ahmad said, "She is beautiful. But I don't like such artificial beauty under which lies devilish motivations. Real beauty is pure and natural; not a beauty which is created by cosmetics."

"You are right", his future bride agreed.

CHAPTER 9

Meanwhile, Fitnah was still scheming about how to get revenge. She felt that her husband did not deeply care for her, but just enjoys himself, yet she knew that she could handle him when she decided what role he would play in her little drama. Finally Fitnah devised a plan in which Hamid could help her achieve her aim. She slept soundly that night and woke up feeling quite happy. She rang the bell to summon her maid, who helped her to bath and dress. Fitnah put on her best silk robe, perfumed herself and walked out of her room. Her maid was surprised, "Are you expecting visitors, mistress?"

Fitnah replied, "Oh, no. How could I greet anyone while I'm wearing these house garments?"

Nadia then asked, "Where are you going?"

Fitnah answered, "To see my husband".

The maid was vexed and Fitnah felt great humiliation when she reflected that her rival was her maid. Yet she considered the great wealth of her husband and knew it was best for her to endure the odd situation.

She knocked at Hamid's door and entered, saying, "May I come in?"

Hamid was just about to leave the home, but he changed his mind upon seeing Fitnah.

"Am I disturbing you?" Fitnah smiled.

Hamid replied, "Not at all. You are always welcome."

"It looks as if you have an important engagement", she told him.

"You are more important than anyone else", Hamid said, embracing her.

"Oh, thank you! You are such a good-hearted man", Fitnah flattered her husband.

In fact, Fitnah was well-aware of his good nature and that she could easily influence him.

They sat down and she began talking about some friends. She was saying, "There is a great struggle going on between the rich man and the artist. Both are determined to get a beautiful girl that I know. Yet I think neither of them will succeed."

"Why not?" Hamid asked.

Fitnah explained, "Years ago there was a similar situation, and she chose someone else."

"Then she is married."

"Oh, no" Fitnah said. "He was her boyfriend for some time, and she gave him up a few months ago."

His curiosity aroused, Hamid asked why.

Fitnah surmised, "Perhaps she is looking for someone more rich, even richer than her present suitor."

"Where do they meet her?", her husband asked.

"Well, at several places. She is clever enough at attracting men to her. Sometimes she claims she is married or engaged. She also often pretends to be a decent girl and a pious Muslim."

Hamid was intrigued by the description of this girl.

Fitnah left his room without saying anything more about her. She returned to her room and thought to herself, 'I can lose nothing in this game. It makes no difference to me whom Hamid has affairs with. In any case, his other mistresses are of no use to me, while this one will help me achieve my revenge. Yes, I will get back at Ahmad, his belief and his morals. This proud beauty, my cousin, can be trapped by Hamid's immense wealth and charm. All women adore money. Since I cannot bring Sumayah to my group, I'll at least show Hamid the way to her. I don't care whether Sumayah or Nadia is his lover. As long as his wealth is under my control, I won't feel jealous. Hamid is nothing to me.'

'Sumayah is a simple-hearted girl, and she has never heard words of love from a stranger. It will be very flattering to her and surely she will soon give in to Hamid's declarations of love. I think she may soon regret her engagement. The last time I spoke with her, she was very quiet. My words have affected her. I'll go on talking until I take off the mask that Ahmad has covered her with. Now I must know where she spends her free time. It's best that I wait until Ahmad leaves again for Europe. If he is nearby, he will spoil my plans.'

CHAPTER 10

Ahmad's next trip was drawing near. He enjoyed the few days that remained with his fiancée. He took her to a public park near a mosque. They sat and watched the people walking by and were pleased to see several worshippers enter the mosque.

"How wonderful Islamic prayer is," Sumayah said. It causes one to feel security and happiness."

Ahmad agreed, "That is quite true. Mosques are the best places for Muslims to meet and to manage the affairs of an Islamic state, as it was at the advent of Islam. Decisions were reached in the mosque and the laws were created which ruled half of this globe. The eternal call of *Allahu Akbar* to prayer echoed throughout dozens of Islamic countries."

Sumayah mused, "How wonderful those days must have been."

"Yes, and it is useful to study them. Since we are committed Muslims, and we live according to Islamic instructions, we are happy. Our happiness is to be derived from our firm stand against all deviated ideologies. It means a lot when we defeat the evil intentions of the self." The Prophet (S.A.W.) says, 'Whoever adheres to my Sunnah when the ummah is corrupted, has the reward of a hundred martyrs.' "

"The early Muslims were the masters of the world", Sumayah remarked.

Ahmad corrected her, "Actually they were leaders, since Islam considers all people as free human beings. There are no masters or slaves in Islam. A Muslim is evaluated only with regard to his piety and righteousness. The early Muslims did not want to dominate and exploit others. They wanted to guide people to the right path, to purify their thinking. Islam is a universal doctrine, and is beneficial for all ages and all countries."

"Dominating or enslaving others cannot result in a nation's progress. With such ideas, the Muslims reached the Persian Court and the Roman Imperial fortresses."

"Did any women play significant roles in the early days of Islam?" Sumayah inquired.

Ahmad told her, "Of course they did. Woman participated in shaping Islamic history. She proved her ability and personality as a human being entrusted with a mission. She was never less active or less brave than a man."

"What is the difference between the Muslim woman of those days and the Muslim woman of our time?" Sumayah asked.

Ahmad said, "Woman today is misled. Man has fooled her and deprived her of all her innate dignity. She has been pulled down to the bottom of society. Our duty is to awaken her from her slumber. We should save her from this pitiful situation into which she has fallen."

"I am afraid it is difficult to reform the Muslim women who have decided to follow Western ways," she said, thinking about her cousin.

Ahmad said, "A real Muslim woman cannot be fooled easily. She knows the true nature of her religion and is secure in the knowledge that Islam has given her all her rights. Anyway, it is not too late to reform the misled ones. Even a misguided Muslim woman still has good qualities within herself, which can remove her blindness one day."

"When and how?" Sumayah asked.

Ahmad said, "I think the time is drawing near. Women who imitate the West suffer terribly in the end. The breaking up of Muslim marriages has increased due to this blind imitation. Such marriages, if they are unIslamic, cannot be happy ones, or survive for long."

Sumayah said, "Some of the misled women claim that *hijab* is imposed on woman by man and it undermines her status."

Her fiancé replied, "This is mere nonsense and an echo of foreign propaganda. The obligation to dress modestly is not confined to women only. However women are more attractive and can have a stronger influence than men; therefore, her *hijab* is more significance. *Hijab* acts as a sort of protection for women. Islam wants women to cover the source of their beauty, as a means of increasing their dignity. Muslim women at the advent of Islam participated in battles, attended the wounded and encouraged the Muslim combatants. The Islamic modest dress they wore did not hinder them from having an effective role in their society."

Sumayah sighed, "How I wish we were like them."

Ahmad told her, "Every woman can be like them."

Sumayah asked, "How?"

Ahmad said, "Struggling for the sake of a belief has many degrees. A Muslim woman can achieve this any time. The struggle against temptation and corruption and enjoining the good and forbidding the evil can all be forms of struggle for belief. In fact, the struggle against selfish desires is of more use than all other struggles. Imam Ali (A.S.) said, *'To purify the self of corruption is more difficult than any actual struggle'*."

The call to prayer could be heard, so Sumayah and Ahmad arose and entered the mosque to perform their prayers.

CHAPTER 11

Fitnah found out the exact day and time that Ahmad was leaving for Europe, and she was ready to put her plan into action. She began a conversation with her husband, saying, "Do, you remember that beautiful girl I told you about?" It seems she has found a new lover, an older, rich man,"

"How do you know this?" asked Hamid.

"I haven't seen such a girl in the clubs we frequent or at any of the parties of our friends," Fitnah quickly told him, "Oh, you wouldn't recognize her. Sometimes she covers herself completely in a large black coat and scarf. On other occasion she looks like a model from the cover of **Vogue** magazine. She's unpredictable."

Fitnah hoped that such a description would intrigue and interest her husband. She continued, "This young woman is seeing a friend off at the airport tomorrow morning. I might go to the airport myself to see her and introduce myself."

"How will you find her? The airport will be filled with young women", Hamid asked.

His wife said, "Well, I know she is fair-skinned, has large brown eyes and is slender. Her clothing will guide me to her."

Fitnah returned to her bedroom. She thought to herself, 'I'll pretend to feel unwell tomorrow. Knowing Hamid and his interest in mysteries, I will stir him to go instead of me. He will see Sumayah and be captivated by her beautiful face.'

Next morning, Fitnah's plan succeeded, as she complained of a severe headache and she soon saw Hamid backing his car out of the driveway. Meanwhile, Sumayah, her father and Ahmad waited in the airport lounge for his flight to be announced. Sumayah was saddened by her fiancé's imminent departure, and Ahmad told her, "It's difficult to leave you, my dear. I shall return as soon as possible. It's only a matter of a few months' separation. Be strong in faith."

Ahmad's flight was called and they bid each other farewell. Sumayah was almost overcome by tears, an she leaned on her father's arm for support as they walked back to their car.

Sumayah's father tried to distract his daughter's attention, telling her, "There was a strange man who just stood and stared at you in the airport."

She replied, "The world is filled with people like that. Don't let it bother you. We should feel sorry for those who waste their time and energy."

They reached their car and soon arrived at their home.

CHAPTER 12

Two days later, Fitnah visited Sumayah and they sat in the garden talking. Fitnah told her cousin, "I usually have a walk in the morning. Does Ahmad allow you to do such a thing?"

Sumayah was annoyed by the question, but she acted indifferently, replying, "Sometimes I take walks in the public park near the mosque."

"You do not go to other places?" Fitnah inquired.

"No."

"Do you go alone?" she then asked.

"Usually, but sometimes I go with my father."

Sumayah said, wondering why Fitnah was asking her. "I thought you didn't go to public places due to religious traditions", Fitnah told her.

"Religious traditions do not contradict polite behaviour. Any action or practice should be in conformity with Islamic ethics," Sumayah replied.

Fitnah sighed, "Oh, what an injustice. How can a pretty girl like you have such a meaningless role in life?

Your beauty is hidden under this long coat and scarf.

Your ideas are buried in the pages of books. You are worthy of the title "Miss Universe", but you do not know your real importance. A teenager cannot understand the influence of her beauty on others until someone whispers words of love to her. Then she will see love all around her.

"Why should you spend all of your time alone while Ahmad enjoys himself in Europe? You avoid the friendship of men in your homeland while he enjoys his time with European girls."

"Fitnah, be serious! What sort of life can a girl have when she becomes the object of men's desires? Most men think that the physical beauty of a girl is the most important aspect, whereas it is only temporary and superficial. Hence a girl's role is determined by men and her development is limited as a result. A girl with sound thinking and wisdom can develop without the influence of men. Religion guides girls and teaches them the meaning of life. A Muslim girl is not deprived of her freedom and she submits to Allah only. A girl who does not respect her feminism and who has no dignity becomes a mere commodity."

She continued, "As a matter of fact, I pity you for having such a life. I think you are a slave to fashion and cosmetic sellers. I don't know how to reform you; perhaps my mother can influence you. I shall call her to come talk with you."

Fitnah stood up, saying, "Oh, no. I am leaving now. I expect some guests tonight."

Sumayah also stood up and walked her cousin to her car, glad that their conversation had ended. Fitnah went straight home and told Hamid he could sometimes find Sumayah at the park. As she had predicted, Hamid thought her cousin was very beautiful, and he assumed that the man who had been with her at the airport was her boyfriend.

CHAPTER 13

Sumayah and Ahmad exchanged letters regularly throughout their separation. He wrote of his love for her and his longing to see her. She wrote to him about how she spent her time reading or taking walks.

One day Sumayah went to the public park and sat on a bench in a quiet corner. As she was reading a book, she felt that someone was standing near her, but she paid no attention. A stranger sat next to her on the bench and said, "Good afternoon."

Sumayah frowned and did not reply. She resumed her reading.

"What book are you reading?" asked Hamid.

Not wishing to be rude, Sumayah told him, "A novel"

Hamid remarked, "I'm certain it is a love story. Love is the most wonderful and sacred thing in life."

"I do not agree. Religion and faith are the sacred things in life," Sumayah said.

Hamid disagreed, smiling, "Love and wealth are essential elements. Love without money is tragic, and money without love has no value."

Sumayah decided to find another bench to sit on, but first she told the stranger, "You are quite mistaken. Money, which you consider to be so important, misleads people and causes regret in the end. Human dignity cannot be found with wealth and a person without dignity is deprived of all things."

She then got up and left the park. Hamid was surprised by her stance. He expected her to be easy prey, and he became more determined to win her. Hamid told himself, 'How stubborn she is! Nevertheless, I know how to seduce her.' He also left the park and drove his car up to the gate. Sumayah was standing at the bus stop. Hamid saw her and decided to follow her home. 'I must learn where she lives,' he told himself.

Sumayah boarded a bus and Hamid followed it at a distance. She soon got off the bus and entered a tailor's shop. Hamid was disappointed, but he felt sure that he would get her one day.

CHAPTER 14

At home, Sumayah found a letter from Ahmad awaiting her and she eagerly read it. She forgot an about the strange young man at the park. That night, she wrote a reply to Ahmad's long letter.

The next day was warm and sunny. So Sumayah decided to take a walk in the public park. Before long, she heard someone say, "How nice to meet you again."

Sumayah turned and saw Hamid, "I beg your pardon! You are mistaken." she said.

She tried to ignore him but he insisted, "I don't think you have such a poor memory. As for me, since I saw you last, I have not stopped thinking of you. And of my wealth, which is in the millions, is at your service."

Sumayah looked at him and said indifferently, "Oh, yes. Now I do remember you! You are the man who lives for money."

Hamid replied, "That's correct. Wealth, as you know, brands the fortunate."

"It is a pity that such men lack any other significant qualifications," she remarked.

"Money can bring other qualifications," said Hamid.

Sumayah said, "None but of fashion, which is very unimportant for a man." Then Hamid said, "Your style is strange compared to your personality."

Surprised, Sumayah said, "What do you know of my personality?! My style, as you call it, is not strange. I don't know why should I answer you. In any case, I have tried to advise you. You may realize one day that money is not everything. If you think that with money you will succeed in life, you are quite wrong."

Sumayah was annoyed to have seen the young man again, and she left as soon as she finished speaking without the least intention of waiting to hear his reply.

CHAPTER 15

Fitnah was eager to know how well Hamid had succeeded in his efforts to attract Sumayah, yet she was afraid to ask him lest he should suspect her game. Hamid spent most of his time outside the home and the maid, Nadia, was vexed. She assumed he had found another lover.

Fitnah decided to visit Sumayah in the hope that her cousin would talk to her about Hamid. Sumayah and Fitnah once again sat in the garden. Fitnah noticed that her cousin was not at ease and she accounted for it according to her imagination. She was certain that her husband had managed to contact Sumayah. Fitnah spoke again about men in general and how they love beautiful ladies. Sumayah remained silent, thinking that there was no use in advising her cousin.

At home, Fitnah noticed that her maid was out and she thought that Nadia might have gone out to look for Hamid. In fact, Nadia had seen Hamid talking with Sumayah at the park, but she was sure that their meeting had been by chance. She continued to spy on him.

CHAPTER 16

Sumayah decided to stop going to that particular park for some time and visited other public gardens instead. As she was strolling through a garden one day, she saw a woman begging for money and Sumayah gave her a substantial amount of money. The woman was quite happy and uttered words of gratitude as she walked away. At that moment Sumayah heard someone say, "How generous you are, Miss...? You should not have given the beggar that much money."

Sumayah was shocked and dismayed to see the same man who had spoken to her on previous occasions standing nearby. She became pale and looked around. On seeing lot of people nearby, she felt safe and said in a loud voice, "How dare you speak to me? Why are you following me?"

Hamid stuttered, "In fact, I ..."

Sumayah told him, "You are a stranger to me, and I don't even know your name. You are very impolite to address me."

The woman beggar was standing nearby and Hamid found it difficult to explain his behaviour. Sumayah's anger confounded him, and he didn't reply.

"Why don't you answer?" Sumayah asked. I swear by Allah I would have called the police, had not it been for this wedding ring on your finger. I pity your wife."

Sumayah left the park, and Hamid saw the woman beggar pick something up off the ground. He grabbed her hand and shouted, "Thief!" Then he quickly asked the waiter to follow Sumayah, since the beggar had picked up a gold coin near where she had been sitting. Sumayah returned and confirmed in front of everyone that she herself had given the coin to the destitute woman.

Hamid was very embarrassed and surprised by Sumayah's behaviour. He thought deeply about her and said to himself, 'In fact, I am not a good person. How worthy it is to do good for others! I never thought such virtuous girls existed."

CHAPTER 17

Sumayah returned home and wrote along letter to her fiancé. A few days later Sumayah and her father went to the public park where her father met some of his friends. Not long after Sumayah sat down, she was addressed by Hamid, who quickly said, "Please Miss, may I speak with you?" Sumayah tried to discourage him with a look of annoyance and disapproval, but he persisted saying, "You are like an angel; you have done me a lot of good. Please do not hold back this light that has removed the darkness around me."

Surprised by his words, Sumayah asked, "What has made you speak like this?"

"I have behaved badly towards you. I ask your forgiveness for my rudeness."

Sumayah was aware of the changed tone of his voice. She looked at him for a moment and felt that he was being honest. She said, "I do forgive you. Actually, I feel sorry for men like you."

CHAPTER 18

Hamid returned home feeling the joy of an awakened conscience. He felt deep regret for all his past actions regarding Sumayah. In the past three weeks Hamid ceased all his indecent behaviour. It seemed as if he had awakened from a deep sleep.

He kept thinking about the things Sumayah had said. He felt he owed her a lot. She had inspired him. Hamid asked himself if he was in love with her, but he was not. His feelings were based on respect and high esteem. He wished he could see her often in order to learn from her strength and good will. He decided to continue visiting the public park in order to see her again.

The next morning, Hamid stayed in his room. He did not allow anyone to disturb him. As he recalled his past life, he was shocked to realize that he had gained nothing from life but the wealth he inherited from his father. He had wasted nearly half of his fortune. What would happen to him in the next ten years, when his money came to an end?

He thought about how important it was for a person to have a decent life and a faithful wife. He knew his friends would give him up as soon as his money was exhausted. Even his wife would leave him if he was not rich. He knew Fitnah loved his wealth and never valued his love. Hamid wished he could escape from his corrupt life and go back ten years in time to when he was quite innocent and pure.

Sumayah's ideas dominated his thinking. He never thought he would meet such an ideal girl who would bring him to such a reality. Since he had met her, he looked with open eyes and realized much more than before. In fact, he had recovered from blindness.

He turned his thoughts to his wife and wondered why she had misled him. He could not justify her behaviour. Could it be from malice? But Sumayah was not her type. In any case, there must be a reason, He was sure she longed to hear from him about his adventures, but he would never satisfy her curiosity.

He was sure she would not ask him herself. Fitnah tried often to begin a conversation to make him mention Sumayah, but he was clever enough to disappoint her. In fact, he was surprised at his firm stand. He used to think he would never have enough courage to resist his wife.

CHAPTER 19

Sumayah felt satisfied by the thought that she had done her best to guide Hamid. Ahmad approved of her efforts. He wrote to her, "...remember that struggle does not only mean war. You have managed to guide a deviated person."

One day, Sumayah visited Ahmad's mother and Hamid happened to see her enter the house. He waited at the roadside until she came out, and he said, "Excuse me. I don't want to annoy you, but I must talk with you."

"What do you want to talk about and why do you follow me?", demanded Sumayah.

Hamid said, "In fact, I would like you to talk and I will listen to you. I have found great comfort in your previous words."

Sumayah then asked, "What does your conscience tell you?"

"It tells me to reform; to give up vices and stick to the right path," was Hamid's reply.

"That is what I had expected would happen. Your inner goodness has been awakened", Sumayah confirmed.

Hamid complained, "Yet, I still feel as if I am lost."

Sumayah answered, "Why do you have such doubt?

You based your worth on money. Now your money can serve you. It won't control your life." She then suggested him to read few books. The bus arrived and Sumayah began to board it.

Hamid begged her to stay a bit longer to talk more.

Sumayah shook her head saying, "You should keep on reading those books, and you will learn a lot."

"Can I have your address to contact you when I face a difficulty?", Hamid asked.

"Oh no. That's not possible," she replied.

"But I feel as if you are my saviour. You are the light that illuminated my inner soul. I have much to tell you." Hamid pleaded.

Sumayah looked at him questioningly, "Such as... ?"

"Well, private matters that I can't speak about at the roadside", Hamid said.

Sumayah boarded the bus and advised him, "I suggest you keep on reading worthy books. I am sure you shall learn a great deal."

Hamid stood at the bus stop for a moment, deep in thought. He wondered why he didn't follow her in order to learn where her house was. Was it dignity or honesty that stopped him? He went into a nearby bookshop, bought some books and returned home.

Looking through the window, Fitnah saw Hamid enter carrying a package. She thought the parcel was clothing. She never imagined that her husband would buy books one day. In the past few weeks Fitnah had noticed a change in her husband's behaviour. He stayed alone in his room more often than usual and seemed to have given up attending clubs, parties and theaters. She was at a loss to explain his new conduct. Fitnah reasoned that even his failure to get Sumayah, could not have caused such a change.

Fitnah also noticed that her maid, Nadia, had become pale and quiet. She was glad to see Nadia suffering from jealousy. She called her to get some information.

"Now Nadia, I want you to be frank. Tell me what are you hiding from me?" Nadia looked surprised but said nothing. "I have noticed that Hamid has been acting strangely recently," Fitnah remarked.

"What do you mean?" asked Nadia.

Fitnah said, "Oh don't play the fool. I know about the affair between you two. You know that I want to know everything about my husband. Now tell me what is the matter with him." Nadia remained silent.

Fitnah persisted, "I won't tell him anything. I won't tell him you spy on him because it is in my interests that you do so."

Nadia began, "I only saw him by chance..."

Fitnah interrupted, "I know it was not by chance. Now tell me what you have seen."

"Well, I saw him in a park with a young lady. I could not believe my eyes. She looked decent and respectable, but...", Nadia hesitated.

"But what," Fitnah said with excitement.

Nadia told her, "I saw them again and he was listening to her talk."

Fitnah demanded to know, "What did they say?"

"How do I know," Nadia replied, "I was outside the park. Then I saw him once again with her at a bus stop."

"Did he give her a lift?", Fitnah questioned.

Nadia replied, "I didn't see since I left for fear he might see me."

"Thank you Nadia. Go now, and tell me everything about him that you learn in the future."

Fitnah was pleased at the news. She imagined that her revenge plan had succeeded. She anxiously awaited Ahmad's return so that she could congratulate him on his choice. She decided to leave her husband unquestioned until Ahmad returned. She then turned her thoughts to her new lover, the young engineer.

.

CHAPTER 20

Hamid continued to read the books he had bought. Slowly he acquired spiritual and religious knowledge. He enjoyed reading the books Sumayah had recommended, and he hoped to meet her again. Wherever Hamid went, he took a book along with him.

The next time he visited the park he saw Sumayah again and greeted her politely. Hamid asked her to allow him to sit next to her and she did not object. Hamid began the conversation by saying, "I have read the books you advised me to read. They have given me much to think about."

"That is wonderful," Sumayah replied, "How do you feel now?"

"I feel as if I were newly born. All my ideals have changed," he said with feeling.

Sumayah nodded approvingly, "That is good. Forget your past and think of the future."

"I am trying to rid myself of the past, but...", Hamid looked down.

"What is it?", Sumayah asked.

"My wife, whose ring saved me from a scandal when you refused to call the police. Her lifestyle reflects my past.", Hamid replied slowly.

Sumayah inquired, "Can't you reform her?"

Hamid sighed, "I can hardly do that. She is quite deviated. She...".

Sumayah guessed, "Is she an unfaithful wife?"

"Yes. She is like a butterfly, always chasing her wishes and desires," Hamid confessed.

Sumayah thought for a moment and said, "An unfaithful wife is harmful for you. Why don't you give her up?"

Hamid said, "As a matter of fact. I love her."

Sumayah disagreed, "You are mistaken. If you truly loved her, you would not let her behave in such a way. You only feel the powerful influence of her physical beauty. You love your house, yet do you allow strangers access to it? You love your money, do you allow other to share it with you? This feeling towards her is not of love. Love is something sacred that overwhelms a pure, innocent soul. If you think carefully you will find that you actually dislike her because of how she is."

Hamid confessed, "I fear her."

Sumayah explained, "That means you do not love her. A lover does not fear his beloved. The weak fear the strong. Now you are no longer weak, because faith and virtue are stronger than vice and indecency. You are now a believer. Try to free yourself of her influence."

Hamid said, "As long as I am with her, I can't get rid of my past. I must leave her."

"I advise you to try to reform her," Sumayah said.

Hamid replied mournfully, "It is impossible."

Hamid changed the subject, "Can I ask who the old man was who was with you in the airport?"

"You saw me there?" Sumayah was surprised, "That was my father. We had gone to see off Ahmad."

"Who is this Ahmad you have just mentioned?", Hamid inquired.

"He is my fiancé. We are engaged," she answered.

Hamid was very amazed by this information and he had much to think about as he slowly drove home.

CHAPTER 21

Hamid felt a great struggle taking place within himself. He thought about how to free himself of his wife's domination and start a new, clean life. He reasoned that he wouldn't succeed until he was free of Fitnah's influence.

Hamid had previously believed that all people were corrupt to some extent until he saw the goodness embodied in Sumayah. The experience had started as a failure, but it led him to ultimate success. He felt very hurt by his wife's behaviour, and he wondered if he really could still love her. Could he go on living with her while she had no concern for morals?

A few days later, Hamid decided to visit his grandmother, who lived in a nearby village. Fitnah saw him packing a suitcase and getting ready for a trip. She asked, "Where are you going, Hamid?"

Hamid told his wife, "I'm going to pay Grandma a visit. She has been seriously ill recently and has asked for me."

Fitnah asked sarcastically, "Are you a doctor who can cure the aged?"

Hamid answered, "I am not a doctor, but I am all that she has. I'll get her a good doctor."

Fitnah continued in her sarcastic tone, "Since when do you think of others with such concern?"

Hamid stated, "Since I recovered from my blindness."

Fitnah didn't understand what her husband meant, but she thought he was joking. "How long will you stay?" she asked.

"As long as she needs me," he replied. "I may stay longer than a week if necessary. I haven't seen Grandma for ages," Hamid said as he carried his bags to the car. He got in and sped away.

Fitnah said to herself, "I know that you are not really going to your grandmother. Enjoy your week with Sumayah. Let this be a farewell week. Ahmad is coming back soon."

Hamid was truly concerned about his grandmother's health. He drove at a high speed to reach her before it was too late. He hoped to be able to ask her for her forgiveness. At last he arrived at her home and knocked on the door.

A servant opened the door. "How is she?", Hamid asked as he brushed past the maid. She told him that the old woman was dying. Hamid explained that he was her grandson and the servant said, "Oh you are Hamid! She has been asking for

90

you often." The maid led him to a door, Hamid entered and found an old friend of his grandmother's at her bedside.

She recognized him and said, "At last you have come. This will mean a lot to her."

Hamid asked, "Has a doctor seen her?"

"Oh yes," answered the maid, "but he cannot help her."

Hamid bent over his grandma and kissed her hand.

He cried, and the sick woman moaned. He called her gently, "Dear Grandma, it's me, Hamid. I have come to see you." With great difficulty, the old woman opened her eyes and a smile appeared on her face.

"Grandma dear, I am very sorry that I did not come sooner. Would you forgive me?" Hamid said as he held her hand gently.

The old woman nodded her head slowly and seemed to be whispering a prayer. Hamid held her hand until it became cold. At last she died and Hamid was grieved. He attended to her funeral ceremonies the following day and returned home at a late hour.

The house was engulfed in darkness, except for Nadia's room. Fitnah's room was empty and he was sure that Fitnah had gone out. He tried to sleep but uneasy thoughts kept him awake. He went to his wife's room to see if she had come. It was after midnight. Hamid called for Nadia to ask about his wife.

"Where is your mistress," Hamid questioned her. Nadia did not reply and he repeated his question.

Nadia decided to get revenge. She was no longer interested in staying in that house since she had lost Hamid's love. She told him, "Fitnah left the house yesterday evening."

Then Hamid asked, "Do you know where she has gone?"

Nadia answered, "No, she told me nothing."

"Be frank. Don't you know where she is?" Hamid persisted.

"She went to the theatre," Nadia said.

Hamid asked, "Alone?"

Nadia answered, "No. With Salah."

"How do you know this?" demanded Hamid.

Nadia admitted, "I followed her and learned everything."

Hamid asked the maid why she spied on his wife.

"She has destroyed my life. She made you leave me."

Nadia told him with tears in her eyes.

Hamid replied, "Oh no. You are mistaken. She had nothing to do with that. Now tell me, did Fitnah spend the night in Salah's house?"

"Yes. I saw them both. They were drunk." the maid said.

"Do you swear to that?" Hamid asked.

Nadia said, "I swear by God that I have seen them. You can go now to his house and make sure for yourself."

Hamid was very angry. Although his wife had flirted with many men in the past, she had never been so openly disrespectful and careless enough to do what she had done that night. Hamid decided to dismiss Nadia, and to make up for the wrong he had done her. He said, "Nadia, you are clever and young. I'll help you find a suitable job.

Tomorrow I'll give you two week's pay and you may leave."

Nadia thanked him and went back to her room.

Hamid waited anxiously for his wife to return. He felt he should try to advise her as Sumayah had suggested, even if his wife was unlikely to change. At last he heard Fitnah's car enter the garage. As soon as she entered her room, Hamid knocked on her door and entered. Fitnah was surprised to see her husband standing in front of her. She murmured, "Hamid."

"Yes, Hamid the cheated husband." Hamid said.

Fitnah tried to control her feelings and spoke calmly, "Oh, you are back soon. How was your trip?"

Hamid ignored her question and said, "Yes, I have come back soon, to find that you spent the night in your lover's house. You have lost all your pride and self-dignity for the sake of your desires."

Fitnah asked, "What is the matter with you? Are you drunk'? Do you talk about pride because you failed?"

"I am not drunk, rather, I am more aware than I. I have ever been before. I am trying now to advise you," Hamid told his wife.

Fitnah said with contempt, "Keep your advice for your own self."

Hamid asked, "Where were you last night? When did you leave your boyfriend?"

"What has that to do with you'? I am free to do what I like," she retorted.

Hamid spoke, "Freedom does not mean cheating or deviation."

Fitnah laughed, "The cheating one claims he has been cheated. Why don't you tell me where you were last night?"

"I have nothing to be ashamed of," Hamid stated. Fitnah tried to change the subject. She asked, "Why have you come back so soon? Have you quarreled or has the traveler returned?"

Hamid said, "I don't understand what you are talking about. I am back, and that is enough. I can't tolerate your behaviour any longer."

Fitnah sneered, "Why are you so angry? Is it because of your failure in your love affair with Sumayah?"

Hamid was shocked, "What love affair!? What failure'? Who is this Sumayah you have just mentioned?" Anyway, I have decided to rid myself of you, and the disgrace and shame I feel due to you."

Fitnah continued, "How soon you forget her name?"

"I don't know a name to forget. Now I want you to justify your indecency and give up your disgraceful behaviour." Hamid said.

His wife exclaimed, "You are indeed crazy! Do you think a young, beautiful woman like me can be content to live with you and stay at home, to spend her life serving you? I am free and have the right to enjoy myself! I won't waste my life for a husband like you."

Hamid became angry, "Instead of apologizing, you speak like this to me!?"

Fitnah shouted, "I won't apologize! What are you going to do? We both have affairs and all of a sudden you sit in judgement against me!?"

Hamid was more calm now, "I am your husband. I'll make my decision now unless..."

"Yes'? Unless what? I won't change. We are both free to go where we please. I'll see Salah whenever I choose," Fitnah said defiantly.

Hamid asked, "Do you know what that means? Are you aware of the consequences of what you are doing?"

"You're sounding like an old man who repeats out-of-date expressions. Have you learned them from your girlfriend, Sumayah? She is Ahmad's fiancée", Fitnah said angrily.

Hamid finally realized whom she was referring to. He shouted, "How dare you talk of her!"

Fitnah glared at Hamid, "Now you confess that you know her."

Hamid said, "I didn't know that was her name until now, since you mentioned Ahmad's name. She is an angel in human shape. She is truly an example of virtue and goodness.

Fitnah was taken aback, "What do you mean?"

Hamid said, "You wouldn't understand. How can someone like you know such a virtuous girl?"

Fitnah asked, "Isn't she now your mistress?"

Hamid exclaimed, "I seek refuge in Allah. She doesn't even know who I am. She is a pure, chaste girl and she has her own man, who is no doubt worthy of her. You have tried to lead me along a deviated path. I was in darkness and now I am no long lost. This girl whom you falsely portrayed as being a corrupt person like yourself, is an angel. God has purified my soul. I am no longer a deviated, sinful person."

"You never tempted her?" Fitnah laughed.

Hamid insisted, "I am not her lover. I only respect her. She is a torch guiding my lost soul. At first, I was foolish enough to believe you. I tried to tempt her and failed. She could have called a policeman, but she tried to guide me. She felt pity for you when she saw the wedding ring on my finger."

"Does she know of me?" Fitnah asked, frightened.

Hamid replied, "How could she know you? She only knows I am a married man. As I told you, she does not even know my name."

Fitnah, greatly disappointed at this turn of events, remarked, "So you couldn't seduce her."

He replied, "Can the devil mislead the righteous? I have decided to divorce you. I have always been wrong. I have never loved you and I won't love you in the future. I am tired of living as an animal, with animal desires. Now you are nothing to me. I'll give you your dowry, which can help you find another fool. I have tried to help you but you have rejected my attempts. You are still following your deviated ideas."

Hamid left Fitnah alone. She understood that her wicked plan had backfired, destroying her life. She had lost everything.

CHAPTER 22

Sumayah was expecting Ahmad within a few days.

As she finished shopping one day and was waiting for a bus, Hamid stopped nearby and walked up to her. He greeted her saying, "I have been looking for you, sister."

"What for'? Have you read the books?" she asked.

"Yes, I have and I have bought new ones. I spend much of my time reading," Hamid said.

"Then you'll learn a lot," Sumayah commented.

"I have something to tell you. I have freed myself of all my hateful past." Hamid said.

"God bless you, but how?" Sumayah looked surprised. At that moment her bus arrived and she said she'd be at the park the afternoon if Hamid had something to say.

In the afternoon, Sumayah went to the park. On seeing her, Hamid came and sat near her. He began, "I have left my wife. I tried to guide her, but it was in vain."

"How I pity her!" Sumayah remarked.

"Oh sister Sumayah, do not say that. She is not worth feeling sorry for." Hamid said.

Sumayah was surprised to hear him say her name.

"How do you know my name?" she asked, "I don't remember having mentioned it to you."

Hamid said, "That's right. You never did. It is Fitnah who mentioned it to me." Sumayah became confused, "Who is Fitnah?"

"My ex-wife. The one I have told you about." Hamid explained.

Sumayah thought deeply. Could this possibly be her cousin? She asked, "How long have you been married?"

Hamid told her, "Four years. We spent three years in Europe and we have returned only recently."

"Oh, I see," Sumayah could hardly speak.

Hamid asked, "What is the matter? You look pale. Have I annoyed you?"

"Oh no," Sumayah assured him, "What has Fitnah told you about me'?"

"In fact, I haven't been very honest with you. Fitnah herself pushed me into following you. She gave me a very different impression about you. She lied, as a matter of fact. I was quite naive to have believed her. You know the rest of the story," Hamid said.

"Has she really done that?" Sumayah could not believe her ears.

"Yes. I swear by Allah she has done it. She described you for me so that I could recognize you that day at the airport." Hamid confessed.

"What a woman! I never thought she was so wicked," Sumayah exclaimed.

It was Hamid's turn to be surprised, "Do you know her?"

"She is my cousin." Sumayah told him.

Hamid said, "Oh, then you are the cousin she used to talk about!"

"About my old-fashioned ways and out-of-date ideas?" Sumayah asked.

Hamid replied, "Exactly."

"Why?" Sumayah asked.

Hamid explained, "That's just how she is."

Sumayah said, "Please stop talking about her. She is suffering terribly now." Sumayah was quite amazed by her cousin. She wondered why Fitnah hated her so much. She had never hurt her. She stood up saying, "I must leave now."

"Can I ask when your fiancé is coming home?" he asked.

Sumayah said, "He is returning next Monday, God willing."

Hamid asked shyly, "May I be with you to welcome him at the airport?"

Sumayah answered, "Yes you can. I have told him about you."

Hamid smiled, "Thank you and good-bye for now."

On the following Monday morning, Hamid was at the airport with Sumayah and her family. "Do you think he will mind that I've come?" Hamid asked.

Sumayah assured him, "He will think of you as a brother."

Ahmad arrived and Sumayah introduced Hamid.

Hamid offered them a lift in his car. Along the way, Hamid praised Sumayah's efforts for his guidance. He mentioned his ex-wife's name and wondered what motivated her to act in such a way against Sumayah. Ahmad reasoned that she meant to have revenge and destroy his life. She never imagined that true faith and belief could protect believers. At last virtue prevails while devilish plans come to nothing.

Sumayah asked, "But why would she plan to get revenge on you?"

Ahmad explained, "She knew me years ago. I had forgotten about her, but I know it's the same Fitnah. She tried to trap me but she failed."

"Oh what a wicked woman," Hamid cried, "It's difficult to believe she's Sumayah's cousin!"

Sumayah said, "Yet she is. I really do pity her. It is not her fault. It is the deviated society that has misled her. Had she been in contact with Islamic ideals, she would not have fallen prey to any corrupted society. There are many people like her. Let us strive for their guidance and hope that Allah may help us."

Ahmad and Sumayah married soon after and Hamid became a good Muslim believer.

THE END

Novel 3

TWO WOMEN AND A MAN

Rihab sat alone, talking to herself about the recent events that had taken place within her home. "….everything is over. Hasanat has achieved happiness, having decided upon a harmonious future for herself. All the guests have left after celebrating the happy occasion with Hasanat, whose finger is now embellished with an engagement ring. She has got the man of her dreams and is now thinking of her future happy marriage. Everyone left, praising the bride and groom. What bothers me most is that I now have to go to my room and suffer tortuous boredom and isolation. How cruel it is to have to live in this spiritual alienation.

My family is against me, on the pretext that I am wayward….

In fact they are! With their background and old-fashioned ideas that are the mainstay of their lives, they are all deviated, even my sister Hasanat, who now thinks she's chosen the right path and tries to make out that she's a saint. She is really misguided and abnormal. How could she agree to marry a man whom she has never seen, and who is far away?

He didn't even take the trouble to attend his own engagement party! Instead he asked his father to represent him! They say that he is a committed believer, and then he's the same as Hasanat. Both of them are crazy. How could he ignore beautiful European women and choose someone like Hasanat? He could get the most beautiful girls –he is rich and charming. Anyway, it must be some defect in himself that made him turn to Hasanat and neglect those beauties. In fact, Hasanat is beautiful and educated, but I never thought, she could get such a man. Anyway he is a complexed person -she won't be happy with him."

Rihab tried to dismiss the subject from her mind. She took a book from the shelf and tried to read. The book was entitled '**Nothing Counts**' wrote by an Egyptian Author.

The book read "Nothing is important. Neither dignity nor conscience, not even what comes after death." She enjoyed reading the story, written for people like herself and read till late.

The next morning, Rihab awoke late. She sat listening to the happy voices of her mother and sister in the living room. She dragged herself out of bed and joined them with a forced smile on her face. She saw her sister was wearing a white gown. She was happy and cheerful, satisfied with her future. Jealousy increased in Rihab's heart, but she tried to look normal. She said to Hasanat, "How's the bride today?"

Hasanat said, "All praise be to God, quite well. I hope to see you a bride soon too."

These words angered Rihab and she maliciously said, "Perhaps a man from Africa will send to ask for my hand, just as a man from Europe did! Huh! As if there aren't enough men here!"

Hasanat had no wish to prolong the conversation and said, "God knows what is best sister."

Rihab continued scornfully, "I know how to build my future myself. I won't marry someone I don't know."

Hasanat said defensively, "Why do you say I don't know him? I know everything about my fiancé. It is enough to know that he is a committed believer."

Rihab persisted, "Is it enough to be religious? You are still young. I fear you may understand life too late."

"What do you mean?" said Hasanat.

Rihab replied, "You should be with your fiancé now, so that he won't meet with other girls. You are here surrounded by the four walls, while your man is free enjoying himself living it up with the girls!"

Hasanat said quietly, "I am sorry to tell you that you are wrong. I would not have agreed to marry a man who was playboy. Mustafa is a righteous believer and does not care for loose women; that is why I am happy to have him. Since he is a religious person, he is deterred from such a life. His belief provides him with immunity whether he is here or in some other place."

Rihab was about to respond when their mother stopped the argument saying, "That is quite enough. You both have work to do. We are going to have visitors this afternoon."

The days passed and Hasanat was quite happy except for Rihab's silly comments. For Rihab, the days passed slowly and were boring. She was vexed to see her sister always happy and cheerful, listening to people's congratulations.

A week later, Rihab returned from her office to find the postman at the door, just about to knock. When he saw her, he gave her a letter addressed to her sister Hasanat. It carried a European stamp. She knew it was from Mustafa. She hid the letter in her bag and did not give it to her sister. After dinner she hurried to her room to read it. Wickedness made her open and read, the nicely written letter.

In the Name of God

Dear Hasanat,

Assalamu Alaikum

Despite the long distance that separates us, I have chosen you. This is my first letter to you. I have enjoyed many days thinking of you throughout the past weeks. You are the hope I waited for, and I am overwhelmed with longing to be with you. My dreams came true when I found you, my treasure. These words can tell my feelings of love since I am deprived of your presence. Now that you are part of myself, I can tell you how much I love you. I have loved you though I have not seen you, because I know you love what I love, and believe in what I believe in. I shall always be faithful to you once this holy bond has joined us together. Such a relation would not have existed but for your faith and religions commitment and your acceptance to marry me.

As for me, I think of marriage as a spiritual and ideological relationship with no false materialistic values. I have chosen you as a wife to build an ideal married life, one decorated with the flowers of faith with a torch of Qur'anic rays, supported with the Islamic injunctions of love, compassion and sincerity. We are both devoted to God first and then to each other. May God bless our spiritual unit and protect our love and guide us to His path. I wish I could keep on talking to you, but I fear you might prefer short letters.

My love to you

Yours forever,

Mustafa

10ᵗʰ October, 1970

N.B. *Enclosed is my photo for you. I expect to get yours as soon as possible.*

With great bitterness, Rihab read the letter, with each gentle word, she felt a sting of fire. Her hatred increased to such a degree that she decided not to give the letter and the photo to Hasanat. She spent the day suffering jealousy and was at a loss as how to rid herself of the letter. She read it several times and suffered more and more pain. She wished the letter was addressed to her, and not Hasanat. She spent a sleepless night, and read it for the tenth time. She said to herself "Beautiful handwriting, beautiful photo, nice words that reveal an emotional nature. Hasanat would have rejoiced at reading it, she would have felt happy, her happiness disturbs me…" Rihab decided to tear the letter up. Then an idea flared up in her mind. She murmured to herself, "No, I won't tear it up. I'll burn it and enjoy watching the fire devour his words of love." So saying, she went to fetch a match.

She saw a bundle of small coloured candles in a golden ribbon with the words: 'Happy Birthday' written on them. She laughed nervously and took out one candle. She said to herself, "How nice to burn Mustafa's letter with Hasanat's candle. This is her gift to me for my 18th birthday. I have kept it to burn Mustafa's letter with, I'll burn her happiness…"

Before burning it, another idea came to her mind. She thought there was no use in burning it, as he would inevitably write her another letter and certainly she could not hope to find the postman at the door again. Thus, burning the letter would be of no use. She sat thinking for some time. She would write a letter to Mustafa using Hasanat's name. She would try to destroy his love for her. Also she would give him another address, her friend's address. She decided to keep the letter in case she needed to read it again. She sat at her desk and wrote:

Dear Mustafa

I am grateful to you for your nice letter and loving words. I was also satisfied with a short letter, as I do not like long ones. You said that writing could replace seeing each other. I think that is nonsense. An imaginative person might think in such a way, in order to convince himself of something. But to me there is no use in letters. What can a letter do as I know nothing about you? How you spend your time? With whom? You are in a country with every kind of enjoyment and entertainment. What will be left of you when you come back to me? I think there is no need to be religious. Today there is not such a sharp conflict between the oppressed and the oppressors, or a class struggle. There is not one exploited helpless group that makes us search for a means of saving it, or search in the darkness for a ray of light. Hence we create for ourselves a Supreme Power, which is stronger than darkness and higher than oppression. By such a belief we satisfy ourselves with hope in such a Power. We wait for it to solve our problems and remove our sufferings. For this reason man came to believe in God and, as a result have a religion. Don't you agree with me that we are no longer in need of such a belief since man has found the way to justice? Anyway, I am sorry to write such ideas, but you see I am a frank person, and like to deal with others frankly.

My wishes and regards for you

Hasanat

N.B. Please send your letter through the following address:

To: Miss Mida Naji ………

Rihab posted the letter to Mustafa. She felt a pang of conscience. She was sure she could destroy her sister's happiness, but still she maliciously dismissed her accusing conscience. She waited for the result of her plot. Mustafa was anxious to get the letter. He was overwhelmed with love and happiness. But as soon as he read it he was stunned and greatly disappointed. He could not believe his eyes. He read it again to assure himself of its contents. Was it really from Hasanat, the girl whom his sister, Zainab had often praised for her righteousness and had herself chosen her to be his wife? Could she be the writer of such a letter? Was she the one with whom his hopes would be fulfilled? Yet she spoke frankly enough to confess that she did not even believe in God! How hard it was for him to accept! How could this have happened? How could his sister have been cheated by her? She was her best friend. What could he do? Mustafa tried to control his feelings after the shock of the letter had passed. He first thought of writing a letter to his sister to blame her for the choice of such a girl and to take steps to divorce her. Then he dismissed the idea. He thought of a quick divorce as a means to escape his responsibility towards her. He had to guide her, to enjoin the good and forbid the evil. Perhaps he could guide her to the right path. He could decide later for divorce. The more he thought of the matter the more he found the idea acceptable. He then wrote to her the following letter:

In the Name of God

To: Hasanat

Assalamu Alaikum

I apologize for being late in replying to you. I have tried to overcome the shock that your frank letter caused me, and it was not easy, but my religious duty has caused me to discuss the matter. You say there is no need for religion. Are you serious? Have you been joking? I don't know how you could have such ideas. I think you are the victim of deviation and misguidance. I am writing to you as a brother writes to his sister. I am bound by social and religious duties to you. You claim, in your letter, that there is no need for religion and belief in God. You should know that belief in God is not the result of injustice or oppression. It came into existence long before injustice or class disputes. What class conflict was there at the beginning of human life, when foodstuff and cloth and land were common for all? Belief in God has been known since the beginning of creation and man's first knowledge about life. You may ask for proof of this. Can't you see that everything has its own qualities and features, drawn on the pages of history? History has given us sound evidence of that.

If you want examples you can have them. In Egypt, the Egyptians were the oldest people who believed in the spirit and its renewed life after death, in its punishment or reward. That was at a special level in regard to their concepts. They symbolized the spirit, in various ways: a flower, a bird and sometimes a human face. Such symbols are clear from archeology and history. They worshipped the Founder of everything, as is clear from their prayers. They considered whatever the heart and the tongue comprehended as having been given by the Founder of life. One of their Pharaohs, Akhnatoon, was famous for his meditation and thinking. He tried to reform religious rituals, as is clear from his prayers which history records thus: "How countless are your creatures of which we know nothing! You are the One God and there is no other lord but You, You created earth at Your will, and furnished it with men and animals..." This happened in Egypt. In India, the historians are not sure of the age when the worship of God started. Some say it started fifteen centuries before the birth of Jesus (as). Some say six centuries before that. Max Muller, an authority on European languages, says: "Whatever the age of the gathering of the written anthems was, prior to that age, the Indians believed in One God Who was neither male nor female, nor had any human natural limitations." Muller interprets one of their anthems common five centuries B.C., in the following way: "There was neither day nor night. There was none, but the One.

China knew religion through the worship of the Sun and the Moon and the Stars and the Winds. The greatest of their gods was the God of Heaven, who controlled the universe and decided the life course of every human being. In Persia, Zurradasht mentions Honnuz the Worshipped as following:

"Oh Honnuz the Merciful, the Creator of the World, the most Sacred, who is the Mightiest in Heaven and Earth?" Honnuz answered, "My name, which is dear from the nature of my heaven, is the Mightiest." They also believed in the existence of a passage where good spirits and devils, come together on leaving their bodies (at death), to meet the God of light and King of Justice. They believed that a balance was set up that the spirits were questioned about their deeds and excuses. They believed that one gate opened into Paradise and another to Hell. In Babylon, where in the most ancient civilization was to be found, archeological studies indicate the Babylonians' belief in the Creator. They believed in the God of Water and the God of Heaven and the God of War and the God of Soldiers. In the Hellenistic civilizations of ancient Greece, the idea of one God was mentioned by one of their wise men who blamed his people for their worshipping of several gods, 6 centuries B.C. History proves man's belief in the One God, centuries before the birth of Christ. This itself indicates that the belief in the One God is a very early human idea.

I mention these things without claiming that the idea of religion was clear at all stages, it has always been influenced by the cultural level of the various successive generations and was thus affected by them. Although not monotheism, it indicates a belief in God in a manner that accords to the ideological understanding of those times. I do not wish to disturb you by writing you a longer letter. Perhaps, you could read a book written by the Egyptian writer Al-Aqadd entitled "God". It would give you more information about this matter and help you accept what I have written.

God is our guide, wishing you every good.

Mustafa

Rihab read the letter and spent the night thinking about it. She tried to compare her knowledge with what he had written to her, to see which was the one more firmly based on sound evidence. She could come to no conclusion, and so reverted to her natural stubbornness. She awoke early the next morning to write her reply. She tried to avoid seeing her sister Hasanat, in case she should feel sorry for her and change her mind about spoiling her marriage.

In fact Hasanat, in recent days had been looking more concerned and unusually silent. She hardly laughed at all and her face had grown pale. Rihab knew the reason for Mustafa's supposed negligence, as Hasanat had never read his letter. Rihab was happy to see her sister suffer silently, although sometimes she felt a prick of conscience. This letter she wrote to Mustafa:

Dear Mustafa,

I was sorry to see that my letter hurt you. I was awaiting a similar letter to your first one, but instead, you rushed to defend your ideas, and put aside words of your love. Perhaps you had found me to be worthless of such feelings? Anyway your talk about the origin of man's belief was quite interesting and the historical evidence that you cited were clear. But I still maintain that belief in God is a means for the weak who feel defeated in the face of the strong. Such a weak person who feels he cannot protect himself, searches for an imaginary Power to protect him from danger. This is the basis for belief in God, and religion. I believe, we are not weak and that we can protect ourselves by various means, why then should we attach ourselves to the unknown in order to get the power that in this day and age, we do not even lack.

I am waiting for your answer.

Hasanat

Rihab waited anxiously for the answer. She wanted to hear his answer after she had agreed with nearly his entire first letter. But she feared her plot might be discovered if his sister returned from her journey. Suppose he wrote to his sister and blamed her for the choice; surely she would contact Hasanat, her best friend, and then everything would become clear. When Rihab thought of this, she became very uneasy. She tried to dismiss such ideas from her mind, and continue her 'game'. Soon she got the following letter:

In the Name of God

Dear Hasanat,

Assalamu Alaikum

I was happy to that you agreed with some of my ideas. I hope this will be the start of our ideological agreement. Yet I am still surprised by your ideas about belief in God. Had that been the case, the prophets would have been the weakest of individuals, whereas we see that all of those who called the people to worship God, were in some way or other strong. For instance, Prophet Noah continued calling his people to believe in God for hundreds of years with persistence and great energy. With great effort he built the Ark, despite the mockery and ridicule of the people; he never gave-up. When the great flood covered the whole earth, he and his family went aboard the Ark with peace and security. He neither feared the vast waves nor was he disturbed by the disappearance of his unbelieving son. These are all clear indications of his strong will and mighty character. Then there is the Prophet Abraham (as) who firmly stood up against his enemies, the pagans. He was not scared by their threat to burn him. His great belief in God turned the raging fire into something harmless to him. Doesn't this indicate a strong will and personality? Could anyone dare to say that Abraham was a weak idle person? What about Moses (as)? He entered Pharaoh's court with nothing but his brother and their faith in God. He didn't fear Pharaoh's threatened horrible revenge. Doesn't such a stance indicate firmness and strength. Jesus (as) as well persisted in calling people to the right path. Our Prophet Muhammad (swas) struggled for the sake of God. He never ceased calling people to worship God even when all the tribes of Quraish were against him and bargained with him to give up the message. His reply to them was, "By God, if you were to put the sun at my right and the moon at my left, I wouldn't give up this issue."

Throughout his life, the Prophet practiced heroic actions. I ask you to read his biography in order to learn more about him. Thus, you should come to know that the prophets were the strongest, the most courageous and the firmest among their people. You should read a book entitled 'Faith.' You will surely enjoy it and benefit from it, but I am still ready to answer your questions.

Mustafa

Whilst waiting for Mustafa's reply to her letter, Rihab had sometimes felt uneasy, and had found herself abhorring her wicked behavior. Hasanat bore her pain silently, sometimes feeling depressed and imagining the most awful things. She could not explain her fiancé's behavior. As a matter of politeness he should at least have written her a short letter, and he should have sent her his photo, as she had not seen him before their engagement. Such feelings overwhelmed her at times, although in her saner moments she did not believe the things that came into her mind and tried to find different excuses for him. She thought, he could be busy or even sick. Perhaps he wrote to her, but his letter had been lost in the post. She found such excuse acceptable, and was happy thinking that he had written to her and thought as much of her, as she did of him. Anyway she awaited his sister's return from holiday; perhaps she would know the reason for his negligence. Hasanat busied herself with reading books.

One day Rihab came to her room. Surprised, Hasanat welcomed her sister. Rihab sat near her, not knowing what to do. Hasanat said, "Have you got a day off? Why aren't you at the office today? I hope you are not ill." Rihab said, "I've a bit of a headache, So I phoned my friend asking her to tell the office, I won't be in today. I'm bored and need something to read. Can you give me a book?" Hasanat was surprised, as her sister was not usually interested in her religious books. She said to her, "Feel free to choose whatever book you like." Rihab got up and stood in front of the shelves while Hasanat watched her to see what books she would take. She was surprised when Rihab took one about 'Faith' and a biography of the Prophet Muhammad (swas). Rihab could not explain her choice of books, and so hurriedly left before Hasanat had time to ask her any questions. In fact Hasanat felt happy to see her misguided sister turning to the right path of faith. She forgot her own sadness for a while as she visualized Rihab as a committed Muslim, engaged to a good Muslim such as her own fiancé, Mustafa. Then she remembered Mustafa, she felt sad and depressed. What could Mustafa be? She resorted to her book and tried to concentrate on reading.

Rihab read the two books she had borrowed from her sister and feeling in need of his explanations, she wrote to Mustafa the following letter:

Dear Mustafa

Perhaps I have been a bit late replying to your letter. Reading the books you suggested has kept me busy for quite some time. I have to admit that your style of writing is very convincing. I enjoyed reading a biography of the Prophet Muhammad (swas) (as you advised me), for a few days and thus I learnt the details of his life. I have also started reading the story of 'Faith' that answered many of my questions.

But I still cannot understand why should I worship a God that I cannot see, or perceive through any of the five senses. Isn't much worship really mere tradition, based on illusions? I am sorry to disturb you with such a question, but I feel I need your answer. Such questions cause me uneasiness. I hope your letter can give me some comfort.

Hasanat

Mustafa received Rihab's letter with the intention of deciding his future relationship with her, according to it's contents. If he found her still negative, his relationship with her would have to come to an end as there was no use in trying to guide her. If he found her understanding and positive he would continue his duty of guiding her, not so that she could be his future wife (he no longer wanted her) but as a person going astray. When he found in her letter that she was responding to his ideas and reading the religious books, he wrote her this letter:

In the Name of God

To: Hasanat

Assalmu Alaikum

Thank God that I am now writing to you in optimistic frame of mind. I was happy with what I read in your letter. I am quite ready to answer your questions. They are clear indications of your desire for knowledge. But my answer in this letter will be short and in the form of questions for you to answer:

1. What is the difference between a human being and an animal with regard to comprehension since both have senses?

2. Have you ever considered something to be impossible?

3. Do you believe in the existent and the non-existent?

I would be grateful to you for answering the questions.

My best regards to you
Mustafa

In great eagerness to read the answer to her question Rihab got Mustafa's letter only to find no answer but amazing inquiries. She found it difficult to understand what had prompted him to ask them. Hasanat was in her room so she went to her, hesitantly. The more Rihab became aware of God, the more she felt uneasy with regards to her sister.

She could not find the answers to Mustafa's questions without Hasanat's help and her sister had recently been helpful to her, since she had seen her interest in religious books. Rihab sat near her sister not knowing which book could help her find the answers. She had to ask her sister, but was silent for a while first.

Hasanat said, "I hope you've finished reading the two books?" Rihab answered, "Yes" Hasanat then said, "Did you find them interesting?" "Yes." replied Rihab. Hasanat guessed that her sister was in a quandary about books, as she had nothing else but books to give to her. She wasn't bothered by Rihab's brief answers, and only said gently, "You know you are free to choose any book you want from my library anytime. Do you want one?" Rihab, said hesitantly, "Yes. But I am not sure what books I want." Hasanat said calmly, "History books, science, ethical or religious, what books do you want?" Rihab said, "I want religious books." Hasanat was happy at her choice.

She gave her three books one about '**Faith and Reason**' and the second one about '**Reason and The Hereafter**', and the third was about 'Science and Faith.' She took the books and went to her room. Her sister's nice words still echoing in her head.

Hasanat's help to her in arranging her room, sewing her clothes and offering her books made Rihab condemn herself saying, "What a wicked person I am! Can't I stop this dangerous game? Why can't I leave the poor girl alone? Now, there is no way out but to see it through to the end. I am in need of Mustafa's knowledge to explain difficult issues for me. If I confess the truth, he and the others will scorn me. No! I cannot retreat."

A few days later she wrote:

Dear Mustafa

I tried to understand your aim behind those questions, and looked for books that dealt with these matters you asked about, to get the answers. Actually, I do not want to be your little student waiting for you to answer every small question. I read nearly three books besides the ones you mentioned to me. I must say quite frankly that my aim behind reading has been to comprehend your opinion before you mention it. Anyway the books dealt with various topics and answered some of my own questions. I found them interesting to read, but unfortunately I could not find the answers to your questions. Hence I wait for you to answer them, along with my answers.

1. Of course the difference between men and animals is not in regard to the five senses but is because of Reason. Man can think reasonably whereas animals cannot.

2. Existence and non-existence are matters clear to everyone who can reasonably comprehend things.

3. Impossible things exist, i.e. to say that it is impossible.

Hasanat

Mustafa got Rihab's letter. He was about to tear it even before he'd read it. Could such a doubting suspicious girl become his life-partner? Could she be the golden girl of his dreams? What a bitter experience his sister Zainab had caused him! How could he live with someone who disbelieved in the most sacred values? Yet he did not tear the letter but said to himself, "I should continue since I've got some promising results." He opened the letter and tried to understand what kind of a girl was writing the letter. He thanked God for success in his efforts to guide her. He wrote the following letter:

In the Name of God

Dear Hasanat

Assalamu Alaikum

I got your letter and was pleased to hear that you had enjoyed reading with whatever results you gained from it. You see how valuable such books are. They are real treasures within your reach but you never knew about them. How did you get such books? As for the questions, you agree that the five senses are not everything. They are only the means for the mind to obtain the truth. Hence there are facts that need no arguments though such facts are not perceived through the senses, such as the existence and non-existence. For instance can you see the non-existent with your eyes? Have you tasted it with your tongue, or touched or smelled it? Has it a sound? Has someone else felt it? This is quite impossible.

Yet you and I and any wise person believe in such a thing. How could that happen? If we say it is impossible to see the non-existent, then how could we get such information? Was it through the senses? Of course not! The senses cannot comprehend anything except what exists. Yet we believe in the non-existent because of absolute reason that makes all the difference between the animal and the human being. There is another fact in this regard. Water is a liquid, a fact that needs no argument. But it is not through the senses that we reach the fact that water is composed of two atoms of Hydrogen and one of Oxygen. Such facts have been proved by scientific process independently of sensory activity. A certain scientist says, "...Some facts are reached through the direct comprehension of the senses. But there are many facts that are not reached through the senses; we get the knowledge of such facts through inference. Such facts are discovered facts. What we should understand here is that there is no difference between the facts in these two categories. The difference is that we get the first facts directly, the others indirectly." He also says, "...The senses cannot comprehend the facts about the Universe, except to a limited degree, yet there are other facts that we know nothing about. There is a way to get such facts through cause and effect or through inference. Both are brain methods. We start with a well-known fact to end at a particular theory; something has been here all the time, but we have never been aware of it." There is also the gravity law which can never be sensed, as Newton says: 'It is something mysterious to see something with no life at all, affect another, though there is no relation between the two." So you see that through reasoning and the accumulation of facts we come to believe in the Creator and eventually we attain to the religion of our own. You may consider this letter to be long, but it is to your benefit. If you need more information, I am ready to give it.

Mustafa

Hasanat was hopeful of her sister's return to faith. She increased her care and attention of her and kept showing her tender feelings. But she noticed that Rihab could not respond easily. She often tried to speak frankly to her.

She thought her sister's uneasiness was due to their past unfriendly relationship yet the more she loved her, the more Rihab felt uneasy. She regretted her misdeed and blamed herself more than she feared the discovery of her plot. She feared she would no more get Mustafa's letters guiding her to the right path. She needed those letters more and more. She would confess the truth to him one day. She would also confess to Hasanat, the great wrong she had done to her. She would ask for her forgiveness and pardon. In fact she feared the loss of Mustafa's letters as well as her weakness to face her sister with her confession. She decided to go on writing to Mustafa, and wrote:

Dear Mustafa

You will never know how grateful I am to you. I am also ashamed of having done you so much wrong, while I benefit from your letters so much. I am sure you are a noble person who pardons the one hurting him. Your explanation is wonderful and convincing. Yet I have another question. We understand that we comprehend some facts not only through the five senses but through deductions and inference. Tell me now: How can we prove the existence of the Creator? Thanks a lot for your help.

Hasanat

Rihab finished the letter and remembered that Mustafa, in his first letter had asked for Hasanat's photo, although he had not since repeated his request. Rihab thought she must do something for her innocent sister. If she did not send the photo, then she would be doing her sister another wrong, and Hasanat was a real beauty, just like an angel.

How could she inform Mustafa of her beauty? Had she thought of this from the beginning, Rihab would have perhaps, sent her own photo, since she had hated her sister. But thinking of that now would mean another crime against Hasanat. Now, she must get her sister's photo and send it to him at all costs. She would ask her sister for a photo of herself. She went to her sister's room. Hasanat was happy to see her and welcomed her heartily. She said, "Can you do me a favor, Hasanat?"

Hasanat happily answered, "With pleasure Rihab dear. I am ready for you to ask anything. What do you want?" Rihab blushed shyly and she said, "I want one of your most beautiful photos."

Hasanat was surprised at the demand. She did not want to disappoint her sister, and said, "You can have my album and choose the one you like." She handed her an album from the shelf. Rihab took it in confusion. She turned the pages looking for a clear beautiful picture. She took one, thanked her sister and hastily left the room. She put the photo in the envelope and left the house to post the letter.

The passing of the days and weeks, only served to increase Hasanat's feelings of loss, with regards to her fiancé. However, she still looked calm and in control of her feelings, appearing to be confident in her future. Whenever she saw her sister reading religious books she felt happy, and one day, saw her perform her daily prayers!

She rushed towards her and kissed her warmly, "How happy I am, and how proud I am of you! Oh, how I love you dear Rihab, and how lovely you look in your prayer robe! You look like a nymph. You are really very beautiful!" she said. Rihab could not reply to her sister's feelings. With every word her sister uttered she felt uneasy. As soon as her sister left her, she threw herself on the prayer rug and burst into tears. She murmured, "Oh God! How cruel am being towards this angelic person."

A few days later, Rihab received the following letter:

In the Name of God

Dear Hasanat

Assalamu Alaikum

I pray to God to guide you in this world and the next. It is good that you have asked me to give you proofs of the existence of the Creator. Science has discovered the second law for heat energy that is called the power law. This law proves that the universe is not eternal and that heat is transferred from hotter bodies to cooler ones until both have the same temperature. Energy resources within the Universe are continuously producing heat, yet their temperature is never the same. This indicates that energy resources are not eternal, and are therefore limited. Had it been eternal, with the continuous heat transference of billions of years, the temperature would have stabilized long ago. Some biologists say, "Science has unintentionally proved that everything has a beginning and that nothing can be self-generating. There is the 'primary cause' or the Lord Creator."

Another scientist says, "Scientists believe that the transference of heat will continue until all energy sources are exhausted. It has not reached its final level. Had it happened, we would not have survived until now. There has to be a beginning and an end to this non-eternal universe." There are other scientific proofs to lead us to a belief in the Creator. We can come to know Him through knowledge of the Universe. It would take many pages if I were to refer to all of the evidence that proves His existence. Anyway, I will mention other scientific discoveries that indicate that the Universe has a particular age. Astronomy has proved that the universe is systematically growing larger and that the planets and other celestial bodies are getting further away from each other. These parts that are now moving away from each other were in the beginning, only one mass. Then heat and motion took part, hence the Universe must have an age. It is in a state of continuous movement until one day when it will come to its end. Whatever has an end must also have a beginning. I hope you are not annoyed with my long letter. I do advise you to read the book: 'God and Science' and the book: 'From disbelief to belief'

My good wishes for your success,
Mustafa

Rihab read the letter then went to her sister's room to get the suggested books. She started reading immediately trying to comprehend their contents. She got one week's leave from the office in order to devote all her time to her reading. On completing the books, she felt a strong belief in God. Yet she still had a few questions that needed answers.

She wrote:

Dear Mustafa

I am never annoyed by what you write. You have removed the veil that covered my eyes and caused my blindness, and misguidance. I still need you to write to me about these things. I have read the books that you recommended, and I now feel at ease. However, could you please relate some more facts to me? I have to admit that I am newly born, and, just as an infant needs milk, I need information. I hope you won't get tired of my questions.

Hasanat

Mustafa was busy with his final exams when he got Rihab's letter, yet he still replied to her.

In the Name of God

Dear Hasanat

Assalamu Alaikum

I was very happy to receive your last letter that dearly showed that you have successfully crossed the stage from disbelief, to Faith and certainty. I congratulate you on your new birth, which, I hope, will be a happy birthday for you every year. You should not think that I am fed up with your letters and questions. On the contrary I am happy that God the Great has chosen me to help you on this crucial issue of faith and religion. I am happy to help you discover the truth that had been hidden from you by deviated ideologies. You have already listened to the voice of faith that has taken you from darkness to light. I am happy and ready to write to you, though, the books you have read can furnish you with all the answers to your questions. You still want more evidence about the Creator. Such evidence is related to our bodies. Have you ever thought of the complicated system of telecommunication? Have you ever thought how the voice is carried from one place to another, far away? Of course it is a wonderful system that calls for praise for its designers. Yet why doesn't man think of a yet more complicated device? It is our own nervous system. Our nerves carry, all the time, millions of pieces of information and instructions from side to side without the least stop, day and night. The nervous system carries out its duty of controlling the heart and other organs. Every system has a central control, and the communication systems center is man's brain. There are millions of nerve cells with wires that extend throughout the body. These are called the neurons and they receive and respond to various stimuli and respond accordingly, thus giving instructions to various parts of the body. Through this system we hear, see, taste and think and do our work. Have you ever thought of the brain? Have you ever thought about how it remembers names, numbers, images, and events of the past and countless other incidents? Can we say where such information is hidden, when the brain is so small? Has nature (which cannot itself comprehend) arranged this brain system and made it the central control in human bodies? Can any wise person really believe such a claim? Don't you know that there are countless machines and devices, which are all invented in imitation of what God the Almighty has already created? Can't you see that the camera functions in a similar manner to the eye that also has an outer network and a screen where images are reflected? The film that is sensation to light, in the camera box is similar to the retina where various images are found. Yet, can anyone claim that a camera makes itself. Is there anyone who would dare to say that the delicately functioning eye was established without designer, just by chance? Have you heard that in one of the world universities, they have invented a tool with which to measure the ultra-sound waves of the voices vibration in order to get more information, about floods and earthquakes before they occur? Do you know that some kind of sea-fish have been studied and imitated to this end? They imitated those fish (that are aware of such occurrences) in order to build their apparatus. These are only a few examples. You can find more if you read the books: 'God in Heaven' and 'Medicine and Faith' and 'The Behavior of Creatures'.

Mustafa

Soon after Rihab got Mustafa's letter, she borrowed the books he'd recommended, from her sister. Her faith increased and yet she had some other questions that she intended to ask him; then she would confess the truth to him before the end of the year when he would be back at home. She wrote:

Dear Mustafa

Assalamu Alaikum

You must be busy with your finals, hence I apologize for asking more questions of you, but they are quite important to me. It is a matter of life that has been renewed in me by you. Therefore I have the right to ask you as a sustainer. We agree that God has created everything. Then who has created Him?

Hasanat

Rihab posted the letter and returned home. She asked about her sister and their mother said that Hasanat had spent the day in her room. Rihab knew that Hasanat was worried by her finance's apparently strange behavior. She felt sad for her and went to her room. She found the door locked so she knocked gently on it. Hasanat opened it and although she smiled, traces of tears could still be seen in her eyes. Rihab knew why she had been crying and was about to tell her the truth there and then but hadn't got the nerve to do it. She still felt in need of Mustafa's letters. She entered the room and sat near to Hasanat, "You look sad dear sister, yet you should be the happiest person in the world." Hasanat was silent, but happy to see her sister concerned for her. She threw her hand on her shoulder as if throwing a burden of pain upon her. Rihab tried hard to control her feelings, and said, "Dear sister, there is nothing that deserves your concern. All that is good is waiting for you."

Hasanat gave a deep sign and then said, "How can you say that. Can't you see how I have been engaged to a man for seven months yet not once have I heard even one word from him. This makes me wonder if I was forced upon him when he didn't want me. Within a few weeks, he will be back. What will happen on his return? I don't complain, but I can't stop thinking about my future with a man who doesn't want me."

Rihab could hardly bear to listen to Hasanat's words. She thought she should do something for the sake of her innocent sister and said cheerfully, "No, Hasanat, you are wrong to think like that. Your fiancé is the most honorable and noble of men. He is just right for you." Hasanat said, "I know that, but it seems he is not satisfied with his choice." Rihab said, "I am sure he is satisfied, and that things are nothing like you think." Surprised Hasanat said, "How can you be so sure..?"

Rihab was at a loss as to how to answer. She said firmly, "I know and am quite sure of what I say." Hasanat insisted, "How do you know?" Rihab was about to break down and confess. What could she say? How did she know? What a dirty trick she had played! Yet she controlled her feelings and said, "You have to believe me when I say I know that I am quite sure of this. Within a few days or a week, I

118

will explain all to you. Now you must feel confident of your future husband. You should look at life with hope and high expectations, please dear sister!" She kissed her warmly and continued, "Promise me that you'll be your old happy self? Be sure of what I say .."

Hasanat smiled gently and said, "I believe you dear sister. I can't explain it but I feel much better already." Both sisters left the room and joined their mother in the living room. Rihab continued to spend most of her time with her sister except when she left for her job. She amused her and talked about the future. She helped her with her sewing and knitting, and continued to read religious books, satisfied with what she read.

Mustafa's following letter read:

In the Name of God

Dear Hasanat

I am sorry to be late in replying to your letter. I have been busy with my finals. Concerning your questions I will give you a brief answer and recommend that you read a book called 'The doctrine of Faith' This will give you details. Supposing we see water boils, we ask: Why has it boiled? The answer is: because it is placed on fire. Then we may ask: Why should fire cause heat? Someone may reply: because it is hot. Can we explain why fire is hot? It is not a reasonable question since there is no fire that is not hot. Then don't we, the believers or the materialists, come to know that this Universe was made for some purpose? Everything has an end. Explanations also have an end. But the difference is that the materialists claim that nature and matter or time has created life. While the believers think and believe that God has created it. Here we see two theories for the creation of the world. The two sides confess that there is a specific reason that cannot be explained. So can the Power, which created this complicated world (which is also in harmony with the needs of man) be an unintelligent, power, which cannot see, feel or comprehend, as the matter itself is? Of course not! The life system is in need of a wise designer. The wisdom behind the creation is itself clear evidence of the existence of a Wise Creator. Knowledge and wisdom can only be bestowed by a knowledgeable and wise Creator. Blessed is He the Best Creator.

Mustafa

As soon as Rihab finished reading the letter, she went to Hasanat and borrowed the recommended books. Reading strengthened her faith and she made up her mind to confess the truth to Mustafa. A new idea had struck her mind. Since she believed in God, she should believe in His Book. How could she make sure that the Qur'an was actually the word of God? She decided to write and ask about this before she made her confession as Hasanat felt and seemed much better since she'd listened to Rihab's words of comfort. Rihab wrote:

In the Name of God

Dear Mustafa

You have guided me well to the right path. You have filled my heart with the light of faith, and I feel I am imposing myself on you. You will soon know why! I would like you to answer my last question. I hope you will pardon me for all the trouble I caused you. My question is: How can I be sure that the Qur'an is the word of God?

Hasanat

Rihab got his reply very quickly. She had already started reading the Qur'an with her sister. On that day, Hasanat told Rihab that she had got a letter from her friend Zainab, Mustafa's sister who was coming back soon. Rihab looked happy and said, "Mustafa will also come soon, God willing."

Rihab went to her room and read Mustafa's letter:

In the Name of God

Dear Hasanat

I would like to tell you that I am not annoyed by your letters. They have helped me to accomplish my religious duty. Now concerning your question; Suppose you see a small girl living in a society, which opens no door for her, whereby she might gain knowledge. She neither reads nor writes and has seen no fashion magazines. Then you see this same girl claiming that she herself has designed the latest fashion. Would anyone believe her? Of course not! They consider her too young and ignorant of any fashion principles. She can neither read nor has she ever been to the big Fashion Houses. How could she design such outfits? Thus, there must have been some one clever enough to have designed it for her. Everyone will know that the little girl was not the designer. In regard to Gods mission to mankind, we know that a truthful man was born and bred in the Arab Peninsula, in the desert, that lacked the least scientific information and art or literature. He could neither read nor write. He never left his birthplace except, once or twice when he was a boy and accompanied the merchant's caravans the same as the others did. He never attended schools for studying either ancient or current civilizations. Yet he suddenly produced a miraculous Book of logic and eloquence. Despite the eloquence of the Arab language, they were stunned at its high level. One of their men (who was against the Qur'anic verse) said on hearing it, "By God, I have listened to words, which are neither of man nor of spirits (Jinns). They are sweet with flavor, fruitful and fresh. Superior to all, and which destroy whatever is below it."

The Qur'an is a miracle at various levels. It has mentioned the events of previous religions, such as are clear in other religions, and their books, even though the Prophet had never read those books and he was illiterate. This is made clear in the following Qur'anic verses: **"And you were not on the Western side when We revealed to Musa (Moses) the commandment, and you were not among the witness;" "But We raised up generations, then life became prolonged to them; and you were not dwelling among the people of Madyan, reciting to them Our communications, but We were the Senders."**

"And you were not on the side of the mountain when We called, but a mercy from your Lord that you may warn a people to whom no warner came before you, that they may be mindful." *(Surah Al-Qasas, ayah 44-46).*

What is quite clear is that past incidents were not copied if anyone might make such a claim. The Qur'an mentions the events in their true form free from distortion or alteration.

The Qur'an relates those incidents positively, not for the sake of merely mentioning them. The Qur'an prophesied events that were improbable then but which later came true, as with its reference to the defeated Roman army by the Persians. This caused the Muslims 'great sadness' since the Roman's were people of the Book, whilst the Persians were (at that time) pagans. The Qur'anic verse says: **"The Romans are vanquished; In a near land, and after being vanquished, shall overcome within a few years."** *(Surah Ar-Rum, ayah 2-3).*

You see a few years, (according to Arab Terminology) cannot exceed ten years. And what the Qur'an foretold came true nine years later. Doesn't such information make you sure that the message of Islam is Divine? As for the scientific miracles contained in the Qur'an, you should consider the following blessed verse:

"And We send the winds fertilizing, then send down water from the cloud" *(Surah Hijir, ayah 22).*

Scientific progress has only recently discovered that the winds play a major role in fertilizing the plants. An English Orientalist, a Professor of Arabic language in Oxford University refers to this fact and says, "...the camel's people knew centuries ago that the winds fecund the plants, prior to this scientific discovery in Europe." Science has also proved that the earth is getting smaller day-by-day and that it is shrinking ever since it was splitted from the sun and got colder. Its surface is cracking, volcanoes, earthquakes and gravity and air pressure causes it to get smaller. This is a recent scientific discovery, but the Qur'an referred to it fourteen centuries ago. The Qur'anic verse says:

"Do they not see that We are bringing destruction upon the land by curtailing it of its sides? And Allah pronounces a doom, there is no repeller of His decree, and He is swift to take account." *(Surah Ra'd, ayah 41)*

"When the sun is covered," *(Surah Al Takwir, ayah 1)*

Only recently has science made die discovery that the sun is burning, like a candle, and is fading away. One day its heat will be exhausted, because of the continuous explosions within it. Hence the sun will vanish, the same will happen to the other stars and planets. I don't want to bother you by making my letter longer, to make you sure of this subject, I recommend that you read 'The Qur'anic Phenomenon' by the Algerian writer, Malik Ibn Nabi.

Wishing you every good,

Mustafa

Rihab read the letter several times. She placed her head on the table and cried bitterly. With each tear she recalled the horrible image of her crime, and her difficult situation. She viewed her new situation for the first time. She felt that she was not the same person who had taken the first step in this plot. She was a new person even though she still had the same appearance. She was filled with remorse and sobbed and sobbed. She was not aware of her sister Hasanat who had heard her and had hurried to her room. Hasanat was worried that something had caused her to want to retreat from the path of Islam. She entered the room and took her sister in her arms. She kissed her gently and asked why she was crying. Rihab could not answer. Her sister's affection increased her agony. Hasanat said to her, "Please Rihab, be kind to me, I am your sister, I cannot bear to see you crying..." At last Rihab stopped and threw her head on her sister's shoulder. Hasanat spoke kindly to her to calm her down. She saw the letter with the address of Rihab's friend on the table. She thought that perhaps it had something to do with Rihab's sadness. She said to her, "Did your letter bring bad news? What nice handwriting! I don't think that it's writer could hurt others, your friend has good taste in friends."

Rihab could not keep silent any longer. She burst into tears saying, "I am a criminal, I am unjust, I do not deserve your love."

Hasanat thought that Rihab was referring to those days when she was unfriendly. She said, "Forget it dear sister. You are now on your way to perfection. You need to take just one more step and then you will be better than I. The one who repents is as pure as the one without sin."

Rihab asked, "Am I worthy of God's forgiveness?" Hasanat said, "Yes. Prophetic narration states that, "However many sins a person commits, then he/she repents, God will forgive him/her. God loves those who repent." God not only forgives you, He also loves you and He is happy with your repentance. Imam Al-Sadiq (as) says: *God rejoices at the repentance of His slaves as one rejoices at finding something lost.*" The Qur'anic verse says:

"***Surely Allah loves those who turn much to (Him), and He loves those who purify themselves.***" *(Surah Al-Baqarah, Ayah 222).*

Then how can you doubt God's acceptance of your repentance when you obey His orders?"

Rihab became quiet, she considered her sister's great help to her, and listened attentively, forgetting her own problematic situation. She said, "What step do you mean?"

Hasanat said, "I mean the head cover, the decent hijab. You believe in the Qur'an, don't you? Haven't you read those verses about Hijab in *Surah Al-Nur*? You know the Qur'an is the message from Heaven. It is for us to regulate our lives by and to achieve happiness here and in the hereafter."

Hasanat's words were effective enough to awaken Rihab and make her feel her painful situation. She was quite sure that the Qur'an is the message from Heaven, but how could she achieve such faith? Rihab was sure that Hasanat would not help her, if she had known the truth (about the false letters). Yet Hasanat continued talking about the decent clothes and the social benefits of keeping a woman's body, properly covered. Rihab wanted to know more about the hijab. She was thinking of wearing it herself. After listening to her sister she said, "Isn't the hijab an old Persian tradition?" Hasanat said, "Not at all. The Qur'anic verses about hijab were revealed years prior to the conquest of Persia. It was before any contact with its people. Anyway the hijab recommended by Islam is quite different from the traditional Persian one. The hijab is just a protection as a shelter, not a curtain or barrier that prevents woman from performing her role. The ancient Persian kept women behind the veil. You can be sure if you read the Qur'anic verses in *Surah Al-Nur, ayahs 30-31,* which say:

"Say to the believing men that they cast down their looks and guard their private parts; "

And say to the believing women that they cast down their looks and guard their private parts and do not display their ornaments except what appears thereof, and let them wear their head-coverings over their bosoms, and not display their ornaments except to their husbands or their fathers, or the fathers of their husbands, or their sons...."

"So why are women believers ordered to cast down their looks if they are separated from society and social performance of their role in life? A man is ordered to cast down his looks, which means there is a woman near him, and women are ordered to do that also, which means there is a man near them. Hence in order not to create sexual and social chaos or stir up the feelings of both sexes, the religion of Islam has ordered the decent covering of women as a means for their protection. Preventing woman from performing her role in society or keeping her behind a curtain could cause a lot of psychological and mental disorders. With the decent covering, it is quite possible for a woman to perform her role, side by side with the men. The hijab prevents lots of social problems and disasters that are to be found in societies where there are no limits placed upon the mixing of men and women." Hasanat stopped talking for a while. She waited for her sister to voice her own opinion. Rihab said, "Some say that the 'hijab' is something which came from the monks. It is an image of austerity and a denial of life's pleasures."

'Woman is a part of man's enjoyment, hence man has imposed the hijab on her to comply with the difficult life he has experienced."

Hasanat rejected the idea, saying, "I am sorry to say that you have listened to a lot of distorted information concerning the Islamic decent dress. Islam has never denied the human being, life's pleasures, and has never called people to monasticism or the non-enjoyment of life. On the contrary, Islam wants man to enjoy life. Once the Prophet (swas) saw a man in dirty clothes with untidy hair and a rough appearance, he said to him, *"Religion is to enjoy life."* What the Prophet meant is that life's bounties are created for the sake of man. Imam Ali (as) says: *"God is Beauty, He loves the beautiful."* Imam Al-Sadiq (as) says, *"God has bestowed on you His bounties, do not hide them."*

When he was asked, how, he answered, "Each of you must be clean and with good perfume. His home must be bright and his walls white, his clothes clean. This will increase his earnings."

Hasanat went on, "Three women complained to the Prophet (swas). One of them said, "My husband does not eat meat." The second said, "My husband does not use perfume." The third said, "My husband does not touch me." The Prophet (swas) was sad. He went to the Mosque, got on the pulpit and said, "Some of my companions do not eat meat, or use perfume or enjoy a relationship with their women. Yet I eat meat, use perfume and enjoy my women. Anyone who does not follow my course, has nothing to do with me." The Prophet (swas) used to keep his hair tidy. He looked in a water pot in place of a mirror before he met his companions. He used to say: *God loves His slave to look neat and beautiful in front of his companions.*" Thus you see that Islam does not order monasticism or the denial of life's pleasures. Hijab bears no relation to such claims, as Islam is against monastic ideas. I'll give you a book about chastity, its positive and negative aspects. You can also learn more about the decent covering and the harmfulness of nakedness. Anyway I have a surprise for you. I have prepared an Islamic suit (hijab) for you, when you are ready you can have it. I hope f won't have to wait long,"

On hearing such words, Rihab grew calm again. Hasanat talked about other things and then left her sister's room. Rihab noticed that her sister gazed at the letter on her desk before she left. Hasanat returned to her room. She threw herself on a chair and murmured, "I'm sure I know the handwriting on that letter! It is familiar to me! It looks like Mustafa's handwriting. I remember his words in a book he gave to his sister as a present. Yes, I still have the book I borrowed from Zainab."

She got up and went to the bookshelves to look for it. She soon found it. She opened it and looked carefully at the handwriting. She fell on to a nearby chair saying, "Oh my God! It is the same handwriting! Could it be so similar? How could that have happened? What has Mustafa to do with Rihab's friend? Oh no! Surely, I am wrong!

Many people's handwriting looks the same. Anyway, what does it mean? Has the letter anything to do with Rihab's pain and sufferings? Yet, I cannot imagine Mustafa's insincerity! Why should I?" She took a book and sat reading, but couldn't take in a word. Her thoughts were busy with the letter, the handwriting.... She tried to sleep but failed. She kept thinking and thinking. She spent nearly three hours in her room, then Rihab came. She was happy to have her company, so that she would not have black thoughts.

Rihab stood near her and said, "I have come to ask for", "What...?" said Hasanat. "I would like the Islamic suit that you have prepared for me. I have decided to wear the decent covering from today." Hasanat's face brightened. She got up, kissed her and went to her cupboard. She got the Islamic Hijab and gave it happily to her. Rihab took it with many thanks. She said, "I will always use it. I hope, you won't ever leave me dear sister." Hasanat was bewildered at her sister's words. She said, "How could I do that? Why do you say such a thing. This will never happen whatever the reason be." Rihab said, "Even if you discover something about my past?" Hasanat answered firmly, "Whatever I learn about your past, won't change me as long as you are clean and pure now." But Rihab persisted, "Even if I did you some wrong?" Hasanat said, "Even so. I am happy with your return to Islamic values. This equals all the wrongs of the past. You are my beloved sister, how can I hate you?" "I do hope so" said Rihab "Yet I am not worthy of your love. Anyway thanks a lot." She left the room with tears in her eyes.

Hasanat was amazed at her behavior and the letter and the handwriting. Rihab sat thinking in her room. She made up her mind to end the shameful game. She was ready to face the result whatever it might be. She took up her pen and wrote a new page in her new life. She began to write to Mustafa:

In the Name of God

To Mr. Mustafa

I do not know where to begin. I am quite ashamed of what I am going to write. In fact I am newly born with your help. You have given me lessons, making me believe that shame is less harmful than hell. To feel shame in this world is easier for me than to feel it in front of God, the Almighty. That is why I am writing this letter. I will confess the bare truth, that I (Rihab) have lied for a long time. My confession, here is an indication about my repentance to God, for all my sins. The truth is that Oh! I am sure you will be horrified. You will scorn me and hate me. The important thing is that I am doing my duty to please God, you and my conscience. I have suffered a lot. I do confess that it is I, not Hasanat who wrote to you all those letters. Hasanat could never write such letters. She is a good believer and does not have such doubts about her faith as I had. She is an angel, a beautiful saint. How could she write what I had written? It is I who was lost in the world of deviation and misguidance. Satan controlled me and tempted me until I was tarnished by all of the devils, and all good

126

disappeared from me. I was jealous and remorseless, hence I wrote to you under her name, I thought I could spoil the engagement and be sure of bringing sadness to my sister. I went far into deviation and wrote what I wanted. I even gave you a different address so that your letter might not get to Hasanat. Through your letters, the cloud of deviation was removed from my eyes. I drew nearer step by step, to the righteous road. My conscience awakened and hurt me. I tried to stop and withdraw from your life, but I was in need of your advice and knowledge, so I continued the dangerous game. I turned towards the source of light that you sent me. I noticed Hasanat's great sufferings because she didn't hear a word from you. I felt sad for her. You do not know how gentle she is! I tried to destroy her future, yet she was happy whenever she saw me read a book that could bring me to the right path. She rejoiced at my return to faith. She never knew that my return was at the expense of her happiness. I do not praise her because she is my sister. She is my sister, but I used to hate her. I never knew her value. Now I have come to know the reality and she is worthy of all praise. Recently I sent you her photo, but you never confessed her beauty because you did not want to praise her. She, you thought, doubted her religion. Your photo as well is still with me. I do not know how to give it to her. I think that now you will curse me and you would be within your rights to do so, this is the painful truth. You once asked me, how I got my religious books, and I never answered you. What could I say? In fact, I borrowed them from Hasanat. She allowed me to use her library whenever I liked. Oh, how I hate myself for my shameful conduct. Perhaps this confession will put me at ease for a while and give me some rest. All that matters to me now is God's forgiveness. I wonder will He ever forgive me! You may get this letter while you are doing your final exams and getting ready for your return home. Anyway I hope you will write to Hasanat before you come back. At least she should get one letter from you. You can hate me as much as you like but I do apologize again and I really wish you all happiness.

Rihab

As soon as she finished the letter, Rihab put on her hijab. She hid the letter in her handbag and before she left the house she went to her sister's room. When Hasanat saw her in the decent clothes, she shouted cheerfully, "How lovely you look! Oh look at yourself in the mirror." Rihab said, "Thanks a lot, I have something important to do but I'll be back soon. Wait for me please." She left the house in a hurry and went to the post office. She posted the letter and returned home. She took off her hijab, and went to her sister's room. She decided to confess everything to her. She knew she had caused her a lot of suffering. She was at a loss as to how to start her confession. What could she say? What would her sister say?

Surely she would hate and punish her severely. Rihab feared that she might not be able to confess, so she hurried to her sister, whispering to herself, "I should fear nothing. I am doing this to please God." Hasanat was worried at her sister's strange behavior. She was anxious to listen to her.

Rihab immediately got Mustafa's photo from her bag and gave it to Hasanat, who was surprised when she turned the photo and read the nice words written by her fiancé. She blushed and then said, "When did this come?" Rihab said, "You can read the date" Hasanat read the date loudly then said, "What? The date is some seven months ago. Where has it been all this time?" Rihab said, "I hid it. I am guilty, I am not worthy of your love!" Hasanat said, "Oh, no, I do not agree with you. Just tell me the story of this picture!" Rihab answered, "Well, I have come to tell you that story, dear Hasanat, and then you will have the right to treat me as cruelly as you wish." She told her all the details, while Hasanat sat listening calmly.

She was surprised at her sister's courage in confessing everything. Rihab finished and sat waiting for her sister's final judgement. Hasanat took her in her arms and kissed her warmly saying, "Oh, dear, how great your suffering must have been!" Rihab could not believe her ears. She said, "Is it my suffering? It is you to whom I caused a lot of pain." Hasanat said, "Oh, dear, all my pains are nothing since they have been indirect means of your return to the right path of Islam. I am now twice as happy as I have a righteous sister and a righteous husband."

"Will you forgive me then?" asked Rihab tentatively.

"Of course!" said Hasanat "I'll forget everything and just feel happy with your return to faith and with Mustafa's return from abroad. I shall kiss you to prove that I will always be your loving sister." She kissed her and then looked again at Mustafa's photo.

Rihab said, "Look, how handsome he is!" Hasanat smiled saying, "All that counts is his faith and belief. I never thought of anything except his good conduct."

The days passed by and Hasanat was again happy and cheerful. She cherished her sister and cared for her. Three weeks later, the servant brought the two sisters, two letters.

Neither put out her hand to get them, so she put them on the desk and left. The letters were from Mustafa. One was addressed to Hasanat and the other to Rihab. Rihab was scared to open her letter. Hasanat encouraged her saying, "I won't open mine unless you open yours. I think it is a friendly letter." They opened their letters and each read hers.

Rihab read:

In the Name of God

To: The Noble Sister Rihab

Assalmnu Alaikum

My letter to you now is a different one. I honor and respect you very much and I think you are a courageous person who managed to defeat the devilish instincts by her own will. You have achieved a record in purifying the self and cleaning the spirit in a way that pleases God. You are blessed by such an experience. As soon as I read your last (first) letter, I considered you to be a sister whose happiness is my happiness and whose hurt is my hurt. Please do not trouble yourself with past incidents and be sure that I do not hate you at all, but respect you and hold you dear'. I hope that Hasanat also has the same feelings since she is, as you say, a good and kind person. Finally, I wish you all the best.

Mustafa

Hasanat's letter was full of words of love and emotion to make up for the long months of suffering. She read her letter and looked now and then at her sister. She feared that she might be hurt by Mustafa's letter. But Rihab's expression showed satisfaction at what she read. When they finished reading their letters, they kissed each other cheerfully. Hasanat said, "He is coming within a couple of weeks." Rihab's comment was, "He will always be welcome."

A week later Mustafa's mother phoned the family and promised a visit. The family thought the visit was to prepare for the wedding day, but in fact it was made to propose for Rihab. Mustafa's brother Muhammad had asked for her hand, and soon after, both sisters were married to the two brothers on the same day.

THE END

Novel 4

IN SEARCH OF TRUTH

INTRODUCTION

Sarah, a Christian, was in her third year of college studying for a degree in engineering. She has accepted a proposal of marriage from Mohsen, a classmate who, though Muslim, does not know anything about Islam. In order to ensure that they have a happy life together, Sarah decided to embrace Islam. Mohsen tells this story:

CHAPTER ONE

As soon as we decided to marry, we found a religious scholar to help Sarah become a Muslim. One afternoon, we went to his house and on the way, I imagined that he was an old man with white hair and a wrinkled face. We both thought that we wouldn't understand his sermons. Sarah told me, "You must understand what he tells us!"

"Why?" I asked.

"Because you are a Muslim, too", she replied.

I answered dryly, "Oh yes, I am a Muslim".

When we reached his home, Sarah confided in me, "I'm scared!"

I myself was a bit afraid of the important step that we were about to take. It was the first time I had ever spoken with a religious man. I feared that he would label me as a deviated young man. My friends had often warned me about these religious men who oppose everything-youth, beauty, education and wealth.

Because they do not enjoy such privileges, my friends told me that they behave oddly. My head was filled with these pessimistic ideas, yet I told Sarah, "Why be afraid? This is a very routine affair; within a few minutes you will become a Muslim, the same as I am".

"How did you become Muslim?" Sarah asked.

"I didn't become one-I am Muslim due to inheritance."

I smiled, saying, "What I mean is that I was born in a Muslim family, hence I am a Muslim."

Sarah said thoughtfully, "It seems that you do not really know why you are a Muslim."

I knocked at the door, which was opened by a young child who led us to a room where the scholar was. I was very surprised to see that he was young and healthy looking. He welcomed us politely and I began to feel at ease. I looked at Sarah and could see that she was no longer nervous or afraid.

I told him the aim of our visit and that I wanted him to teach Sarah the *Shahada* (testimony of God's Oneness and of the Prophethood of Muhammad (swas)).

He quietly told me, "But that is not sufficient, my son." I was surprised to hear him address me thus, since he was only a few years older than me.

"What else do we need to do?" I asked.

He remained silent for a moment. I appreciated the silence, because I dislike those who attempt to fill every space with words, yet I was anxious for us to achieve our aim, so I said, "Well?"

He smiled and said, "I want to help you, but as a religious man, I cannot offer Islam in the form of mere words. I have an obligation towards my religion."

I told him that it was a private matter and that he didn't have any responsibility towards us. He sighed and said, "I am not responsible for people, but I have a great responsibility towards Almighty Allah and towards Islam. Do you think religious men are free to act as they wish? As a matter of fact, a scholar has a serious duty. It is not easy to carry such a burden."

His words affected me and I asked, "What do you expect of us?"

"I do not expect anything of you. You want me to witness the repetition of a few words, but I will not agree to this unless Sarah becomes acquainted with Islam and understands its precepts."

At this point, I realized how serious he was and how tolerant. Still, I thought that it was best to do it my way, because I thought Sarah would not be able to comprehend Islamic concepts, since I myself did not. Sarah understood my intentions and told me, "Do not insist any longer. I appreciate his devotion to his duties, and I think we should listen to him. If I can understand my philosophy courses, why can't I understand Islam?"

I turned to the scholar and, feeling a bit embarrassed, said, "We want you to do what is right, and we will pay you for your time."

He shook his head and stated, "We do not barter our religion. A religious person only expects reward from Allah. We should offer our services without expecting any compensation."

I regretted my words, and Sarah admonished me, "You have made another mistake."

"I apologize, but one hears many rumours."

Our religious instructor answered, "One should be sure of the truth and not believe everything that is said." He continued, "Man is in dire need of religion. He cannot live without it."

"Why not?" I asked.

"Human nature is such that man seeks ease and comfort, which cannot be obtained except through happiness. And happiness cannot be found unless it encompasses all aspects of life. Religion is the only system which offers happiness and satisfaction, and abounds with ideals and educational values."

I said, "Are you saying that nothing can be substituted for religion? But don't you believe that scientific progress can take the place of religion and provide man with a comfortable life?"

"No, my son. Even if man replaces religion with science and seeks happiness in it, he will not be able to appreciate the true meaning of happiness. Scientific progress and technology may provide man with material comfort. Man can travel far distances in a matter of hours, listen to foreign broadcasts, view the surface of the moon on television while sitting in his living room. Yet man cannot truly experience happiness, since he cannot put an end to injustice and oppression, which human nature opposes.

"He cannot uproot his inner instincts of hating hypocrisy, aggression and the exploitation of the weak by the strong. He is powerless to end the world's insane race for wealth and power. Everything science offers man is controlled by two factors: good and evil. Man can direct scientific progress according to his desires-a plane, for example, is a device for a comfortable journey, yet it can also be the means of great destruction. Television is a useful means of information, yet it also spreads indecency and corruption in society.

"Explosives are used to build roads, but they also maim and kill innocent people. Thus, man is constantly struggling between what he likes and dislikes. There is no happiness in such a life."

I objected, "Can't an ideal morality replace religion? I mean to say, if morality is highly developed and all-encompassing, then justice can be achieved in society."

He replied, "Such idealism is not sufficient for a person's happiness. It is the result of an emergency situation, not a sound foundation. Compassion, for instance, is a feature of such idealism and a natural inclination in humans. Yet it must be stimulated. A kindhearted man cannot but help a poor man he meets. Only such an incident can stir compassion in his heart. If he does not come across this poor man, his compassion will be useless and society won't benefit from it. Compassion here is just an example of idealism and social sympathy. It is not the outcome of a solid foundation. Hence, it cannot cause a man to feel at ease and happy as it's range is limited." While I was listening approvingly, another question came to my mind.

"What do you think of mutual interests? Can this replace religion and create happiness for man?" I asked. He said, "No, serving mutual interests alone cannot bring happiness."

I asked, "Why not?"

He answered, "Because there are serious gaps due to the different interests of individuals. Often a person's interest conflicts with another's. One may benefit by the loss of another. How often palaces are constructed on the ruins of others! How often towns emerge on the remnants of others! How often someone feels happy at the misfortune of others. Unhappiness won't be uprooted through any law of mutual interests. Happiness won't be fulfilled by such means. Man will still face what he does not like and will pursue his own comfort by all means."

I asked, "Well, can't good breeding and enlightenment achieve that for man?"

He answered, "This good breeding that you visualize, in turn, needs good teachers to supervise the learning process. They, in turn, need be watched and so on, along an endless chain. Breeding does not start at point zero. Zero cannot produce numbers. Hence, an individual remains with an insistent need for religion; a need which can provide all aspects of happiness and an easiness on a firm foundation that never changes."

The scholar stopped speaking and we remained silent, thinking about what he was saying. After a while I asked, "Why have you stopped master?! Have we caused you trouble or taken too much of your time?"

He replied, "No, but I wanted you to have a rest and also to ponder over what you have heard today."

I looked at Sarah, who whispered, "Oh, please ask him to continue. I am quite satisfied and have no objection."

I told him, "Please continue."

He said, "Now you agree that a man is in need of religion, which means he is in need of Prophets and Messengers. But we should know the nature of this religion and that kind of message which brings man true peace."

I told him, "Yes, tell us the message of Islam."

He said, "First, it must be in total harmony with human instincts but not contrary to it. Second, it must be reasonable and within the scope of a human mind's comprehension.

"Third, it must present righteous values and morals with which the life of a good individual can be constructed. It must use good examples and illustrations that will acquaint us with its very essence and aim so that we can follow its teachings. Islam can do this,"

I asked, "How do we know that Islam can do this?"

He said, "This is what I intend to explain, but it will take a long time. Can you be patient?"

Though I was in the habit of glancing often at my watch, for some time, I had forgotten to look. It was nearly 10 p.m. We should have left an hour earlier in order for Sarah to enter the boarding house where she lived before the doors were locked. We stood up to leave and expressed the hope that we would meet again soon. Our earlier thought had completely changed, and we were anxious to come again.

As we left his house we noticed someone following us but we could not see who he was in the darkness.

Sarah was afraid that it was her cousin, who loved her and was jealous, as she had chosen to marry me. I tried to calm her as we walked hand in hand along the streets to the boarding house, where we found the doors already closed.

Sarah and I were at a loss as to what to do. Finally I said, "We must decide now. We can't stand here all the night. I wish we had left earlier."

She answered, "We have not been wasting our time! We need to listen to the lecture. I feel that it was worth staying for. What I fear is that my cousin was the one following us. I am sure he will put obstacles in our way."

I agreed and had the same fear. At last, I suggested that she spend the night in my small home and that I would sleep on the sofa in the living room. She agreed, and when we reached my door, I had a feeling that someone was watching us.

The next morning, while I was on my way to the lecture hall, a first-year student handed me a sealed letter. I opened it and read:

'Do you think I'll let you enjoy life while I am brokenhearted? I will do anything to make you leave my cousin. I shall tell her family about your plans and how she spends her evenings in the homes of strangers and visit Muslim soothsayers.'

The letter upset me greatly. I found an empty corner and sat down to think. "I cannot give up my fiancée. She has become part of my life," I told myself, "Yet I may be risking her life, which I care very much about. I must find a way to keep her out of trouble. This cannot be achieved but by marriage."

I decided that I would not tell Sarah about the letter and that I would ask the scholar to perform his job sooner. I reasoned that when we become husband and wife, her family would not try to interfere. So I never told Sarah about the letter but I found her a bit disturbed that day. I tried to cheer her and told her of my plan to finish the matter quickly. She said doubtly, "I don't think the matter will end soon."

I said, "I'll do everything to make him finish it."

She said, "No, please. Don't forget he has a responsibility for his religion and will fulfill his duties completely."

"You are right Sarah. Anyway, we will see to it. At 5 o'clock I will be ready to accompany you to his house."

At five, I found her waiting at the door of the boarding house. She looked pale and worried. I asked her what the matter was but she smiled and said,

"Nothing." Although I tried to find out why she was so worried, she wouldn't tell me, but insisted on hurrying to the scholar's house. I was afraid that she had received a similar threatening letter. I tried to talk about different matters to distract her attention.

We reached the house and were soon in the scholar's presence. I begged him to start and finish quickly so that we could avoid the previous day's trouble. He felt sorry and apologized but I said,

"Oh, you need not apologize, we were really interested in your lecture, but we forgot to note the time."

He said, "Without hardship, rest can't be appreciated. You do not agree?"

I replied, "Perhaps."

"You are not sure. But haven't you ever drunk water after hours of thirst and did the same at ordinary time? Haven't you noticed the difference? Sometimes you walk for long hours in the sunlight and you look for shade to escape the heat. Can that shade be the same as that in your home?"

"When one falls ill, deprived of movement and unable to enjoy life, and finally he becomes well again, does he not feel more grateful for the health he had previously? In times of sickness, he appreciates the great treasure of health."

We listened to him attentively and I said, "It is exactly as you say."

He said, "That is why sometimes hardships or troubles can actually be to our benefit. Thank God for His bounties. Without experiencing pain and suffering, one cannot experience true happiness."

I repeated, "Thank God."

He continued, "We agree that man is in need of a religion which will suit all aspects of life and must be in harmony with human instincts and wisdom. A religion that can set examples and illustrations; Islam can do so. Islamic theory is handed down to man through Prophethood. It contains all that a human being needs.

The Qur'an says:

Those who believe in the unseen and keep prayer and spend out of what We have given them and who believe in that which has been revealed to you and that which was revealed before you, they are sure of the hereafter (Al-Baqara: 3-5)

"That belief in the unseen is in harmony with human nature. Despite having different attitudes and opinions, man generally feels that there is a great might outside his limited senses. He takes refuge in it in times of hardship. He is similar to a man flying in a plane, when the pilot suddenly announces some damage that may cause the plane to crash. He warns the passengers to get ready and to use life belts or emergency doors. Everyone tries his best to save himself. A crippled person cannot move, even though he finds himself near death, he does not give up hope. He thinks there is a merciful power somewhere that may help him. He believes in the unseen power that exceeds the power of technology or science. Until the last moment, this man hopes for mercy."

"Another example is a mother whose child is seriously ill. Doctors give up the hope of curing him, yet the mother still hopes he will recover. She feels there is some mighty power that can do this. This is what is meant by the belief in the Unseen, a belief that is in harmony with mankind. Another example is a captain of a ship lost in the middle of the ocean. How does he feel at such a time? He appeals to the unseen, highest power that is beyond his materialistic potentials. This is a real factor that man is in need of believing in the unseen. Religion is an instinct that exists among all human races, even the most primitive. Metaphysics and paranormal study, is an inner human inclination. Such an instinct is found even among children who continue to ask about such matters. A child's questions unintentionally express the feeling of this unseen power that he wants to understand."

"This belief in the unseen is essential in religion, as it naturally leads to belief in Allah. Such belief is sometimes clear and sometimes vague, depending on explanations. Another aspect of harmony in religion with the human instinct is the unification of our great universe and the accurate coordination in it."

I looked at my watch. Seeing that we still had some time, I said, "What do you mean by the coordination of the universe?"

He said, "This is a lengthy discussion. I see you are in a hurry, so we can discuss the matter in another lecture." I looked at Sarah, who agreed, saying, "We'd better avoid yesterday's trouble, especially since..."

"Especially since what?" I asked.

"Oh nothing", she told me, "Please schedule our next meeting after Wednesday because I have an exam on that day."

I asked the scholar to fix the date of our next meeting and he said he could not see us until the next Saturday afternoon. I thought about the many long days that would pass without achieving our goal. I begged him saying,

"Please can't you spare one or two hours before Saturday?"

He said, "I am quite busy with teaching, studying and working on various questions raised by others."

I said, "Can't you postpone some of your lessons?"

He smiled saying, "You are convinced that exam cause the delay of other matters. Don't you think my lessons need my thorough attention?"

I was ashamed and remained silent for a moment, then said, "In fact, I did not think that you were busy with studies."

"Knowledge is an ocean. One cannot reach its bottom except after long, continuous efforts. It may take all of a man's life. When one gets some knowledge one tries other doors for more."

I asked, "Oh, do you also do that?"

He smiled and said, "Are we a special group, different from others? We are the same as any other researcher. We study religious sciences and related things that may influence religion. One keeps on studying looking for constructive opinions or better ideas as long as one lives."

I said, "Then you are not confined to the study of *Halal* and *Haram* (the allowed and the forbidden) matters?"

He said, "This is the core of our study, but this knowledge has certain dimensions that require the study of other matters."

"What are these dimensions?"

He told me, "It is necessary for one to know about logic, linguistics, the narrations, the origins and the reasons behind Islamic precepts. One who guides others must first of all know that Allah, the Almighty, is the source of all guidance. It needs great efforts and serious research and investigation."

"I never thought of that," I admitted. "I used to think that a religious man has less trouble, less responsibility and an easier life than most."

"It is a pity. Such feelings are enough to create a gap between religious men and intellectuals. Yet each one needs the other to understand and spread the message of life completely. Perhaps you will understand in the future what you have been ignorant of until now."

I said, "Surely, I will."

He said, "Until we meet again, I want you to read these two books about religion."

I accepted the books, and we left with the promise to meet again the following week.

CHAPTER TWO

The days dragged on as we anxiously waited to meet the scholar again. We were afraid we might not be able to carry out our plans before matters got worse. Sarah and I read the religious books.

One day before our scheduled meeting with the religious man, I received another threatening letter from Sarah's cousin. It was more strongly worded than the previous one, and I spent the night awake, deep in thought. I seriously feared a conflict. When I saw Sarah the next morning, I did not tell her about the letter because I didn't want to worry her. She was eager for that day's meeting with the religious instructor. Sarah was in a cheerful mood, and I realized that her previous uneasiness had nothing to do with her cousin. At the appointed hour, we went to our religious instructor's home and found him resting, as he caught cold. We were going to leave, but he insisted that we stay and that he was ready to continue his lecture- "In the previous meeting, we mentioned the coordination of the universe's parts and its unity," he began. "A human being senses this unity and when he knows that he too, is part of this huge plan, he feels in perfect harmony with all that surrounds him. He then believes that there is a mighty Power ready to help him. This Power has prepared everything for man's benefit. Thus, he does not feel alienated or at loss in the great universe. He comprehends the truth and the reasons for this unity around him."

"Contrary to this feeling, when one does not understand the dimensions of relativity in the universe, where man does not weigh a feather in comparison, he must learn that this great planet, and the sun are at his service; that the sun's heat is designed to ensure his survival on earth, and by this thought, he feels satisfied and proud."

"Had the sun been just a bit nearer to Earth, everything would have burnt up long ago. Had it been a bit further away, extreme cold would have destroyed every living thing. When man learns such scientific facts, he can appreciate the fact of his existence and his role in the world."

"Had night time been longer than it is, the resultant cold would have damaged or destroyed life. This movement of the earth has been calculated to serve man. How does man feel towards the manifestation of such mighty Power? The oceans cover most of the earth; had they been deeper, then all the carbon dioxide and the oxygen on our planet would have been exhausted by water, eventually leading to lack of air. The depth has been determined to fit man's needs, including his safety."

"One may think of this planet as being made up of just stones and dirt. But if one studies its dimensions and its geography, one will be amazed at its grandeur with regard to these huge mountains, hills and the many oceans and rivers. One can actually feel the greatness of our Maker by contemplating on the creation. This earth has been designed for human life. Man is in need of a certain amount of oxygen. When one looks at the gases that surround the globe, one is fascinated by the sky's blue colour in the day and the bright stars at night. Had this layer of gases been thinner, meteors and shooting stars would have burnt through the outer layer of gases and would have fallen to the earth. Such meteors, which travel at speeds of up to 40 miles per second can destroy everything in their path."

"Even the moon has been placed at a particular distance which affects life on this planet, since the moon causes the high and low ocean tides. Had the distance been less, water would have covered the entire globe. Our air, as well, helps the sun's rays penetrate throughout the universe. Our Creator's wisdom has designed the sun's rays with various extents to fit life. Man is, in fact, a vital part of the universe."

The religious man stopped talking. He seemed tired. Though we knew about these scientific matters, we listened to him attentively as he exposed these facts in relation to God and Divine purpose.

He continued, "Now, you can realize that man lives in harmony with nature. Believing in the unseen is not a mere instinct without a particular aim. In fact, it is important that man learns and investigates in order to reach the truth. Belief in the unseen impels man to learn the secrets of the unseen and to study metaphysics. This instinct, which helps man to understand unity, also teaches him about his links with the great universe. When he understands that everything is designed for his welfare, is he not bound to be grateful? Such knowledge will show him that everything is created with amazing accurateness. Man then may wonder: Since everything is arranged in order in this huge universe, be it the smallest atom or the largest planet, and all is regulated, can man, the best and most worthy creature be left without a master plan of life? Even an ant or a bee has a regulated life. When man recalls such facts. he asks: What is the best order for human life ?"

Then he asked, "Now, have you read the books I gave you?"

We both answered, "Yes" He then gave us another book and said, "I have explained this aspect of the matter for you. I stated previously that religion should be in harmony with a human being's nature and mind; however, science can also help man to progress. The religion of Islam is in thorough agreement with mental,

144

as well as spiritual progress. There are many facts that can prove this." He started coughing and I felt sorry for him.

I said, "Please rest now. You look tired. We can wait for a few days until you get well again."

He smiled, saying, "But you were in quite a hurry."

I replied, "Yes, but not if it will affect your health!"

He said, "But I don't know how long it will take me to get well again."

I told him, "In two or three days, I will call to ask about your health"

He said, "Then we shall decide at that time when your next visit will be. I hope you will finish this book in the meantime." He gave us another book about Islam

The next day I returned home early and Sarah visited me with some women friends. I started reading the religious book after I finished my studies. It was an interesting book and I recorded some facts in my tape recorder. At about 10 p.m., the doorbell rang. I did not expect any visitors, and I wondered who it could be. I was annoyed, but thought it might be an old friend. Carrying my book and recorder I went to open the door. I wanted to show the visitor that I was quite busy. When I opened it, I saw a young girl standing surprised at seeing me and said, "Oh, I am sorry. I have made a mistake again." I asked her, "Who are you looking for?"

She replied, "Oh, I am a stranger in this city and I was given this address, but I have knocked on all the doors here and yours is the last one. I think I have been given a wrong address. Oh, what shall I do?" I said, "Let me see the address."

"It is this street and the house is nearby." She started crying and asked, "Where shall I go? Am I to spend the night in the street?"

I saw that she was young and pretty. I feared she might fall into the clutches of some wicked person, yet I found it difficult to invite her into my home. I hesitated for a while then said, "Look, I live alone in this house. I can let you spend the night and I will find somewhere else to sleep." She calmed down and said, "Where will you go?"

I said, "Never mind, I can manage." She said, "Oh, no please, I don't want to trouble you." I stepped outside the door and asked her to enter. I told her that I was leaving the house and that she could stay until morning. At that moment I saw a sudden flash of light, but could not tell its source. I looked around and asked her, "Did you notice that sudden light?"

"Yes, perhaps it is from a car's headlights," she replied. Then she said, "But I am afraid I cannot sleep alone in the house."

I said, "What do you suggest then?" She said, "I suggest you sleep in your bedroom and I sleep in the living room."

I said, "No, you can use my bedroom and I will sleep in the living room."

She said, "Thank you so much."

She entered and I went to sleep in the living room that night. Just then I realized that my small recorder was still on. The tape had finished, and I left it in its place as I was quite sleepy. I was worried about the telephone, which was in my bedroom. What if someone calls? Then I dismissed the thought, since it was nearly midnight. At seven a.m. I woke up and saw the girl waiting for me at the bedroom door. She told me, "Thank you very much for your hospitality, but please don't tell anyone about my stay in your house."

I said, "How can I tell anyone? I don't even know your name."

Oh, yes, I am Maryam," she said. I replied indifferently, "Happy to meet you."

She left and I returned to my bedroom. I saw cigarette butts lying on the table and noticed that Sarah's picture was no longer in its place. I said to myself, 'surely this girl knew I did not care for her.' I wondered how freely the girl had behaved in a stranger's house! I changed my clothes and left for the college. There, I saw Sarah walking with some classmates, so I went directly up to her and wished her a good morning, as usual. She answered me in cold tone and went on chatting with the others, as if I was not there. "What's wrong?" I implored. She replied, "Oh, nothing."

I asked her, "Have you spent the night reading? You look tired."

She gave me a long sad look and then said, "What about you, have you spent it reading?"

I had nearly forgotten everything about the previous night. I said, "Oh, no, I slept well."

She gave me a bitter smile and said, "Surely it was a comfortable night."

I was about to tell her about the strange visitor, but I remembered my promise to the girl not to tell anyone about her. I hesitated, then said, "Oh, no, it wasn't at all."

She looked at me sadly and said, "I hope you will enjoy your future sleep." Then she turned away and left me standing there alone. I tried to see Sarah that afternoon, but she avoided me. The next day I looked for her at the college but I could not find her. I phoned the boarding house, but they told me she was busy. I went to see her at her home, but she wouldn't come out. I returned home feeling quite miserable and I couldn't sleep that night. The next morning, I hurried to the college to see Sarah, but when she saw me she turned and walked away. I asked her, "Sarah, are you angry?"

"Yes!" she said angrily. Shocked and dismayed, I sat on a bench as she walked away without waiting for me to ask her the reason for her anger. I felt like crying and had to return home since I could not pay attention to my lessons that day. I had no idea why she was angry. The incident concerning Maryam came to my mind, but I brushed it aside, since no one knew about it. I decided to tell Sarah about that girl.

The next day I went early to the college, but Sarah did not come. I was at a loss as to what to do. Walking aimlessly through the streets, I remembered the religious scholar and decided to visit him to ask about his health. I was in need of his help. A young child answered my knock, and I asked about the scholar. He told me he was well and would receive me. I felt as if I were drowning, without any hope of being saved, and then suddenly a bright light shone, giving me hope. The child looked at me and asked,

"Why haven't you come together? Sarah was here earlier today."

I was surprised to learn that she visited him. "She did not enter, she just asked about my father's health and left," the boy said.

I saw that the scholar looked much healthier. We talked about different matters. I was at ease and wished that I could tell him of my trouble but I felt shy. I thought he would talk about Sarah, but he didn't. I asked when our next meeting would be, he looked surprised and then said,

"Tomorrow afternoon at 4 o'clock." I thanked him and left directly to phone Sarah and tell her of the date, but there was no answer. I felt hopeless until I recalled the scholar's words of the power and strength of faith. I thought, 'I have a God to worship and to whom I turn to in times of trouble.' Then I remembered that I hadn't finished the book about religion. I tried to read, but Sarah dominated my thoughts, and I could not understand a word. I closed the book and wrote a few words in the hope that I could give the letter to Sarah the next morning. 'Oh dear Sarah,' the letter said. 'How I wish the entire world be against me except you! After writing the note, I felt better. I thought that everything would be all right once we resumed communication. I got up early the next morning and gave the letter to a friend of Sarah to pass it on to her, but she refused to take it. I thought that she must have had a good reason for such behaviour, thus I was not angry with her.

I spent the day in the college and at the appointed hour, I went to the scholar's house and saw Sarah at the door. I walked up and greeted her, but she answered indifferently. I noticed that she looked pale; as if she hadn't slept the previous night.

I asked her "Is it really you?"

She did not reply and I continued, "It is good that we are both attracted to the scholar. It means we are actually united."

She said, "Though we both want to continue our studies, it may not mean we are united."

I said, "Please Sarah, be kind to me! You know I cannot live without you. You are my whole life. Why are you treating me in this way? You know your own feelings."

"Whatever I know makes no difference!" she replied.

I said, "But why my dear Sarah? I cannot understand your anger." she was silent then said, "You don't want to understand."

I said, "Oh, no, I really do. I am ready to listen to whatever you say."

"In any case, it is the time for our meeting", she replied. She knocked on the door and we both entered.

CHAPTER THREE

As soon as we sat down, the scholar asked us if we had read the book he gave us. I felt embarrassed because I had not finished it. Moreover, I felt shy when Sarah answered that she had read it and had written some notes for explanation. She handed him the notebook. He looked pleased and said, "This is a good sign. I will have a look again later."

He turned towards me, and seeing that I had not answered, he began his lecture, saying, "We previously said the best religion is the one which is in harmony with human instinct. We also discussed belief in the unseen and the unity of the universe."

"Religion is a matter of choice. Man is free to choose his own religion. It is a doctrine firmly implanted in the deep inner recesses of the mind. If not, then it will be mere rituals and habits. Thus religion is an individual choice that cannot be made through compulsion. One cannot be compelled to practice his religion correctly. As for belief, there is no use in compulsion. Man can choose the best religion and can be convinced through discussion. Choosing the right religion with a profound knowledge of truth and perfect awareness is a matter concerning the individual himself. Hence, religion is a choice based on thought and reasoning. The Holy Qur'an calls for thinking and reasoning, as in these verses:

Say: Consider what is it that is in heavens and earth; and signs and warners do not avail a people who would not believe. (Yunus: 101)

Do they not then look up to heaven above them, how We have made it and adorned it and it has no gaps! *(Qaf: 16)*

"Throughout the Qur'an, the verses encourage man to think wisely and give the mind freedom of choice after presenting facts and evidence. In order to make one believe you, you must have sound evidence as a proof. Islam comprises all these aspects in the Qur'an. It is safe to say that Islam is the only religion that has such a quality. Every religion has been in need of a miracle to prove its authenticity. The miracle of Islam is embodied in the Qur'an's miraculous eloquence. The best, most literate men failed to produce anything equal to it. The Qur'an challenged them to produce it's like, as in this verse:

Say, if men and jinn should combine together, to bring the like of the Qur'an, they could not bring the like of it, though some of them were aiders of others. (Al-Isra: 88)

"Then, when they failed, the Qur'an challenged them to produce a few chapters themselves:

Or, do they say: He has forged it. Say: Then bring ten forged chapters like it and call upon whom you can besides Allah, if you are truthful. (Hud: 13)

"When again they failed, they were challenged to produce one more chapter of its like, as in this verse:

And if you are in doubt as to what We have revealed to Our servant, then produce one chapter of its like, and call your witnesses besides Allah if you are truthful. (Al-Baqarah: 23)

"They failed, despite being masters of language and literature."

"Every religion is in need of a message and proof of that message. Islam has both in the Holy Qur'an. All kinds of sciences, whether social, economic, natural or related to man's biological construction, can be found in the Qur'an. Many a scientific fact has been recently proved in science, though the Holy Qur'an referred to it fourteen centuries ago. Still other facts have not yet been discovered by science but were revealed to the Prophet, who had been illiterate. Islam elaborated various social topics centuries ago. Some have been recognized only recently by the world, such as the 'Human Rights Charter', which states: 'Abolition of slavery, and economic solutions to prevent monopoly and exploitation.'

"You can find many similar facts in recently written books on Islam. Islam's message is independent except regarding its own concepts. In Islam, man is free to choose with dignity. The mind is not imprisoned in ignorance, nor in feelings of humiliation and regret of a sin (referring to the first disobedience of Prophet Adam). Islam does not call for ritual worship only, but also calls man to pay attention to his everyday affairs. In the Holy Qur'an you can see legislations and good foundation for life. All aspects have been tackled and solutions are applicable anytime and anywhere. Clear evidence of this is found in the Holy Qur'an. Some Chapters are named after animals, such as:

The Cow, the Bee, the Ant and the Spider. Some refer to natural phenomena and elements such as: The Thunder, The Smoke, The Moon, The Sun, and The Iron; Some refer to political and social stances such as: The Parties, The Faithful, The Counsel and Women.

"There are also Chapters that refer to historical events such as Alay-Imran, The Prophets, Yunus, Hud, Yousuf, Ibrahim, Muhammad, Al-Rum (The Romans), Maryam, and Noah. Others refer to the Hereafter and the Day of Judgment, such as: *Al-Haqqa*, *Waqiah*, and *Al-Qariah*. Some Chapters refer to economic matters, including: The Spoils (*Anfal*) and the Food (*Maidah*). There are Chapters that refer to morals and good conduct, such as: *Abasa* (He Frowned), *Humazah* {The Slanderer) and *Al-Mutaffifin* (The Defrauders). Other Chapters refer to religious rituals, such as: *Al-Hajj* and *Al-Sajdah*. In conclusion, we see that 32 Chapters concern living creatures, and natural phenomena, 29 Chapters concern belief and ideologies, 27 refer to social and political stances and 17 concern history and philosophy. Four Chapters concern behaviour and morals and four concern materialistic and economic subjects, while two only concern religious rituals. Thus we see that Islam is a complete religion that covers all aspects of life. It does not merely link man to his Creator.

On the contrary, it links man to the Almighty by linking him to all of humanity. So religion's scope is wide enough to cover all aspects of feelings and behaviors, be it struggle for the sake of Allah or a smile in the face of a brother believer.

"Islam can meet the physical and spiritual needs of an individual and it is a perfect religion when it is performed correctly. Islam is in conformity with life and does not neglect the other side."

The scholar ended his lecture, and we fixed a date for the next morning. We bid him farewell and left. Outside the door, I implored Sarah to allow me to accompany her, but she refused. I told her, "But I have something to tell you. You know, my dear, that I cannot tolerate this unfriendly behaviour. Please, tell me what is the matter? I am sure there is something very wrong."

Sarah replied, "I am going to the boarding house, and I do not want to stay here one more minute."

"Then, let me walk with you to your home." I told her.

"No, I can walk by myself, as I came by myself," was her response.

Then I asked, "But why do you still come to the lectures?"

She said, "I am interested in the subject. Now I am a person in search of truth for my own benefit. What about you? Why do you come? The Truth is clear to you!"

I said, "It has never been clear to me. I knew nothing about Islam; perhaps even less than what you know."

"Then let us continue together for the sake of knowledge," she replied.

I said, "And for my sake, dear Sarah."

"For your sake!", she exclaimed.

"Yes, don't I deserve it?"

She slowly answered, "You did deserve such a thing in the past."

"And now, what has happened to make you change your mind? You know how important you are to me. Life is meaningless without you. At least please take this letter from me. Perhaps it will clear up the matter. Please, take it, it won't do you any harm. A small lie should not destroy our whole future together."

She said, "What small lie? A lie that is proved by evidence?"

"If one is quite sure of something, one's confidence cannot be easily shaken", I said, surprised by her allegation.

She said, "But one sometimes doubts one's feeling."

"Then one must be frank and reconsider the matter in order to be certain. Why don't you be frank and tell me the source of your anger?"

She said, "Give me more time to think."

"Please at least promise that you will read the letter."

"I will do that", she told me. "Good-bye for now."

I returned home a bit calmer than before. I picked up the book to finish it, but I put it down again to look among my papers for poem I previously copied from a book of poetry. I had intended to give it to Sarah, but I could not find it. Moreover, I could not find a photo Sarah had given me at the beginning of our friendship. My own photograph was also missing. I used to keep all these in the drawer near my bed.

The next morning, I went to college but I didn't see Sarah that day, or the next day. After three days, I met her at the door of the scholar's house. Upon seeing me, she knocked on the door and gave me no time to even offer a word of greeting. We entered and were asked to wait for the scholar. I was about to speak when she said," Mohsen, can you tell me what you saw yesterday?"

This question of hers was the first line of the missing poem. I wanted to be sure, so I said, "What do you mean?"

"I mean, whom did you see?" she asked. I said,

"Whom could refer to many, but I am sure I saw no one but you, though I did not actually see you."

She interrupted me angrily, saying, "Please, that's enough. This is not the first time you are saying it."

I said, "But I have not said it to you except now!"

She answered, "Yes, but you have said it to someone else."

"But you know I don't talk to any girls except you!" I protested.

"Yes, but you can write," she answered.

I said, "Can writing be enough?"

She said, "Yes, if it is well composed."

"Sarah, why don't you be frank and tell me what you are talking about."

She said, "I wish I could be brave enough to speak. In fact, I am afraid, so you should be the one to speak."

I said. "But, I do not know what is the matter yet."

She said. "Oh, it can't be! You certainly know what is bothering me."

"Call me stupid or anything, yet I do not know the reason for your anger. I am ready to die in order to know it." I replied earnestly.

She asked, "Then you have not guessed?"

I said, "No, but there is a certain incident I thought of, then put it aside!"

"What is this particular incident?" she asked.

I started to tell her about the strange girl, but our teacher entered the room at that moment. I stood up and welcomed him absent-mindedly. I decided to tell Sarah about that girl when the lecture ended. I was not ready to lose her on account of a promise to a stranger. The scholar apologized for the delay. He asked about our reading and gave Sarah her notebook with some explanations written in it. Then he began his lecture.

CHAPTER FOUR

"We have previously stated that Islam is a complete religion. Islam links an individual with his Creator through various means, whether social, economic, political, or emotional. Hence, all of the actions of an individual, however large or small, are in harmony with Divine Law. Performing prayer, paying *zakat* (religious tax), refraining from injustice and abandoning all vices are aspects of this religion. Spiritual rituals, such as fasting, create good morals, and giving charity and religious alms can direct the behaviour of a Muslim and regulate family affairs", the scholar ended his lecture.

"Does worship also include these aspects?" I asked.

"Yes my son. Islam is a religion broad enough to cover all that I mentioned. Each aspect is clearly stated. Now we should determine what Islam has achieved in showing the norms that can mould a righteous person."

I asked, "What do you mean by norms?"

"I mean religious instructions", he replied. "Islamic laws are constructive in regard to an individual's character, which is shaped with the knowledge that he is an important part of humanity. Islamic laws take such a fact into consideration, in the interest of the individual as well as the community. Islam forms a comprehensive, unified whole; all the parts of which are in harmony with and support each other."

Here Sarah asked him to illustrate his point and our teacher said, "For example, gambling and intoxication destroy the human personality, therefore, they are forbidden in order to protect both the individual and the society and to prevent the various crimes that result from these two evils. Another example is the religious order to observe decent dress and covering with regard to women."

Sarah asked eagerly, "I have been anxious to know the reasons for the imposition of *hijab* on women."

The scholar smiled and replied, "I'll explain why Islam insists that women observe modest dress when in the company of men to whom they are not forbidden in marriage. Islam does not state that woman should be kept hidden from society, it simply calls for covering her beauty. The word 'hijab' is mentioned in one particular Qur'anic verse addressing Muslim believers with regard to dealing with the Prophet's wives:

...And when you ask of them any goods, ask of them from behind a curtain... (*Al-Ahzab: 53*)

"This concerns the respect which was due to the wives with such a status."

"Then Islam does not require that women be confined behind the walls of their homes," Sarah commented.

"Of course not. A clear indication is in the Qur'anic verse about modest dressing as mentioned in Chapter *Al-Nur,* which states:

Say to the believing men that they cast down their looks and guard their private parts; that is purer for them, surely Allah is aware of what they do. And say to the believing women that they cast down their looks and guard their private parts and not display their ornaments except what appears thereof; and let them wear their head covering over their bossoms and not display their ornaments except to their husbands or their fathers... (*Al-Nur: 30-31*)

"You can see that Islam orders both men and women to cast down their eyes and guard their private parts. This fact proves that woman is present in the arena; otherwise, there would not have been any need for this Qur'anic order. Men would not have found it necessary to cast down their looks as well.

Sarah nodded approvingly and the scholar added, "In the early days of Islam, woman's role in life proved this fact. Women participated in all activities for the sake of religion. The first Muslim martyr was a woman- Summayah, the mother of Ammar Bin Yassir and the women were present in all the battles and wars for the sake of Islam. They nursed the wounded, supplied water for the soldiers and gave them courage. In fact, the call for Islamic modest dressing is intended as a protective measure to keep the society, of which woman is a part, safe."

I asked, "How?"

He answered, "It is a well-known fact that a woman possesses attraction and can excite a man's innate feelings, to such a degree that he may come to a crucial crossroad; either he responds or restrains these feelings. In both cases, a man may seriously suffer. A free release of his emotions, without regard to religion or social conduct means sexual chaos and the destruction of families and social tragedies. Statistics in countries that encourage sexual freedom prove this fact. Such statistics show a high incidence of rape and other forms of sexual abuse.

"In Sweden, some researchers discovered that 15% of the Swedish population is unwell psychologically and that a large percentage of that country's income is spent trying to cure them. This is the result of sexual freedom in one of the Western countries. A report issued by the American Association of Family Services stated that the breakdown of the family in the U.S. has reached epidemic proportions and is a major social problem. Every year, divorce separates one million people. The U.S. divorce rate has increased rapidly, as has the number of illegitimate children. Such facts are the result of sexual freedom."

"On the other hand, if man restrains his feelings, then he may suffer physical and psychological disorders. Restraint in the presence of exciting beauty is difficult for many men. We can relate that to exposing a hungry man to a sumptuous banquet. The delicious aroma of food arouses his appetite, and yet he is forced to stay away from the food. He may obey, but we cannot remove or change his desire to eat. The display of feminine beauty in front of a male will certainly awaken his innate desires. The best way to protect society and avoid a harmful reaction is for women to cover their beauty. Thus woman, as well as man, can avoid harmful consequences."

Sarah said, "Then observation of decent dress is a precautious step to the interest of society." The scholar said, "Yes, it is like that. Moreover, it is to the interest of a female to keep herself from turning into a cheap commodity devoured by the hungry looks of men."

Sarah commented, "But I have heard that the covering of a woman is a Persian tradition that mingled with Muslim tradition."

The scholar said, "Covering and decent dress are legislated by Islam years prior to Islamic conquest in Persia. Moreover, the decent dress mentioned in Islam is different from the Persian tradition."

Sarah added, "I have also heard that it was imposed for economic reasons."

The scholar asked, "What do you mean?" She answered, "That man wanted to enslave woman and exploit her, hence he imprisoned her in the house for his own advantage."

The scholar said, "This is not the case in Islam. Islamic legislations guarantee the woman's rights in full. She keeps as her own what she gets by work. The Qur'anic verse states:

...men shall have the benefit of what they earn; and women shall have the benefit of what they earn...(Al-Baqarah: 32)

Man cannot benefit from her work since she is the owner of her property. By the way, such a right has only recently been granted to the European woman, who used to get half wages a man received for the same work."

Then Sarah raised another question. She said, "In regard to *hijab*, has it anything to do with self-denial?"

The scholar answered, "In Islam, there is no such thing!"

Here for the first time, I exposed my being a Muslim, so I said, "The Prophet of Islam says: There is no monkery in Islam."

The scholar smiled and said, "Here is a Muslim who knows such a fact, there is also a Qur'anic verse in this regard:

...and (as for) monkery they innovated it, We did not prescribe it to them... *(Al-Hadid: 19-25)*

In Islamic history it is related that one of the Companions wanted to spend all his time for the worship of Allah, so he gave up all earthly pleasures, including his wife. The wife complained to the Prophet (swas), who was annoyed at the husband's behaviour. He went to the mosque, got on the pulpit and warned his Companions, saying: "Three matters have been made enjoyable to me in this life: all that is good, women and my beloved prayer."

Sarah asked another question, "What is the status of woman in Islam? Has she the same rights as man?"

The scholar told us, "She has equal rights, but they are not identical to man's. Similarity is impossible, while equality is justice. Women's rights in Islam are no less than man's rights with due consideration of the differences between men and women. Imagine that a wealthy man who owns many properties wants to divide his wealth among his sons. He will surely consider their qualifications and give the fertile land to the one interested in farming; business management to the one interested in business, and so on. The man is aware that his sons will get equal shares, though not similar. In regard to woman, she has the right to work and keep her earnings for herself."

"She will be rewarded for her good deeds and punished for bad deeds in the hereafter, the same as man. Man and woman follow the same life course towards Allah, the Almighty. They have equal rights in the Divine Legislations. I will list some books about this subject which should help you understand more about Islam and women's rights."

"I'll read them," Sarah said. "Another question I have is this: Does Islam consider woman (Eve) as the source of all evil, and that she tempted Adam to eat the forbidden fruit?"

He replied, "Absolutely not. Islam does not blame woman for this disobedience. When the Holy Qur'an narrates the story of disobedience it refers to them both suffering from the trick of Satan. The Qur'anic verses state:

And We said: Oh, Adam dwell you and your wife in the garden; so eat from where you desire, but do not go near this tree, for then you will be of the unjust. But Satan made an evil suggestion to them that he might make manifest to them what had been hidden from them of their evil inclinations and he said: Your Lord has not forbidden you this tree except that you may not both become two angels or that you may not become immortals. And he swore to them both; Most surely I am a sincere advisor to you. Then he caused them to fall by deceit, so when they tasted of the tree, their evil inclinations became manifest to them and they both began to cover themselves with the leaves of the garden and their Lord called out to them: "Did I not forbid you both from that tree and say, to you that Satan is your open enemy?" (Al-Araf: 19-22)

"You see, they were both exposed to temptation and they both succumbed. Eve alone is not accused of the first disobedience."

Then Sarah said, "They say woman was created from man and for the sake of man. What does Islam say in this regard?"

The scholar said, "This is not correct either. Almighty Allah could have created man without any innate desire for woman. Yet Allah created woman as an independent creature whose existence is related to man, just as his is related to her. The Qur'an says:

...they (women) are an apparel for you and you are an apparel for them...(Al-Baqarah: 187)

Another verse states:

He has created you from a single being then made its mate of the same (kind)." (Al-Zumar: 6)

Sarah's final question concerned children, and if Islam considered woman just as means for producing children.

The scholar said, "Islam gives the mother a supreme status and grants her full rights to her children in addition to recognizing the important role a mother has with regard to bearing and raising her children. Islam has confirmed through the Prophet (swas) that Paradise is reached through a mother's satisfaction. Hence, Allah's pleasure stems from a mother's pleasure."

Then it was time for the evening prayer, so we asked the scholar to schedule the next meeting. We left the house and stood outside for a few moments. I saw a couple of men who were walking by admire Sarah and I felt quite annoyed for the first time. She was also bothered by their looks and bid me farewell, although I pleaded with her to stay and talk with me. She stopped a taxi, got in, and left me at the roadside broken-hearted.

I was excited and did not know what to do. I walked along the streets, bought the books recommended by the scholar and returned home exhausted, both spiritually and physically. I started reading and gradually I felt better. I never ceased thinking of Sarah, who was not only a dear friend, but my whole life.

CHAPTER FIVE

I spent the days waiting for the meeting on that day. I reached the scholar's house before Sarah. After she arrived, he began by saying, "Today we shall elaborate on the constructive ethics of Islam. For example Islam has forbidden Muslims to pray on any usurped property. This has two dimensions: The first is related to a special aspect; the second to a common one. The special aspect is linked to worshipping. Prayer is the most important ritual in Islam. In prayer, an individual's spirit is released from this earthly world. Man reaffirms his submission to the Almighty Allah. Hence his prayer should be sincere and pure and at a place not taken by suppression or injustice. So, when one's soul is clean, his prayer is also clean. But if he prays on usurped land, he will either be angry at the injustice or satisfied with it. Both cases spoil his prayer."

"As for the common aspect, the refusal to pray at a usurped place means denouncement of injustice. Thus private property, which is a human right is protected."

Here a question came to my mind so I asked, "Why has the Chapter *Fatiha* (Opening of the Book) been chosen to be read during all the daily prayers?"

He replied, "*Al-Fatiha* comprises all the Islamic doctrines. Praising the Creator, glorifying Him, obedience to Him, monotheism, belief in the Day of Judgment and the creature's constant plea for guidance. This Chapter is rich with ethics."

"Why do the last three verses only address Almighty Allah?" I asked.

He said, "In order for man to comprehend that his prayer is for his own benefit, and not for Allah. Man will benefit spiritually, ideologically and mentally from regular prayers."

Then I said, "By the way, a verse of the prayer prohibits indecency and evil, yet many who pray do commit such forbidden actions."

"Yes, prayer prohibits evil as the Qur'an says:

...and keep up prayers, surely prayer keeps (one) away from indecency and evil... *(The Spider: 45)*

"But it does not prevent man forcibly from committing evil. It preaches and supplies man with ways to keep him away from indecency. Yet it is up to him to accept this and behave accordingly. Some understand the essence of prayer and avoid evil practices. Some do not comprehend this concept and hence behave otherwise.

The Prophet (swas) says in this regard: "You gain nothing from your prayer but what you comprehend."

I said, "Now I understand that all worship is for man's benefit."

"That's right", he said. "If you take a look at the Qur'an, you will understand that all Islamic laws have humanitarian aspects. Its message is not confined to one particular country, race or class. This religion has come as mercy to the whole universe."

"In the Holy Qur'an, there are upstanding examples indicating that Islamic laws can cause a righteous person to be followed in society. All individuals are responsible in society. A hadith states: 'You are all shepherds and are responsible for your flocks.' Every individual is given the chance to construct his personality and participate in society. The difference is great between a society nurtured on selfishness and idleness and a society based on both personal and communal responsibilities. Laws give responsibility and cause him to know his moral duties. The Prophet (swas) says: 'I have been sent to uphold good morals. The best of you in faith is the one who is the most well-behaved.' "

Our teacher looked at his watch and our time was over, so we bid him farewell and left.

Outside the door, I noticed that Sarah kept her head covering on which was not her habit. I tried to talk to her but she quickly handed me a letter and left at once. I was about to open it and read it, but I prepared to read it at home, so I hurried back to home and read the following:

Mohsen,

Assalamu Alaikum

I hesitated before I wrote this letter. The situation has become so serious that it has affected my own life. I have expected many things, but not that which has happened. Why have you betrayed your promises? Why have you weakened so much as to consider our relation indifferently? You have destroyed our hopes for the future. I think you know what I mean. You will find with this letter, clear evidence in addition to the fact that I have myself heard about what you have done. Anyway, I don't want to keep a token of your insincerity. You must be sure that I have suffered a lot. Had it not been for this new light of Islam that engulfs my heart, my suffering might have destroyed me. Be sure that when I give up your love, I am not turning to anyone else, because you are the only one I love.

Sarah

In the other envelope I found the missing photos of Sarah and me as well as the poem that I had intended to give to Sarah. There was also a photograph of me welcoming the strange girl into my house. Everything became clear. I was the victim of a well-designed conspiracy. I had been a fool. Sarah's cousin had prepared all the drama. Surely Sarah had been informed of the incident as soon as the girl came to my door. I felt sure she had phoned and heard the girl's voice in my bedroom. I felt dizzy. I made up my mind to fight for my girl.

I immediately left the house to find Sarah, but stopped when I realized it would be difficult for me to prove my innocence. I returned home quite desperate. My eyes fell on the Holy Qur'an, which I always kept on the bookshelf. Feeling it was my only hope I opened it and read a few Chapters, after which I felt a bit relieved.

Then, suddenly, I remembered my recorder and the tape on which the incident was recorded. At last I had some evidence to prove my innocence. I decided to give the tape to Sarah the next day. I praised Allah for His bounties and slept soundly that night.

The next morning I looked for Sarah in the college, but I could not find her. Her friends told me that she had left for her hometown. I was surprised, since it was not a holiday. The days passed by, and whenever I asked about Sarah, I was told she was still away.

On the day of our next meeting with the religious scholar, I took the tape and wrote a letter explaining every detail to Sarah. I hoped to see Sarah there, and I did.

I was surprised to see her wearing black clothes and a black scarf. My love was so great that I wished no man but me would ever see her.

Pointing to her black dress, I asked, "It is nice to see you again, but why are you mourning?"

Her eyes filled with tears as she told me, "My father has died." I was saddened by the news and felt like crying. I expressed my condolences and said, "We are all from Allah and to Allah we return." I kept silent and she turned to the scholar and said, "Please start your lecture. I have a lot of things to do, but I wanted to come and hear you. Despite my sadness, I have read the books you recommended. I consider Islam to be an important part of my life."

The scholar replied, "May Allah bless you, my daughter. I pray to Him to give you patience and reward you well for your righteous feelings and desire to pursue the truth. You have made it easy for me by reading those books."

She said, "Had I not a wish to hear from you more and more, I would have told you that I am quite satisfied with what I have learnt from you. I am anxious to hear about the good examples of Muslims throughout Islamic history."

The scholar told us, "No legislations or ideas can be successful unless examples exist. Otherwise, it would be impractical. Islam presents the Prophet (swas) as a good example to be followed. The Qur'an reads:

Certainly you have in the Apostle of Allah an excellent example far for him who hopes in Allah and the Last day and remembers Allah much. (Al-Ahzab: 21)

"To talk about the Prophet alone would take months. Other examples are his cousin, Imam Ali (as), and the eleven Imams (as). You can read many books about these great men. There are also other Islamic characters in history known for their righteousness such as: Salman Farsi, Ammar Bin Yassir, Abu Dhar Al-Ghaffari and Maitham al-Tammar. When you read the books about these Muslims, we shall hold a final meeting, by the will of Allah."

We thanked him and left. I asked Sarah to stay and listen to something important I had to tell her. I said,

"I'll prove to you that I have always been faithful to you and I am quite innocent."

She looked surprised and said, "How will you prove your innocence?"

I said, "Oh, I'll tell you everything, but not at the roadside! "

"Where then?"

"Any place you suggest," I said.

She thought for a moment and said, "There is no better place than the scholar's house. Since he is our spiritual father, we can discuss the matter in his presence."

At that moment the scholar appeared at the door; he was on his way out. Upon seeing us still there he was surprised, so we told him our problem and he invited us back to the same room in his house. He apologized for not being able to stay, but he promised to return soon.

We entered the room, and I found myself feeling very shy, despite my great love for Sarah, I could not even look at her. I kept silent for a while then from the depth of my heart the words poured out. I explained everything to her. She listened to me attentively. Truth and sincerity were obvious in my voice and manner, and she believed me without even asking for proof. I asked her, "Don't you want any proof of what I said?"

"No. I believe you all the same. Thank God you are now more truthful than before."

I said, "But I do want you to listen to this tape on which details of the event are recorded."

She said, "Oh, no, I do trust you. There is no need for it."

I insisted, saying, "Please, at least keep it for yourself."

"Okay, I will take it just to please you." she agreed.

When the scholar returned, he was delighted to see that our problem was solved. We both thanked him and left, feeling greatly at ease, a feeling that we had missed for so long. We read all the books he told us to read. The more we read about Islam, the more surprise I felt at my great ignorance of my own religion. As for Sarah, she was careful to observe *hijab*. We both started our daily prayer at their fixed times. When we finished the books, I phoned the scholar for a meeting at the soonest opportunity. When we visited him, he asked us if we had read those books.

We both answered "yes". Then he asked, "Have you acquired good knowledge of Islam and its righteous exemplars?" I replied for both of us, "yes". We wish we could follow in their footsteps."

Then the scholar said to Sarah, "Now, my daughter if you are convinced, you can become a Muslim."

I said, "Please, Seyyed, I would like to become a Muslim also.

He asked in amazement, 'you'?"

"Yes. I must become a Muslim, since I knew nothing of Islam except in name. "The scholar looked at me in the eyes and said, "But you need not repeat the *Shahada* (testimony that Allah is One and Muhammad is His Apostle); it is enough for you to have true faith in Islam in words and deeds."

I replied confidently, "I have true faith."

"Are you ready to sacrifice everything for the sake of Islam?" he asked.

I said, "Yes, everything."

"Give me an example." he said.

I looked at Sarah and told him, "Had I not known that Sarah has become a Muslim believer, I would have decided not to marry her, although she is the most precious thing in my life."

He turned to Sarah and said, "And you, my daughter?"

She said, "I feel the same way. I would not accept Mohsen as a husband if he were not a Muslim, even though he is very dear to me."

The scholar then said, "Allah bless you both and guide you to His pleasure in being righteous seed for a righteous generation."

Sarah then gave her testimony to the scholar. He gave her a golden-lettered Qur'an as a gift. We left him feeling as if we were a newly-born couple. Soon we married and lived happily. We named our first child after the scholar as a token of our gratitude and esteem.

Is he who was dead then We raised him to life and made for him a light by which he walks among the people, like him whose likeness is that of one in utter darkness whence he cannot come forth?... (Al-An'am: 123)

THE END

SHORT STORIES

INTRODUCTION BY THE AUTHOR

Dear Readers,

To embody the general concepts of the Islamic viewpoint concerning life is the aim behind these stories. I believe concepts at the theoretical level cannot produce a change or an effect as they can when presented in the form of events or incidents from real life. Thus the Holy Qur'an gives examples and values through pictures with details of the events in which prophets and the righteous suffered for the sake of Allah. If these short stories are knitted of imagination, they are certainly taken from the depth of present-day Muslim girls' lives. Hence, any girl may read in these stories, incidents she has experienced in some way or directly.

In each story, there is the positive stance of an Islamic viewpoint. The difference is great between this pure and sublime Islamic stance and the impure, corrupted stance of non-Islamic views.

Bint Al-Huda

THE HOMELESS AUNT

Khadijah listened as her aunt tearfully complained to them about her miserable situation. She was saying, "So you see, I have received nothing for my trouble. Both of my children disregard all that I have suffered for their sake. I sold my last gold ornament to send my daughter abroad. I have mortgaged my house twice to enable my son to become a doctor. I sold a valuable carpet so that I could buy a colour T.V. to please my daughter. Do they appreciate or even remember such sacrifices? No. My son wants me to stay away from his home since his wife can't tolerate my presence in the company of her aristocratic visitors. She says she wants to be free in my son's house, as if I deprived her of her freedom."

"I thought that my daughter would be happy to have me live in her house. She is my only daughter. You remember how I helped her to live a life free from worry. Do you know how she treated me in return? Like a maid in her service who should clean her house for her and look after her child while she and her husband spent their time at theaters and clubs. Yesterday, she was out until one in the morning. Her child cried and cried and I couldn't calm him. When she finally came home, I was tired and complained about her behavior. I wanted her to treat me like her mother, not like a servant or a baby sitter…."

"Can you guess what she said to me? Without any shame, she told me that since she gave me shelter and food, I had no cause to complain. She also told me that she valued her freedom and was not ready change for the sake of either her child or her mother."

She wept bitterly, unable to continue. Khadijah gave her something to drink and Khadijah's mother tried to comfort her sister. Khadijah told her aunt gently, "…It is a pity that you have taken so much trouble to raise your children. You have brought them up in such a way that you yourself produced the present state of affairs. You thought that your daughter's happiness could be found in unlimited freedom, and, as a result, she did not learn what her responsibilities were towards you. You helped her neglect her religious duties. Your methods have backfired. She enjoyed life to the utmost without the least concern for Allah, and she forgot the high position Allah the almighty has assigned to a mother. She forgot the Qur'anic verse: *And your Lord has commanded that you shall not serve but Him, and goodness to your parents. If either or both of them reach old age with you, reprimand them not, nor chide them, and speak to them a generous word. And make yourself submissively gentle to them with compassion and say: Oh, my Lord! Have compassion on them as they brought me up.* (Al-Isra: 23 and 24)

And the Qur'anic verse: *"...and keep up prayer, surely prayer is timed ordinance for the believers"* (Al-Nisa: 103)

"You should have taught her the verse in the Holy Qur'an concerning hijab," continued Khadijah, *"...and let them (women) wear their covering over their bosoms and not display of their ornaments.."* (Al-Nisa: 31)

"The result of being raised with no regard to religious duties is always deviation from the right path. There is a great difference between one who spends long hours watching television and indecent films and a person who spends his nights reading religious books which tell him that caring for parents is equal to worshipping Allah, and that Paradise lies at the feet of mothers. You have sold your gold ornament," she continued, "and sent your daughter abroad, but you have forgotten that such travel can uproot all good instincts still buried within her conscience. She has returned to you a figure empty of compassion."

Her aunt sighed deeply and said, "You are quite right, Khadijah. It is my own fault, but I have realized this too late. I followed my husband's advice, which was to raise my children free of all complexes, and to allow them to have whatever they desired. Now, I see how mistaken I have been. Your parents, who brought you up with much attention to religious instructions, are quite happy with you." Khadijah replied, "They are happy as well with my husband and with my brother's wife. My husband encourages me to fulfil my duty towards my parents in order to please Almighty Allah."

Her aunt then said, "I wish I had chosen a righteous husband for my daughter to help her rid herself of all deviation. She should not have married a man who gambles and drinks."

Khadijah then asked, "Why did you agree to such a marriage?"

"It was his expensive car that attracted my daughter, and the high dowry impressed me and prompted me to accept him as a son-in-law," replied her aunt. Sorrowfully, Khadijah said, "Oh, how frank you are, dear aunt! It is a pity that you have realized the truth too late. May Allah save you from this loss, since you admit your fault."

The aunt spent a week in her sister's house, and during that time neither her daughter nor her son showed any concern for her well-being. Khadijah's mother wanted her sister to live with them, but their house was small. The aunt was seriously pressed for a place to live. One morning, Khadijah and her husband said to her, "Please come and stay with us. We really would like to have you. Don't disappoint us."

"Oh, I am a broken-hearted woman. What can I do for you?" her aunt replied. Then she accepted their kind offer gratefully. Khadijah mentioned a narration of the Prophet of Islam (swas) in this regard, which states: A Muslim believer came to the Prophet (swas) and asked what he could do to please Allah. The Prophet (swas) asked him if he had a mother, and the man said: "No". Then the Prophet (swas) asked if he had an aunt, and he answered: "Yes". The Prophet (swas) recommended that he should look after her and love her because she had the same position as mother. The aunt feared that she would be a burden to them.

But Khadijah's husband said, "Please do not say such a thing. I lost my mother too early in life to enjoy her love and care. Perhaps Allah has sent you to make up for that loss. You can live with us and you can receive your son and daughter here whenever you like."

Khadijah's mother, who was seated nearby, said, "They are quite serious about wanting you to live with them. I would be very happy to know that you are near my daughter."

The aunt moved to her new home and was comfortable and at ease for the first time in her life. She never felt like an intruder, and Khadijah accompanied her when she attended religious meetings. The aunt benefited very much from these meetings and enhanced her religious knowledge. She compared Khadijah's happy marriage to her daughter's. She could feel the harmony and spiritual understanding between Khadijah and her husband, and recalled her daughter's life, which was full of quarrels resulting from jealousy, selfishness and indifference. She could easily differentiate between the normal, healthy life of her niece and the disturbed, unnatural one of her daughter. She could do nothing but pray to Allah to guide her daughter and son to the right path.

Early one morning a few months later, the doorbell rang continuously, and Khadijah hurried to open it. She was surprised to see her cousin standing at the door, carrying her child in her arms. Her eye was black and she looked pale. Khadijah welcomed her cousin and took her to her mother's room. The mother was surprised to see her daughter, and she rushed towards her to take her in her arms. She thought that her daughter longed to see her and she had regretted her past behaviour. But her daughter sat down on the nearest chair without the faintest idea of her mother's feelings.

The daughter said, "My husband has turned me out of our house, as if I were a piece of used furniture that could be replaced." Her mother's face grew pale and she said, "He turned you out? When? How?"

Her daughter replied, "Oh, mother. You know how he is. He returns home late every evening, quite drunk. He throws himself on the bed dead with sleep. When I object to his behaviour, he reminds me of our deal that we should respect each other's freedom. I can do nothing but keep silent, since this idea of freedom was my wish from the beginning. But things have grown worse recently. He has started to help himself by my salary and deprived me of my rights in my house.

"Yesterday he said he would no longer tolerate the chains of marriage and made me leave my own home. I spent the night in the garden. I have nowhere to go! My only brother won't allow me to stay in his house. I have none to turn to but you."

Her mother did not know what to say. She thought her niece was kind enough to have her in her house. Could she bring someone else to live with her? It was too much a favor to ask. Khadijah, who had heard everything, knew of her aunt's hidden suffering. She decided to save her the trouble. She told her cousin, "You have done the correct thing by coming to your mother. She will be happy to have you with her until things get better."

The distraught young woman thanked her cousin for her kind help and said, "Oh, how grateful I am to you, Khadijah! You have been so kin d to my mother. Now you are doing me a great favor."

Khadijah smiled and said, "Oh, don't say such things. You should consider this house as your own." The aunt was so moved that she rushed to Khadijah and kissed her. She said, "How wonderful you are, my dear! What great faith you have."

Khadijah whispered into her ear, "Please aunt, tell your daughter to wear her hijab as long as she is in our house." The aunt answered immediately, "Oh, yes, I have already decided to do so."

She settled herself near her daughter and said "I have never felt such comfort in my life as I feel here. I have found in your cousin Khadijah and her husband love and care that I never found in you and your brother. You are my own children, but you showed ingratitude towards me, while my niece and her husband flood me with kind feelings. I wish you knew the reason." She was silent for a while. Then her daughter said, "Oh, mother, surely it is faith in Allah and His Pleasure that dominates their life, while we lack such faith."

"Praise is due to Allah the Almighty that you have realized the truth by yourself!" said her mother. "Therefore, you should start to show regret for the past and return to religion by first wearing your hijab." The daughter looked down at the floor and was silent. Then Khadijah said "..I think she has found out what happens when one neglects one's religion. She now feels the importance of Islamic ethics."

Her cousin looked up at her and said "You are right, Khadijah. I am tired of this life of pretense. I need someone to lead me and teach me true faith and real salvation with no submission to other's wishes and desires. But I can't help wondering what people will say about me."

Khadijah replied, "You always tried to please people in the past, which made you their slave. You have gained nothing from that but false happiness. You have wasted years, running the wrong way. Now, it is time for you to come back to your religion and understand Islamic values in order to gain happiness in this life and the Hereafter."

"Will Allah accept my repentance after years of deviation?", her cousin asked.

"Yes, of course, Allah loves those who repent and hates those who insist on doing wrong." Then Khadijah recited the Qur'anic verse: ***Do they not know that Allah accepts repentance from his servants and takes the alms, and that Allah is All Compassionate? Say: Work and Allah will see your (good) work and so will His Apostle and the believers ...*** *(Bara'at: 104, 105)*

The cousin spent a few weeks with her mother. She was greatly affected by Khadijah's strong faith. Khadijah did her best to help her, and she gave her some Islamic books that she read and discussed later. Khadijah's cousin eventually became a good Muslim, and she knew she could no longer live with a man addicted to drinking and gambling. She filed for divorce. She gave up all her rights to her home in return for keeping her only child. She intended to raise him to be a good believer.

A MUSLIM STUDENT'S DIARY

I was feeling depressed yesterday because of Layla's words. She tried to prejudice the class against me, saying that my Islamic dress was nothing but immature behavior designed to attract attention. Her words were cutting and left me spiritually hurt. How difficult it is when a woman doubts her purpose in life! She often acts harshly towards Muslim women. I was shocked, dismayed and hurt by her words.

I thought about the matter at home and sought guidance from Allah. I realized that I was not immature, as Layla had claimed. In fact, being an adolescent is but a stage of an individual's physical and mental growth. At this stage, knowledge flourishes and rids itself of childhood confusion. One becomes used to life's contradictions.

Hence, my attitude towards hijab is not abnormal. I rationalized that attracting attention is not accomplished by wearing long garments, but through dressing without hijab. I used to go out in public without Islamic dress before Allah guided me to the right path. I could actually feel the sharp looks of men wherever I went. I always noticed and was embarrassed by their looks and their obvious pleasure at seeing an unlimited exposure of beauty. Now that I have my hijab on, what can they be attracted to? If they look, they see nothing to excite them. This hijab reminds them that a Sacred Law protects the blessed creatures of the Creator.

I have come to a conclusion: Layla does not understand her words and I only feel sorry for her. Her beauty may become spoiled by this corrupted society. I pray to Allah to help me guide her in understanding Islam.

February 7th, 19...

Yesterday I was waiting for my friend, Wala, to come over so we could study for exams together. She did not 15 show up, and I became worried. I waited for her to phone me but she didn't. She has just now phoned to apologize and to tell me that she isn't feeling well. I wished her a speedy recovery.

I like Wala very much because she is a good Muslim. Our beliefs, dreams and hopes are the same. We became friends at the beginning of the school years. Harmony in beliefs and ideals brings strangers together, while disputes always leave close friends apart.

Today we are going to have our weekly Islamic meeting. We shall recite some Qur'anic verses and try to understand their meaning, than we will discuss religious subjects. I wonder if Wala is coming.

February 12th, 19...

Our meeting last week was a real success. Despite her illness, Wala attended and gave an interesting lecture about religion's sublime aim. I, in turn, spoke about the issue of obedience and disobedience in regard to Islamic instructions. One of the sisters complained of her mother's insistence that she not wear hijab. This Muslim girl wondered if she had to obey her mother's orders, since obeying parents is a religious duty. I explained to her that she should obey her parents' orders as long as their rules did not violate religious instructions or cause Allah's displeasure. She can disobey her mother and keep her hijab to please her Creator.

March 2nd, 19...

I have really tried hard to make Layla listen to me. She has often been unyielding; however, I won't give up. I feel she has changed a bit. I gave her some Islamic books about why women should dress modestly. She accepted the books and promised to read them and discuss them with me.

When I visited Layla's home yesterday, she gave me a warm welcome. I shall never regret this visit. We discussed the Islamic books and she asked whether she could continue her high school studies with hijab. I assured her that Islam has ordered both men and women to seek knowledge. The Prophet's hadith relates: "It is an Islamic duty for men and women to learn."

March 11th, 19...

How happy I am! I have seen Layla wearing her Islamic dress in school. She has become a good Muslim girl. In our history lesson today, the teacher claimed that if the Holy Qur'an were revealed today, it would not order woman to wear hijab, since woman today plays a significant role in society. She cannot be isolated within the house. I asked the teacher to allow me to answer her point of view. I told the class that: "Throughout history woman has been involved in society. In fact, she played a significant role in ancient civilizations. Women were queens and empresses. In the Holy Qur'an, for instance, the Queen of Saba is mentioned: *Surely I found a woman ruling over them and she has been given abundance and she has a mighty throne.* (Al-Naml: 23)

"History also tells us of Cleopatra, who ruled Egypt and resorted to suicide when she was defeated by the Roman invaders. However, past civilizations generally considered women to be inferior to men. Some religions considered woman to be unclean and did not allow her to perform religious rituals or enter places of worship.

I continued, "Islam neither isolated woman nor belittled her contributions to society. On the contrary, Islam has given a woman equal rights, as is clearly stated in the Qur'anic verse: *I will not waste the work of any worker among you whether male or a female; the one of you being from the other...I will most certainly make them enter gardens beneath which rivers flow; a reward from Allah, and with Allah is yet better reward.*" *(Aale-Imran: 194)*

"In another Qur'anic verse concerning hijab, Islam does not address women only; men, as well, are ordered to cast down their eyes. Had Islam aimed at isolating woman, there would not have been the necessity for such an order: *Say to the believing men to cast down their looks and guard their private parts... and say to the believing women to cast down their looks and guard their private parts and not to display their ornaments except what appears thereof; and let them wear their head covering over their bosoms and not display their ornaments except to their husbands or their fathers or their sons... and turn to Allah all of you, oh, believers, so that you may be successful. (Al-Nur: 37)*

"Islamic history illustrates the role of women in the Muslim community. Women were present at the Prophet's battles. They nursed the wounded and supplied water and food to the believers. Some even carried a sword and defended Islam. The Prophet (swas) appreciated their role and gave them their share of the spoils. We also read in Islamic history that Muslim women held meetings to recite and interpret the Qur'an. Such evidence indicates that Islam never isolated women or negated their role in the community...Furthermore, *hijab* is necessary for woman and is in harmony with her nature and man's nature too. Men are inclined naturally towards women and women are inclined to draw men towards them. Hence the exposure of woman without hijab in society can arouse the inner instincts that lead to sexual relations that affect not only individuals, but the family and the community as well. One illustration of this is in the Western so-called civilized societies where corruption and immorality are increasing and more and more homes are being broken."

March 26th, 19...

I have noticed recently that my dear friend Saffia does not look well. Though she has not missed our meetings, I feel something is wrong with her. I wish I could help her. I know nothing about her family. May be she needs money and does not want others to know about her hardship. She is quite wrong. Muslim believers do not care for an easy life, and they are kind to each other. What counts are good, righteous deeds as mentioned in the Qur'an: *As for the scum, it vanishes as jetsam, what profits men, abides in the earth.* (Al-Ra'ad:17)

April 20th, 19...

At last I have discovered the reason for Saffia's uneasiness. She lives in a humble house and thinks this may cause her to be ashamed among her friends. I managed to make her change her opinion. I told her our great Prophet (swas), the greatest man in history who achieved the most sacred mission, was a poor man. He could have lived as a king or an emperor, but he did not. Fatimah (sa), his daughter, lived in a humble house with a minimum of furniture. The Prophet's companions lived the same sort of humble life. History relates that a great fire broke out in Al-Madyin (in Iraq) when the companion, Salman al-Farsi, was the ruler. People rushed to save their valuable possessions, but Salman carried nothing but a small bundle of clothes, a Qur'an, a prayer rug and a water pot. He was heard to have said, "In this way, light travelers are saved."

May 2nd, 19...

I came across an old friend of mine the other day. She used to be a very optimistic and active girl with tremendous belief in Islam. She never hated others or harbored any ill intention towards anybody. She trusted all her friends and was ready to help them in order to please Almighty Allah. Anyway, it had been a long time since I last saw her. I was so happy to meet her again, but I was shocked to see that she had changed into a different person with a pessimistic view towards life. She was sad to see that those around her never differentiated between good and bad deeds. She had nearly lost confidence in everything and had resorted to living a solitary life, avoiding both friends and relatives. She was spiritually depressed. When I saw her in such a state, I realized she had been a victim of our deviated society. I told my friend, "Do you really regret your good deeds? "I felt the question put her at a loss. I hoped she would say "No", but she remained silent. I said to her gently, "Say, no, please. Doing good is something wonderful and gives spiritual satisfaction. Never regret good actions. It is enough that you can examine your deeds and find that nothing shameful stains your record. Allah will surely reward you. Don't regret anything and don't be hopeless. Life is filled with promise and there are those who appreciate good deeds. Please don't let disappointment with society cause you to hate it. If you fall, try again and remove this cloud of doubt in order to see more clearly. Keep on being a good righteous believer, think of Allah's reward and you will feel much better': she listened to me attentively and I hope my words will be of some help.

May 22nd, 19...

Today a Muslim sister has asked me to explain a phrase in Du'a Kumail: "...Oh, Allah! I appeal to you by your Holy Names to make me pray to you day and night...

The sister asked, "How could one pray continuously day and night? We live in an age that requires cooperation with others in order for us to carry out our various jobs and daily work. How can we put aside our duties and resort to du'a all the time?" I said to her, "Be at ease, sister. We are not supposed to pray day and night. Though it is a good habit that gains reward, this is not everything. Many people glorify and praise Allah with their tongues but forget Him in their deeds. We can enrich our lives with prayer easily and without neglecting our duties. "Religious rituals, such as daily prayers, can be reflected in our actions. If you are a good housewife, then you are a righteous individual glorifying God day and night. One of the Prophet's traditions relates that a woman came to him and asked "what women could do in that way of *jihad*." The Prophet (swas) said, *"Righteousness and good house management are features of good Muslim woman and are well-rewarded by Allah. A woman, whether a housewife or a young girl, can be in the service of Allah all the time, if she gives a helping hand to the needy for the pleasure of Allah. Any help to others for the sake of heavenly reward is a du'a and a prayer to Allah the Exalted. Any hardship endured for the sake of elevating the Word of Allah is a prayer. Any good idea on behalf of the community's welfare is an act of worship."*

Reference to Allah's bounties without the notion of *kibr* (self-pride), can be a prayer. A smile without the intention of flattery or pretension can be a prayer to Allah. But telling a person's secrets or someone's defect without the least necessity and for non-religious aim is disobedience to Allah's orders.

Our final exams are drawing near and we should schedule our time wisely in order to pass them successfully and prove that Islamic activity can not hinder study or prevent reading. In fact, it can widen the scope of the brain and deepen thinking.

CHOOSING A WIFE

Seeing that his mother was in a good mood, Ahmad sat near her and said, 'Mother, I have an idea which should bring you much joy." His mother answered eagerly, "My son, all that you give me makes me happy. What is on your mind?"

"You know," he told her, "I have finished my studies and can afford to begin a family. I have decided to marry."

His mother's face brightened with a smile. "This is very good news! I have long awaited such a day," she told him. "How often I have wished you would marry one of your cousins. Praise be to Allah that you have made this decision before it is too late!." Ahmad exclaimed, "Before it's too late? What do you mean?" "Your cousin Maryam is now old enough to marry. Every day there is someone visiting her home, seeking her hand."

Ahmad sat silently for a moment and said, "Then why should we bother her suitors?"

"What do you mean, Ahmad?," asked his mother, dismayed.

"My cousin Maryam is not fit for me."

"Why not? No, my son, you're mistaken. I shall go and see about your engagement tomorrow," his mother told him.

Ahmad frowned and said, "No, mother. Please do not do such a thing. I will not agree to this." "When she becomes your fiancée, you will feel love for her. Put aside your fears. Maryam is beautiful, and she has a respectable job."

Ahmad disagreed, "No. This matter only concerns me."

Ahmad's mother thought for a moment and said, "If you dislike Maryam, then there's my brother's daughter. She is as beautiful as Maryam, and she has inherited a large sum of money from my brother.

"Mother, please think about this matter from my point of view. I need someone to share my life, not a business partner."

His mother became angry and sharply asked, "What's wrong with my niece? Why isn't she good enough to be your wife?"

Ahmad replied, "She is not a practicing Muslim. I want a Muslim wife."

Ahmad's mother laughed sarcastically and said, "You speak as if you were an angel who could only marry another angel. Why don't you stop saying such nonsense, my son? You are an educated young man, you should give up your impossible ideals."

"I am neither an angel, nor do I seek a saint for a wife. I am a Muslim believer looking for a girl who also believes in Islam." replied Ahmad.

Ahmad's mother told him, "I don't know any girls who share your ideals."

He said, "I know someone who measures up to my expectations."

Startled by this admission, Ahmad's mother asked, "You know someone? Who is she? Since when do you begin friendship with girls?"

Ahmad answered quickly, "I didn't mean that I know a girl personally, but I know of her." "I see," she said. "You have already chosen your wife. Who is this lucky girl?" "Mother, please be more understanding. I hope you will take my side and persuade father to agree with my choice."

This appeal to Ahmad's mother softened her, and she said, "I swear that I think only of your welfare. I'll help you. Tell me, what are this girl's qualifications?"

Ahmad told her, "Nothing matters except the religious aspect. She is Muslim, and wears complete hijab." "Oh, then she is uneducated!" "No, she has a high school education and her religious knowledge is extensive."

Then his mother asked, "What family is she from? Do I know them?"

"She is from a good family known for their piety", Ahmad told her. "Of what use is a well-known family if a girl has no Islamic morals?" He silently beseeched Allah to give him the patience to overcome his mother's resistance. "A happy marriage doesn't depend on fame or wealth. Happiness stems from spiritual nearness and mutual understanding." Then, in a different tone of voice his mother asked,

"What does her father do for a living?" "He is a grocer," Ahmad replied.

"A grocer?!" she exclaimed. "Yes. He is a grocer and a very righteous man. He is the head of a happy and virtuous family."

Ahmad's mother interrupted him, "You are the son of a wealthy man; with your college degree you wish to marry a grocer's daughter? What a shame! Yet you ask me to assist you! If I had chosen the daughter of a jeweler, how would you feel?"

His mother replied, "There is a big difference between a jeweler and a grocer."

"The only difference is with regard to the substance. The former sells rings and the latter sells sugar. Both work in order to earn money," Ahmad answered.

His mother lamented, "Imagine your father's reaction to this news!"

Ahmad said firmly, "This is my desire, either you help me or I'll do it myself."

He spoke so seriously that his mother laughed mockingly, saying, "Does the matter require a great effort? The least move you make, they will give their daughter to you gladly."

Ahmad shook his head in doubt and said, "Wait and see!"

"What an odd situation this is! Am I to present my son to a grocer's daughter? What special beauty does this girl possess to make you blind to every other consideration?'

"I have not yet seen her," Ahmad said.

"Then how do you know she's not ugly?" asked his mother.

"I know she is not. As far as good conduct is concerned, physical beauty is of little importance."

"Oh Ahmad, my amazement never ceases."

The next morning, Ahmad told his father of his intentions. His father became angry, but Ahmad remained determined to marry the woman of his choice. Finally his father agreed and Ahmad asked his mother to visit the girl's home to make the proposal and overcome any obstacles.

The following afternoon Ahmad's mother, accompanied by his oldest sister, went to the girl's house. On the way there, Ahmad's sister asked her mother what the girl's name was. Her mother replied, "I forgot to ask him! "When they knocked on the family's door, they were surprised to see a beautiful young girl open it. The girl was surprised to see the two unfamiliar women, but she showed them into the living room and went to tell her mother that they had visitors. Her mother welcomed the guests and waited for them to explain the reason for their visit. After exchanging greetings, Ahmad's mother asked who the young girl was who had opened the door. "It was my daughter, Zaynab," she replied. "Do you have any other daughter?" asked Ahmad's mother. "No, she's my only daughter", replied her mother. Ahmad's mother and sister were delighted to learn that the beautiful girl was Zaynab. Just then, Zaynab entered with coffee for their visitors. She sat next to Ahmad's sister and they soon found much to discuss. Then she collected the empty coffee cups and left the room.

Ahmad's mother began, "We have come with a blessed aim. We would be happy to have your daughter Zaynab as a wife for my son." She praised her son for his intelligence, his good looks and his wealth, but she neglected to mention his firm Islamic beliefs, which was very important to Zaynab's mother. Therefore, Ahmad's mother was stunned when Zaynab's mother shook her head slowly and said, "I'm very sorry. It is difficult for me to agree to this proposal; in fact, it's impossible." With much surprise, Ahmad's mother asked, "What is impossible?"

"My daughter is still young. I'm sure your son can find a girl who suits him." Ahmad's mother protested, "But Zaynab suits him well! Would you be kind enough to justify your refusal?"

"I only have one daughter, and I should be sure of her future married life."

"But Ahmad is well-off financially," said his mother. "He is an engineer!"

Zaynab's mother replied, "Zaynab would not marry someone because he is wealthy or has a college degree."

Ahmad's mother was at a loss for words. "Then what will ensure your daughter's happiness and consent?"

"When a mother looks for a wife for her son, she should mention her son's conduct." said the mother of Zaynab. "My daughter is a committed Muslim. She wants a Muslim husband, and remember, my daughter wears *hijab*, and your son may want a modern wife, who dresses like his mother and sister."

Ahmad's mother laughed with relief and told her, "You're correct. I haven't mentioned his conduct. I thought that other aspects of his character were of more importance. My son is a faithful Muslim. He is, in fact, looking for a wife who observes *hijab*. Be sure that my appearance (un-Islamic clothing) is not to Ahmad's taste."

Zaynab's mother also smiled and said, "You should have told me earlier! Please give us your address so we can visit you and learn more about your son."

"We hope you can come early next week," said Ahmad's mother.

Ahmad was waiting anxiously for his mother's return. As soon as she and her daughter returned home he asked, "Well, mother? How was your visit?"

"It was very strange," she replied.

"What was strange?" he asked. "Has anything bad happened?"

"Oh no, Ahmad! But I never expected such a thing," she answered. "Then they have refused?" Ahmad's father said, "How could a grocer's daughter refuse a wealthy young man?"

Ahmad's mother turned to her husband and said, "They did, in fact, refuse..."

"What! they refused?" asked the father. "I spoke about Ahmad's good qualities, but I didn't mention his Islamic morals. My appearance also caused her to decline my proposal because her daughter is a very faithful Muslim. When I realized their objections, I told them that you are a true Muslim as well. I have come to respect them very much. They don't care about status or wealth."

"Have you seen the girl?" asked Ahmad's father.

"Yes, she is lovely and polite. Ahmad is a lucky man to have made such a choice."

The following week, Zaynab's family paid a visit to Ahmad's home and plans were made for the upcoming wedding. They were soon married and there was much rejoicing.

A VISIT TO A BRIDE

After finishing her morning prayer, Fatimah usually sat down to recite a chapter from the Holy Qur'an. She always found great pleasure in reading each verse as she thought about the sublime meaning of the Divine words. At such times, she felt as if she was existing on a higher plane, a spiritual world with a sacred atmosphere. The words taught her lessons and flooded her life with new light when she read the Qur'anic verses:

And one of His signs is that He created mates for you from yourselves that you may find rest in them... and He put between you love and compassion. Most surely, there, are signs in this for people who reflect. (Al-Rum: 21)

And,

And they who say: Oh our Lord! Grant us in our wives and our offspring the joy of our eyes and make us guides to those who guard (against evil). (Al-Furqan: 74)

The words reminded her of famous Muslim believers. She gave a deep sigh. She really felt quite sad when she saw some Muslims failing to continue striving towards perfection. However, there were still promising examples. She thought about her friend, Khadijah, who had just begun her married life and was visiting some holy shrines during her honeymoon. Khadijah was a good Muslim sister who chose her partner carefully and according to religious measures. She rejected all anti-Islamic traditions that distorted the meaning and essence of marriage. She always said that, according to Islam, marriage is the first brick of a foundation in raising a generation of good believers. Fatimah beseeched Allah to guide her dear friend along the right path in her new life. She had barely finished her prayer when one of her Muslim friends rang the doorbell. She had come to tell Fatimah that Khadijah had returned from her honeymoon and that she had settled in her new home. Fatimah rushed to put on her hijab to go and visit her, but the sister told Fatimah it was too early to go that day, and that Khadijah was not quite ready to receive visitors. Fatimah was surprised. How could Khadijah refuse a Muslim sister's visit? She felt sad and said, "I can hardly believe this. Why don't we go and clear up the matter?"

The sister replied, "Oh, perhaps Khadijah will be annoyed for some particular reason."

Fatimah said, "Yes, it may be so. Otherwise, she would not refuse her sister's visit simply because she lacked furniture or some similar reason. She has never been concerned about materialistic things."

Fatimah spent that day depressed. She feared Khadijah might yield to the false values of society, yet she knew that her friend was a good believer and would not change easily.

At nine o'clock that evening, the doorbell rang and Fatimah went to open it. She was so pleased to see Khadijah standing there that she could hardly believe her eyes. They exchanged kisses and words of welcome and Fatimah congratulated Khadijah, and told her of her desire to visit her. Khadijah expressed surprise at the delay in visiting her, but Fatimah said, "Have you not announced that you are not ready to receive friends?"

Khadijah replied, "Why should I? I have missed you all so much and have been waiting for your visit since my arrival."

Fatimah said, "Well someone said that your house was not fit yet for visitors."

Khadijah was surprised and said, "Oh, dear! Since when have I cared for such trifles? How can you believe it?" Fatimah was pleased to hear this. She said, "Praise be to Allah! How happy I am to hear you say this! But such un-Islamic rumors should be stopped. We are quite happy that you have begun your married life in harmony with your religious beliefs. We shall soon visit you, God willing."

Khadijah warmly replied, "You are all welcome any time. The sooner, the better."

The next morning Fatimah phoned the other sisters and told them of her proposed visit to Khadijah on that day. While she was thinking about telling her cousin, she heard her talking to her mother. Fatimah went to her and asked her to join them, but her cousin said, "Oh, thank you, but..."

Fatimah was surprised at her cousin's answer, and asked, "What is the matter with you? Didn't you say that you wanted to go with us?"

Her cousin replied, "Yes, but it is clear that you do not want me to accompany you."

Fatimah was amazed. "What makes you think so?" she asked.

Her cousin answered, "How can you inform me of the visit on the same day? How am I to get ready when I need at least two days to get a new dress and buy a nice present? Do you think I can go without a gift?"

Fatimah said, "Not necessarily. A present can enhance friendship and is recommended in our religion. But buying a present should not cause financial strain. Otherwise, it seems as if it were a tax to be paid. A present can be something simple and still special. Our Prophet (swas) used to accept even a cup of milk as a present."

Fatimah's cousin retorted, "Don't you think it would be shameful to give her a cheap present?"

Fatimah said firmly, "A gift is not valuable because of its price, but by its being given. A useful book, for instance, is a good gift. As for anew dress, I suggest you visit Khadijah in your old dress and you can buy a new one another time."

The cousin thought for a while, than agreed to go. On that day, the new bride Khadijah was busy with her daily work. She baked a cake for her expected visitors.

She was active and at ease. Thinking of the upcoming visit, she recalled pleasant memories of the past. The doorbell rang and one of her relatives, who also happened to be her neighbor, was at the door. Khadijah welcomed her and invited her in. They sat down and chatted a while.

Her relative told Khadijah about their district, most of the inhabitants of which were wealthy. Khadijah said, "I do not care much for this aristocratic district. A true Muslim does not change his or herself to fit in with any particular class of people."

The relative answered, "Well, I just wanted to tell you about some matters concerning the district where you have settled."

"Does it really matter?" asked Khadijah.

"The style of your *hijab* is not accepted here. You look peculiar."

Khadijah proudly replied, "I am happy to look different in my decent Islamic dress."

Bewildered, her relative asked, "Why should you be happy to be so different from the rest?"

Khadijah said, "First of all, my aim is to obey my Creator and gain His pleasure. Also, when I wear my hijab, I surely remind others of Allah and their obligation to worship Him cording to the Qur'anic verse:

And I have not created the jinn and mankind except that they should worship Me. *(Al-Zariat: 56)*

"My duty is to enjoin the good and forbid evil. Through my appearance I call people to Allah's religion. In any case, thank you for your advice."

Khadijah's relative could not believe her ears. She changed the subject, saying, "You are expecting some guests, aren't you? I smell fresh cake."

Khadijah smiled and said, "Yes, I expect some of my sisters in faith."

"It is pity you have not furnished your home yet,"

Khadijah's relative remarked, looking around the living room. "Since you have no chairs, I can lend you some, and any other things you might need."

"Thank you very much, but I do not need to borrow any chairs. I can manage without them. I consider such things to be of little value. I believe in the Qur'anic verse:

...And the embellishment of gold, and all of this is naught but provision of this world's life; and the hereafter is with your Lord; only for those who guard (against evil)." (Al-Zukhruf: 35)

That evening, Khadijah entertained her friends, who enjoyed the visit and were warmly welcomed by the bride.

DETERMINATION

It was a gloomy, overcast night. The wind was blowing and it was going to storm. Khadijah and her three young children were sitting on an old worn carpet in their room Khadijah looked out the window often, trying not to draw her children's attention. She was worried that the storm would break before her husband arrived. Finally, hearing the key turn in the lock, she quickly got up, telling her children to go welcome their father.

"Oh mother", said the youngest child, "Has he brought us food?" She gently scolded him, saying, "This is not important. Don't ask him this question." The children ran towards their father and, although she was upset, Khadijah, too, greeted him with a smile. Her husband had brought a few pieces of bread and cheese, which he handed to his wife. She soon served the simple meal on plates that had lost their colour through long use.

Khadijah spoke cheerfully while they ate and later the children slept, dreaming of sweets, toys and games. Their parents sat quietly for a while.

"So this year is about to end," Khadijah's husband, Hassan, said bitterly, "And I still haven't found a job. We have spent our savings and sold what we could of our furniture. We have nothing left with which to fight our hunger."

His wife replied, "We still have faith and determination, which are the keys to all which is good and brings happiness."

"What good thing or happiness has our faith brought us? Our children are wearing torn clothes and are hungry. It is this very faith that has made life difficult for us, and it is guidance, which has led us to poverty! In the past we were living in luxury..."

Khadijah interrupted her husband, asking, "What kind of luxury was it? Since when has gambling been a way of providing for one's family! Allah has said that gambling is forbidden to Muslims. How could we have been happy knowing that the food we ate and the clothes we wore would send us to the Fire in the Hereafter? Our gain caused others to go hungry and naked!

"Yes, Khadijah," Hassan said. "I know you are right. For these very reasons I gave up gambling, but it has brought us nothing. I thank you for helping me out of that bottomless pit. All praise belongs to Allah for His guidance. Still, poverty is bitter and the shamefulness of being needy is almost unbearable."

Upon hearing these words, Khadijah consoled him saying, "Oh Hassan, it is only temporary. Allah says that with every difficulty comes relief. The life of the Hereafter is the real and endless one. We still have hope. This future, everlasting life is the one we should care about and make ready with good deeds. Don't regret what has passed; instead, thank I Allah for possessing the means of obtaining His forgiveness. Happiness belongs to those who are patient while facing hardships and avoid disobeying Allah."

"Oh Khadijah, I am not without hope, but I'm afraid that Satan will cause me to sin- then I will fall and lose everything."

"I still have my gold wedding ring," his wife said.

"Tomorrow I shall sell it and we will have money for a while. Almighty Allah will help us. Be confident that you will find a job, with Allah's help. Allah doesn't leave those who worship Him without hope of His compassion. You will surely see how the future will brighten for you, and how generous Allah is to those who believe."

With a sigh, her husband replied," If you think so, I will believe you but what is the wisdom behind our hardship?"

"Oh, Hassan!" She cried. "Don't you know the Qur'anic verse: *And we will most certainly test you with what you fear, and hunger, and loss of property and lives. Therefore, give good news to the patient?"* (Al-Baqarah, 155)

"But when will this hardship end?" he asked.

"As soon as we pass our test successfully," she replied. "Through patience, prayer, and avoiding sinful ways of getting money, we shall succeed."

At this point, the couple stopped talking and fell asleep, putting their trust in Allah. At dawn they awoke for their morning prayers. Afterwards, Khadijah began preparing breakfast and her husband sat down to recite some Surahs from the Qur'an. When the children woke up, their mother poured tea for them. One of the children asked for bread. He said, "My friend and his brothers have eggs and butter every morning."

His mother, feeling great pain in her heart, smiled, kissed him and said, "'Tomorrow, by Allah's will, you will have whatever you like."

The child innocently asked, "Why do you say: 'By Allah's will'?"

"Because," she replied, "It is Allah Who gives us everything and helps us to do our work. Without His will, we can't even breathe."

"Mother, does that mean Allah will give us eggs and bread for breakfast?"

"Yes, my son. By the will of Allah it will happen." The father listened to his wife. He was greatly surprised by her strong faith. He began to feel hopeful and confident. He started talking with his children about the days to come and how Allah would help him to find a good job. Then he would buy whatever sweets and fruits they like. Then there was a knock at the door. Wondering whom it could be at such an early hour, Hassan went to find out. When he returned, his face was shining with happiness. Upon seeing this, his wife said, "Hassan, I feel our test is over."

In a voice choking with emotion, he replied. "Yes, my dear wife, Allah, the Exalted, has ended our test. Praise to Allah, it has happened with your patience, efforts and faith. There is a hadith which says: 'A good woman is better than 1000 men.' Our hardship is finished by the grace of Allah and your strong faith."

"Was it the messenger of Hajj Sahib?"

"No, it was Hajj Sahib himself. He said that he had been looking for someone to manage his business and heard about our situation and my past experience. Allah used him as the way to save us from despair and to give us hope, as Allah promised to the patient believers. Hajj Sahib said to me, 'You are now cleaner and purer than all of us. You are now as one newly born.'"

THE LOST DIARY

It was by chance that Tuqa found a small diary lying on the ground outside the public library. When she picked it up and opened it to the first page, she read the following lines:

4/8/87

"Am I strong enough to hold onto these tiny threads of hope? Can I continue in spite of these difficulties and reach the source of light behind these clouds? Who can give me a helping hand so that I can endure this cruel life? Oh God, what darkness surrounds me!" Tuqa read another page:

26/8/87

"Again I resort to my diary to complain about my suffering. I feel as if my nerves are about to shatter ...I have no one to talk to; no one at all. Oh, why can't I sleep? The moon and the stars gaze upon me as if mocking my dreams." Tuqa looked for an address in the diary but she could only find a name Huda Najafi. She went into the library and asked to see the list of book borrowers of the past week. Finally, she found the name she was looking for. Huda's address was written next to her name, so Tuqa decided to pay her a visit to return the diary and see if she could help this troubled sister.

The next day, Tuqa went to Huda's house. As she rang the bell, she wondered if she was doing the right thing. But since she knew that her intention was pure, she was at ease. A young girl opened the door, and Tuqa asked to see Huda. The girl asked her to enter and showed her to Huda's room. Huda was surprised to see an unknown visitor, but she welcomed Tuqa with a warm smile. They shook hands and sat down. Tuqa took the diary out of her purse and gave it to Huda, who was very happy to see it. She held it close and said, "Thanks God I have it -at last! Thank you for bringing it to me!"

Tuqa introduced herself and said, "Please excuse me for reading a few pages of your diary. I found it yesterday on the ground, near the library."

"There is nothing to apologize for! I have suffered greatly since I lost it. I was nearly heart-broken when I realized that my diary was missing."" Why should you be so upset at the loss of a few pages?" asked Tuqa.

"These words reflect my innermost feelings; they are like a part of my soul," replied Huda.

"But such reflections are but a small part of a person's thoughts, since life is an enormous theatre comprised of countless images. Life is like a wild garden wherein various kinds of flowers fill the air with their fresh scent. Yet there are also trees and thorny weeds in the garden, which may hurt a person. The earth from which flowers emerge nourishes weeds as well."

Huda listened attentively, and then said, "Thorns cause one to bleed, and weeds hinder the growth of blossoms." "It isn't always so," replied Tuqa. "Hopes and disappointments follow each other in turn. This is a natural law of life. However, great one's sufferings are, one still hopes for the dawn which follows even the darkest night."

In a weary voice, Huda said, "But this dark night may be so long that it causes one to lose hope." "You can counter feelings of hopelessness by having true faith in Allah's help and guidance. A life of hardship is of no value if one forgets about Allah and His Compassion. Master yourself, and you can direct your thoughts and actions towards the right path." "But some things are beyond a person's control and cause pain and disappointment," Huda persisted.

"Still", said Tuqa, "Disappointment is not in itself evil. If a believer has strong faith, a new door opens when another is closed. Never give up hope."

Tears formed in Huda's eyes and she said, "I don't know. Perhaps Allah has sent you to save me from my despair."

Tuqa recited a verse from the Holy Qur'an:

"...and despair not of Allah's Mercy; surely none despairs of Allah's Mercy except the unbelievers" (Yusuf: 87)

Then Tuqa stood up, saying it was time for her to leave in order to reach home and perform the evening prayer. Huda begged her to stay a little longer and suggested that they pray together. After praying, they resumed their discussion and Tuqa reminded Huda of the Qur'anic verse:

Do people think they will be left alone saying: We believe, and not be tried? And certainly we tried those before them so Allah will certainly know who are true and He will certainly know the liars. (Al-Ankabut: 2 and 3)

Tuqa added, "I all that we experience during our brief lifetimes prepares our soul to control itself through using good will. Some losses are considered to be disasters while, in fact, they are disguised blessings. A calamity which disrupts a happy life may be a means to crystallize thoughts and can direct a person towards faith in Allah and obedience to His orders."

"My dear friend Tuqa, I thought that I was a good believer in Almighty Allah, but I was about to fall apart."

Tuqa firmly stated, "Faith will defeat earthly concerns through submission to Allah and acceptance of His Will. Failures can teach us many useful lessons. Hardships can make a person wise if they stand firm."

Thinking that she had given enough advice for one afternoon, Tuqa tried to change the subject, "Aren't you going to ask me how I found your home?" Huda replied, "I believe Allah sent you to me, no matter how you found you way."

It was time for Tuqa to leave, and Huda made her promise to visit again soon. The next meeting between Tuqa and Huda took place a few days later. This time, Tuqa decided it was better to let Huda do most of the talking. Huda talked about her younger sister, whom she said had a great desire for learning. Huda said, "She studies continuously, but I fear that she may one day give up her studies."

Tuqa asked, "What makes you think so? I think that she may become even more interested in acquiring knowledge as she gets older." "But life is not generous enough to help one achieve one's dreams and wishes,"

Huda replied. "Pessimism should not dominate anyone's thoughts. If evil has an effect on a person's life, goodness is still more effective. Rays of sunlight can penetrate the thickest clouds," Tuqa said. She felt that her friend still needed encouragement, so she added, "Muslims know the origin of life, the story of creation. Almighty Allah gave all human beings the opportunity to perform good deeds in this life and has given them the chance to worship Him. This worshipping of Allah gives us the opportunity to evolve into more, which will benefit us in the next life, the Hereafter. Therefore, if one comprehends the aim behind this worldly life, the death of a dear one can be tolerated.

"As for suffering due to material poverty, a wise person should know that true poverty is embodied in spiritual shortcomings, which can bring about various illnesses," Tuqa concluded." Nevertheless, poverty can cause one to be ashamed,"

Huda said, "There is nothing shameful about poverty,"

Tuqa told her. "One should be ashamed to be rich and dishonest. A poor man who remains virtuous and rejects dishonest means of living enjoys self-respect. Poverty not only is not a source of shame, it is an aspect of the lives of righteous believers. As Allah states:

And We will most certainly try you with something of fear and hunger and loss of property and lives and fruits,' and give good news to the patient. (Al-Baqarah: 155)

Tuqa continued, "A Muslim is not envious of another's good fortune. He feels optimistic that he will have his r turn one day. A wise believer has a strong will, and if he is betrayed by a friend he will not regret the loss of such a person. Perhaps such an experience will cause him to choose his friends more carefully."

"But one can be hurt by ingratitude or even aggression when one tries to help another."

Tuqa answered, "This is not the case with a true Muslim who does not trade his good deeds. He is ready to help purely based on his good faith and expects nothing from anyone but Allah. It's better that good deeds be rewarded in the Hereafter."

"What you're saying is true. You have been so kind and helpful to me that I can hardly find a way to express my gratitude", Huda said.

Tuqa told her, "There is a narration from our Prophet (swas) *'If one cares for a fellow believer, one should manifest one's concern.'* The best thing you can do is to respond to Islamic ideals and think over my words. As material concerns bring about unhappiness, so do spiritual values lead to happiness. Imam Ali (A.S.) says: *'If a man behaves properly in matters concerning himself and Allah, Allah keeps proper the matters between him and other people; and if a man keeps proper his affairs for the next life, than Allah keeps proper for him his affairs of this world...'* " (Nahjul Balagha)

Feeling much better, Huda said, "Due to your helpful words, I feel optimistic about the future. I shall never feel hopeless again. I will use my faith like a weapon to confront hopelessness and to strengthen my will."

Tuqa happily replied, "Faith produces security and calmness. Faith itself is obedience to Allah's commandments. Through faith, earthly concerns are shaped and invested with various meanings. Hence, sickness can alleviate sins and disappointment can lead to victory. The Qur'an says:

Surely We have made whatever is on earth an embellishment for it, so that we may try them (as to) which of them is best in work. (Al Kahaf: 7)

"We are tested by Allah throughout our lives. Now that you have helped me out of my difficulties, will you remain my friend?"

Huda asked: "Of course! Our common faith has sealed our friendship. The best sort of friendship is based on spiritual harmony and righteous ideals. Such a foundation is unshakeable. The faith that floods a believer's heart is enough to flood the entire universe with mercy and compassion."

"Have you noticed how few establish relations based on faith and common ideals?" asked Huda.

"Yes that is precisely why the majority fail and friendship so often turns into enmity. But since we are inspired by faith and we have good intentions to reform society, Allah will surely help us."

INGRATITUDE

Waiting is often a source of annoyance. The longer the wait, the greater the feelings of hopelessness. Aminah was waiting for her friend. Huda, who had promised to visit her that day. It was nearly nine o'clock in the evening, and Huda still hadn't arrived. Aminah could not stop worrying. She knew that something important had kept her friend at home. She tried reading a book, but couldn't concentrate. At half past nine, the telephone rang. Aminah rushed to answer it, and Huda was on the line, apologizing for not coming. She promised to come the following day. The next day, Aminah was so happy to see Huda that she hardly noticed her paleness. They sat together to talk, and Aminah noticed the lack of warmth and animation that was usually evident in Huda's voice. She was saddened by her friend's unspoken distress. Huda was not only a sister in faith for Aminah; she was also a torch that lit the darkness for her. Huda's strong belief and worthy ideals attracted the admiration of others. She was calm and wise when she advised her Muslim sisters.

Hoping to discover what was wrong, Aminah asked her friend, "Now, what prevented you from showing up yesterday?

"Sometimes I am unable to keep my promises," Huda replied, sighing.

"That is not unusual," Aminah told her. "Various reasons can prevent a person from carrying out his plans sometimes."

Aminah saw that Huda was too upset to even speak. "Are you crying?", she asked. Tears should be shed for the sake of Allah. What is important enough to make you so upset?" Do you imagine that I would cry for any reason other than His cause? In fact, my sadness is for the sake of Allah."

Aminah tried to reassure her friend, "Then you have no reason to be upset, because you are on the right path. You should find comfort and solace in your faith. Shouldn't a Muslim feel happiness knowing that she is hastening towards Allah with a clear conscience? Such a person hearkens to the Prophet's (swas) words: *How I long to meet them-the true believers.*"

"That is exactly the source of my sorrow," Huda replied. "I am afraid that I may stop in the middle of the road and that I will fall to meet the Seal of the Prophets with an unblemished record." "Do you feel that you are performing your religious duties inadequately?" asked Aminah.

"Oh no, I always do my best. But, sometimes one is forced to ...", Huda broke off her sentence." Forced to disobey religious' commandments?" I would never do such a thing, even if the world pressured me to do so!", asserted Huda. "My discomfort arises from the thought that I cannot increase my Islamic activities so that I may reach a higher stage. I sometimes feel depressed when I think that I'll never reach perfection."

Aminah admonished her friend," How can you feel depressed? Don't you know that it is unbelievers who despair of Allah's Mercy and Forgiveness?"

Huda replied, "Of course, I do not despair of Allah's Mercy, but when I encounter ingratitude or unfair treatment, I feel that it is due to my inadequateness or to a lack of faith on my part. Hence, I feel at a loss and do not know what to do. I fear that such self-doubt may endanger my spiritual strength."

"All aspects of a Muslim's life are based upon adhering to religious principles. One should recognize one's faults and weaknesses and work to correct them. Strive to increase your Islamic activities and efforts," advised Aminah. "I have thought deeply about this matter", said Huda, "but I have come to no conclusion. This is why I have confided in you. A Muslim is like a mirror, which can reflect a fellow believer's faults and also show how they can be corrected."

"But I haven't seen any faults in you," Aminah answered. "So I can only advise you to continue on the right path; the one which you are on now. You have the ability to plant seeds in every sort of soil. If anyone doubts or mocks your good intentions, another person will benefit from the fruits of your knowledge. An important aspect of a believer's life is suffering which brings him or her closer to Allah. When one has a divine aim, the negative reactions of others are not of any value. For Allah, a good deed will be rewarded tenfold. Such efforts will inspire others. Please don't allow any pessimistic thoughts to dominate your thoughts. You are young and active, so don't lay down your weapon or leave the field. Have confidence in yourself and you will surely overcome all difficulties."

"Thank you so much!" Huda exclaimed, embracing her friend." Your words have brought me tremendous relief. I feel sure now that I will continue on the correct path and that Allah will help me to do so."

INNER DEBATE

As Samia was anxiously waiting for her favorite television program to begin, unusual feelings were dominating her thoughts. Although her eyes were fixed on the T.V. screen, her mind was elsewhere. She was not feeling quite like her old self. She was disturbed and felt uneasy and the lively music of the television did not cheer her up as it normally did. Samia said to herself, "They were only few words yet they have spoiled my evening. Why should I take the matter so seriously?" She tried to concentrate on the program, but the words still echoed in her mind. She listened to the music, but she heard a voice telling her, "This is the real loss and the ultimate weakness. Why should one let a song or a show influence one's life? One should be affected by a good deed or a wise saying. A useful word can elevate the spirit of its recipient."

Samia was troubled by this inner dialogue. It conflicted with her usual thoughts. She told herself, "This discomfort is the result of Sana's words, which are still ringing in my head. Why should I care about what she said? I have been living such a life since my childhood. I like to dance and listen to music." She moved to a different chair and settled closer to the television.

Samia tried her best to forget Sana's words and to enjoy the program, but tears involuntarily came to her eyes. Again the inner voice whispered to her "What weakness! A few minutes ago, you were laughing for no reason. You were happily enjoying the music. Now you are crying. What is this? Are you living in a world of illusions? or is it some gloomy sadness which causes you to cry for no special reason?" She recalled the unlikely source of her uneasiness. She was not used to hearing such an inner dialogue.

Could it be the result of Sana's words, which might be truth and guidance? The music on the T.V. ended and Samia still felt an inner struggle. She tried to forget her friend's words and keep to her usual behavior, yet the word *haram* kept echoing in her mind. What could *haram* mean? Disobedience? Allah's displeasure? Hell?

Oh, yes. She remembered Sana's recitation of some particular Qur'anic verses:

...then be on your guard against the fire of which men and stones are the fuel, it is prepared for the unbelievers. (Al-Baqarah: 24)

Most surely the righteous shall be in bliss; on thrones they shall gaze; you will recognize on their faces the brightness of bliss. (Al-Mutaffifin: 22-24)

Oh, you who believe! save yourselves and your families from the fire whose fuel is men and stone. (Al-Tahreem: 6)

Samia seriously thought about how she had been spending her time in un-Islamic activities and concluded that such practices would displease Almighty Allah, and that she would eventually suffer for her actions. She might suffer the following day or years later. She remembered how much it hurt when her finger accidentally touched the bottom of a hot iron and how she ran to find relief. Would there be a remedy in Hell?

Again she recalled some verses from the Qur'an:

...And as to him who is given his book behind his back, he shall call for perdition, and enter into the burning fire, surely he thought that he would never return. Yea! Surely his Lord does ever see him. (Al-Inshiqaq: 10-15)

Samia left the living room and returned to her bedroom. She felt as if someone was mocking her innermost feelings.

"How shameful for one to enjoy this worldly life and forget the everlasting one! It is a sign of the utmost weakness to allow desire and fun to dominate one's life without the least consideration for Allah's instructions" the voice told her.

Confused, Samia sat down and thought seriously about the various thoughts filling her mind. Sana could advise and guide her towards the right pat. She made up her mind to see her soon. She suddenly felt great comfort and relief at this idea. She fell asleep dreaming of the next day's meeting and the meaning of true repentance.

SOCIAL MEASURES

The lady of the house, dressed in the latest fashion, was waiting impatiently for her daughter Zaynab to get dressed for the wedding party. The lady was impatient, and walked up and down the room. Now and then she stopped in front of a mirror to have a look at her image. Her daughter was a bit late, so she rang a bell and a pretty maid came in the room. She was wearing a short dress and had her hair done.

The woman admired the attractive maid and said, "I see, Samia, you have finished before your little lady. Go and tell her to hurry up. We have no time to spare.. It takes an hour to reach the bride's house."

The maid replied, "Yes, my lady." Samia left the room and soon returned, saying that Zaynab would be getting ready now. Zaynab's mother became angry and exclaimed, "What has she been doing all this time?"

The maid answered, "She has been praying."

"Praying?! Oh, what an abnormal girl she is! Go again and tell her to hurry up."

The maid went out and came back to announce that Zaynab was coming.

The mother said, "What did you say? How could she get ready in such a short time? Surely she will bring disgrace to me at this party. How I pity her. She is spoiling her beauty by negligence and indifference." Admiring herself again in the mirror, she saw her daughter enter with a smile on her angelic face.

The daughter said, "Here I am mother, quite ready."

Her mother gave her a sharp look, and said ironically, "Of course you are ready! What is this? Are you going in this long dress? Where is your make-up? Is there a girl of your age who does not know how to color her lips or put on eyeliner except you? I have been waiting all this time while you did nothing but pray. Now you say you are ready!"

Zaynab waited for her mother to finish, then she said politely, "Yes, I have performed my prayers since it is my religious duty, and I cannot pray at the party which will end after prayer time. My dress is not that long, but it certainly is not a mini. My hair is tidy, with no need to waste my time at a hairdresser to be polluted with chemicals. As for the make-up, of course, I know how to color my eyes and my lips, but I feel this is not necessary. I like to show myself as I am, with no mask on my face. "

Her mother turned her head away, disapproving of her daughter's logic. She said, "Let us leave before you get on the pulpit and give us a long sermon, as is your habit. But I feel bitterness when I see the maid exceeds you in her good appearance."

Zaynab replied, "If such measures are the true criterion, I agree that she does exceed me." The mother stated," In fact, I don't know how you are going to face the famous people there. You will appear so poor and humble among the men and women."

"The party is not for both sexes," Zaynab replied.

"Had it been like that, I would not have agreed to go. In any case, there will not be any singers or music of any kind."

The mother laughed in a mocking tone and said,

"Then the party is for giving a religious speech on the decency of hijab."

Zaynab answered quietly, "No! There is no religious speech. It is only a formal farewell party to a bride starting her honeymoon."

The mother feared delay, so she said to her daughter, "Come on; tell me the details on our way to the party." Zaynab put on a long black coat and a scarf on her head as she always did. They got into their car, with the maid carrying a box of her mistress's cosmetics.

While they were driving, Zaynab's mother asked her daughter, "How do you know that the party is not for both sexes?" Zaynab answered, "It was supposed to take place at one of the clubs, according to the bride's mother. But my friend, the bride, is a good believer, as you know. Thus she refused to have her wedding party according to western values, or in defiance of religious morals. Quarrels started between the mother and daughter. But the groom took the side of the bride, and my friend insisted on canceling the celebration. Finally her mother gave in and agreed to have a simple farewell party."

Zaynab's mother was astonished and asked, "Does the groom have the same reactionary beliefs as the bride?" Zaynab tried to smile at her mother's cruel words.

She said, "Of course he has the same beliefs, and he is of equal moderation. Otherwise, she would not have agreed to marry him. A good believer does not marry a playboy who is totally different in beliefs and ideals. Disputes in such matters are a serious threat to a marriage. How can you brand such ideals 'reactionary' while they are the essence of our religion? They are clearly elaborated in the Holy Qur'an. Our belief is the right path, while the non-Islamic way is the reactionary one, since it goes back to the primitive stage of humanity when there were no Divine creeds or human values."

Her mother was affected by the argument and she said," You are right, but civilization requires something different."

Zaynab replied, "Oh, mother! What civilization is this? Tragedies and disasters are under the surface. Bright masks hide devilish motives and inhuman desires. Oh, mother! We should not be fooled by this civilization."

The mother spoke in a sorrowful tone, "This is the general attitude of the day and the social measures that count."

"We shall try to defeat such perceptions," Zaynab said. "We will prove that in a society, a young girl can show herself through her real personality -not by her make-up or her fashionable clothing. When she has an independent personality, she will taste the sweetness of victory. It is contrary to woman's true nature to expose herself in a framework of fashion or make-up, which is only a means for public exposure."

They arrived at the house of the bride. The mother tapped her daughter on the shoulder and said, "May Allah bless you. I wish I could have your strong faith and self-confidence."

THE RED ALERT

When Ahmad returned home, his wife Maryam was still out. He sat down next to his children and joined them in their game. Afterwards, he picked up a book and passed the time reading. Finally at 10 o'clock that evening his wife returned home. She did not even allow Ahmad to greet her, but quickly rushed passed him to her room and took off the mask that transfigured her natural form. She looked less beautiful but more gentle. From her behavior, Ahmad knew that she had something to tell him.

As soon as the children went to bed, she said to her husband, "Oh, Ahmad, you have not asked me about my visiting today."

Ahmad smiled and said, "I hope you have enjoyed yourself."

Maryam said, "...I had a wonderful time! The house and the garden were magnificent, and their table was rich with delicious foods. My friend, Hana, had the most beautiful wig. Dr. Iram's wife wore an expensive suit. It was quite beautiful."

Her husband smiled ironically and asked, "The suit or the Dr.'s wife?"

"Oh, the suit was wonderful! But I was too embarrassed to enjoy the visit," she added. Ahmad silently beseeched Allah to give him patience and said to himself," This is just the beginning; Allah will help me in the end." He did not answer his wife's remarks. She continued, "It seems as if you do not care for me. Am I nothing to you? You do not ask the reason for my uneasiness. You regard me as if I were a stranger."

Maryam seemed truly upset, so her husband said to himself, "I place my affairs before Allah. If I do not ask her the reason, she will cry."

He gently asked her, "Why do you think such a thing? You are my dear wife and the mother of my children. Why are you upset? Were you embarrassed by your clothing?"

"Oh no, although it was not as beautiful as the Dr.'s wife's suit. I can buy a better one in the future. The source of my uneasiness has been in my failing to ask my friends to visit me. It has been a long time since I last invited them to my home. How would they account for such delay? Surely they will think it is due to some financial hardship, or that you are a miser or ignorant of social formalities. Such ideas hurt me, since I know you are an excellent husband and a good father."

"Thank you for the compliment. Now what exactly do you want?"

Maryam replied, "Today is the fifth of the month. I can fix a day for their visit as long as we can afford to spend some money."

"You talk as if the event is a victorious battle in need of great preparation," Ahmad said. His wife laughed, "No. it is not like that, but it doest cost...."

Ahmad said, "But how can we manage until the end of the month if your party will be expensive? We are already in debt. Now you want to make matters worse." "You can borrow some money from your friends," his wife suggested. "You know I have borrowed from many of them. How can I ask for more?"

"Oh, how miserable I am! I was brought up in a rich family and lived a luxurious life. Now I cannot even afford to invite my friends over for an afternoon. Oh, what a shame! How am I to face them? Can I show myself in society? This means I must isolate myself and give up all of my friends." Maryam started crying, while her husband tried to convince her of his viewpoint. She never listened to him, but said, "Oh, surely I shall suffer from sickness. If I stay two days at home, I shall suffer a nervous breakdown and lose my appetite."

Finally, Ahmad gave in and agreed to his wife's demand. His wife arranged everything for the special day. She asked her sisters to help her arrange the rooms for the occasion. She would have never imagined that the outcome of her party could be the destruction of her family life. On the day of the party, Maryam asked her husband to stay out until a late hour and she sent her children to her mother's house. She got herself ready for her guests, who arrived shortly before sunset. They were all dressed in the latest fashion and with full makeup. The home was soon filled, and gossip and idle speculation dominated the conversation. Each was criticized by the other. One's dress was not to the taste of the other; and this hairdo was not nice as another's. Silly talk and jokes filled the air.

At 8 o'clock, Maryam called her guests to dinner. Suddenly the phone rang and one of the guests was called. As soon as this lady put down the phone, she came to Maryam and apologized for having to leave at once. Her husband had warned of a red alert and she had to reach home before the lights went out. Upon hearing this news, the other guests rushed towards the door. They left without even a good-bye. Maryam emerged from the kitchen to see that her guests had all disappeared. She was shocked and dismayed to see her party come to such an end, especially when she thought about all the trouble she had gone to and the dispute with her husband about the matter. She had hoped to make a good impression on her friends. She sat down and wept bitterly. She wished her husband would come home early, before the red alert sounded. She waited to hear its wailing but there was none.

At 10 o'clock Ahmad came and was surprised to see the house empty. His wife told him the whole story. She feared that he would be angry, but he was quite at ease. He said, "It may be a lie. There is no need for an alert since there are no impending raids. Anyway, I hope you have learned a lesson."

The wife said, "Indeed, I have. I won't undergo such an experience again."

The next day, Maryam's friend phoned and apologized for the previous evening. Her husband had lied to her in order to get her home early since her child had been crying for his mother.

Maryam told her friend that it had been a silly joke, but a good lesson too.

STRUGGLING WITH CONFLICT

As Fatimah walked along the tree-lined street, thoughts filled her head and mocked her sensitive emotions and delicate feelings. She hurried to reach the source of pleasure, security and light in her life. She wished she could overcome this nagging doubt, but she was weak, and in need of support. She told herself, "I will tell her everything. I will explain all of my difficulties to her. I will confess to her my fears." When Fatimah reached her friend's home, she knocked anxiously at the door. She feared disappointment; not finding her friend Aminah at home. Aminah came forward to welcome her, they shook hands warmly and then entered a room where they settled to talk. Aminah chided her friend gently, saying, "Oh, I have missed you. Welcome again, dear friend." Upon hearing her friend's warm voice Fatimah felt at ease and nearly forgot the aim of her visit. She remained silent, so Aminah gave her a smile of encouragement and said, "You do not look like your usual self, Fatimah. Tell me what is bothering you." Her question helped Fatimah to speak. With a trembling voice she said, "Oh sister, something is very wrong with me. My courage has failed me. I thought I was well protected against Satan and whatever troubles in my way to reach my goal. But..." Fatimah silently thought of the right words to express her suffering, but Aminah was quick to understand her pain. Aminah asked, "But what, Fatimah?" Fatimah replied, "I have lost courage; I can no longer endure these difficulties I am facing as a religious instructor."

"What difficulties are these, Fatimah? Tell me about them. I am your sister in faith."

Fatimah told her, "Being a Muslim, I believe in our responsibilities towards our beloved religion, Islam. I have tried my best to guide misled Muslim girls; to save them from our deviated society. But society, Oh, Aminah…."

"What about society?" asked her friend.

"It is a corrupted one, with no morals. Everything is measured with materialistic values. Living in this society has made me feel a bitterness I never dreamed I could feel."

Aminah admonished Fatimah, "Did you think that the road of religious guidance was strewn with flowers and empty of obstacles? We should not deny these difficulties. But we are told not to worry about troubles and hardships as long as we are on the right path for the sake of Allah. Haven't you heard the words of one Muslim woman believer: 'Whatever difficulty we encounter in the way of Islam is not a difficulty, and whatever bitterness we may feel is not a bitterness.' Now tell me Fatimah, what specifically has happened to upset you?"

Fatimah sighed, "It is not anyone particular incident."

Then Aminah told her, "So you feel cowardice in front of deviated currents, and you fear harmful ideologies."

When Fatimah heard these words she cried, "No, I am never afraid of such things. It is only troubles and obstacles that have shaken my faith in myself, as well as my lack of experience and understanding."

"What else bothers you, Fatimah? Tell me everything so that I can be of help to you."

Fatimah said, "From the beginning, I had a strong desire to serve my religion by all means and at all levels. I believed also that Islam knows no limits...." Fatimah stopped, as if not knowing what to say. Aminah explained, "That is why it hurts you so much to find that society is still under the yoke of false measures that a person is judged through a materialistic view point and within a frame of pseudo-measures. But had society been a Utopia believing in Islamic values, considering an individual through realistic measures, then our cause (Islamic guidance), our responsibility would not have purified our souls and increased our determination to surmount any difficulties. Had we been struggling in a virtuous society, guiding our fellow Muslims in an ideal environment, flowing with the tide instead of having to oppose it as we do today, then we would not have been among those referred to in the Holy Qur'an as patient men and women:

Surely men and women who submit, and the believing men and the believing women, the truthful men and the truthful women, and the patient men and patient women... Allah has prepared for them forgiveness and a mighty reward. (Al-Ahzab: 35).

"Fatimah then said, "But Aminah, our enemies rejoice, they mock us when we are distressed or are facing hardships." Aminah smiled and asked, "Haven't you read the Qur'anic verse:

You shall certainly be tried respecting your wealth and souls... surely this is one of the affairs determined upon. And the verse: Don't think of those who rejoice for what they have done... and they shall have a painful chastisement. (Aale-Imran: 185 and 187)

"The Holy Qur'an has clearly revealed everything. It has lined the path with thorns and obstacles, but the aftermath with bounties and blessings. We must be sure of ourselves, in order to stand firm and avoid collapsing in the face of difficulties. We must always remember the early days of the Message of Islam and all the hardships that faced the great Messenger of Allah (swas) when he called on people to give up the worship of their idols and to worship Allah. The One, the Almighty." Aminah continued, "The Prophet toiled to prune a primitive nation which was overgrown with wild traditions such as unprovoked attacks, the plundering of properties, murder, the drinking of alcohol and the committing of adultery as well as other indecencies. He planted and nurtured Divine values and morals in the people in order to make them the best nation ever found among nations. We should remember Muhammad, son of Abdullah, the offspring of the best family in the Arab Peninsula and he noblest member of the Quraysh tribe. All of the people, young and old, high and low in society, agreed that he was a truthful, honest person. We should try to imagine the responsibility this great man assumed when he was chosen by Allah to carry His Message. All of the tribes rose against him and joined forces opposing him. They threatened him and barred any trading with him. Standing firm, he neither relinquished his divine duty nor stopped calling on the people to worship Allah. He and his followers were isolated, as if he was a deviated person. He endured every kind of insult and mockery. They called him a wizard while he was the Prophet, and called him a liar while he was the most truthful honest person in their midst. They said he had been taught (by someone) while his knowledge had been revealed to him by Heaven. They accused him of madness while he had the greatest prophetic wisdom."

"We should keep all this in mind, and remember as well the Prophet's Du'a (words of prayer) to Allah when he was in the village of Al-Taif calling people to worship God. The people of that village sent their sons to throw stones at him, make fun of and insult him. He took refuge by a wall and stretched out his hands towards the sky, praying to Allah, *'Oh, God to you I complain my weakness, my lack of means and the scorn of my people. Oh God of the oppressed and of mine, to whom do you leave me? To a wrathful relative or to a foe, to whom you gave control over me? If You are not angry at me, I don't care whatever happens to me; Your compassion is great enough for me.'* "

Aminah went on, "Fatimah, we must remember the Prophet's words after his painful suffering. As long as we are certain that our ideas are right and our belief is true, we should not be daunted by falsehood and fear. Fatimah, remember the honorable Zaynab (sa), the daughter of the Leader of the Faithful, Imam Ali (as), when she stood near the body of her slain brother Imam Husayn (as) on the Day of Ashura. He was to her not only a brother, but a supporter and a defender, yet she put up her hands and said: 'Oh, God, accept from us this sacrifice.' Yes, Fatimah, we must remember all this in order to remain devoted to Allah."

As soon as Aminah stopped speaking, Fatimah cried and said, "Oh my dear friend Aminah, may Allah never deprive me of your friendship. You are a guiding light for me. Your words have revived my spirit, which I nearly lost. You have helped my faith to remain firm and steadfast. How stupid I was to have lost all hope!"

Aminah told her, "No Fatimah, you are neither stupid nor had you lost hope. These are feelings that arise as result of many reasons. The best evidence of your sincerity is your firm stand and faith. You have come directly to me to help you overcome obstacles which are the result of this deviated society and which you have no hand in producing. Oh Fatimah, have you abandoned reading as you have abandoned visiting me?"

"I never abandoned you; I was trying to solve an inner conflict (of feelings) and I was afraid."

Aminah said, "You were afraid to speak frankly to me, but you did not fear the serious results of remaining silent?"

She smiled at Fatimah, who said, "You should be quite sure that I will never feel weak again, and I will always admit my fears and my hopes to you. You will be my guiding angel as you have always been."

Aminah embraced her, saying, "Oh Fatimah, I am not an angel. I am only a loving, advising sister to you and to all Muslim girls."

FIRM STAND

As the first rays of dawn shone on the horizon, Sumayah awoke. She had spent the previous night in tears. Sumayah felt certain that the dawn had come to dispel her bitter suffering and open the door of hope, through prayer, to her; a door which would direct her towards her Creator. She hurried to get ready to pray, as if she were on her way to meet a loved one. Forgetting the suffering and pain she had experienced for many years, Sumayah merged with her prayer, giving all of her attention to Him.

Sumayah finished her prayer and thought once more about the two paths open to her-one leading to I happiness in this temporary life; the other ending in spiritual happiness in eternal life. She was well-aware that true peace could only be found by remaining a faithful Muslim and adhering to Islamic principles, thus avoiding any deviation from Islam.

The first path would take her to a world of luxury filled with misleading comforts and illusionary happiness. The other road would guide her along the path of Islamic guidance. By following this path, she would taste victory and be crowned with the laurel of firm belief and determination. Since she was a Muslim, naturally she rejected the first, misleading road. But still, Sumayah sometimes felt weak in the face of threats and temptation.

Sumayah silently beseeched God: "Oh God, You know I am an orphan who lost her parents at an early age. My only brother is studying abroad. Europe, with its so-called civilization, has trapped him. He has forgotten me and is busy running after amusements. God, Your blessings caused my soul to be flooded with the light of Islam. My conscience is clear. You have armed me with the weapon of strong faith, which enables me to remain steady and have a pure heart neither stained by pseudo-civilization nor attracted to the glittering results of false progress.

I am not fooled by any poisonous, imported ideologies. Oh God, help me to be content. Help me to find joy in assisting misguided Muslim girls so that I forget my own unhappiness and the painful loss of my parents. Such happiness, the result of helping others, can compensate for my uncle's cruelty."

Sumayah's troubles had begun when a stranger a young man, had become acquainted with her uncle, who was her guardian. The young man was wealthy and fascinated Sumayah's uncle with his fast cars and various properties.

This man had made life hell for Sumayah ever since he had become attracted to her and had asked her to marry him. Sumayah never let herself to be influenced by his wealth. She avoided his company because he was careless and wild. Her uncle was trying to pressure her into marrying the young man by describing how happy she would be with every imaginable earthly comfort. He built palaces for her based on his wishes and hopes.

Sumayah's uncle ignored her objections, and she was afraid that if she gave in to her uncle's demands, she would be deviated from Islam. Would my brother take my uncle's side if he was here?' she wondered. She thought about how much she needed to see .her brother. She always remembered him in her prayers, and asked Allah to guide him.

Sumayah's uncle had locked her in her room for two days in his attempts to pressure her. As she sat in the room, she said to God, "O God I am afraid of what may happen, but I will stand firm. I shall keep on struggling until you help me by Your mercy." Her prayer put her at ease. She reasoned that only real submission to God could cause her to feel such calmness and then she slept, exhausted from the previous sleepless night.

Suddenly her uncle's sharp voice awoke her. He was knocking loudly on the door, saying, "Are you still asleep, you woman from the Middle Ages?" Sumayah sat up, shaking, and answered meekly, "Yes, I had been asleep."

Her uncle opened the door and tried to speak in a friendly tone, "You look happy this morning, Sumayah. I'm certain that you have returned to reality and have given up your impossible dreams."

"Uncle, I have always lived in reality."

"Yes", he replied. "The reality of ancient times! Now were living in the twentieth century, and if you give up your old ideas, I will keep the door unlocked."

Sumayah told him, "Oh uncle, I don't want you to open a door for me which leads to worldly pleasures and close the door to God's blessings and forgiveness. Please be kind enough to let me manage my own affairs."

Her uncle angrily retorted, "I won't let this opportunity pass by. I don't want you to stay hidden in your room constantly reading and writing. You have disappointed me greatly."

Sumayah answered him quietly, "I will always be as I have been and am now. "

"Then you must leave my home. I won't let you trouble me."

"Are you serious?" Sumayah anxiously asked.

"Yes!", replied her uncle." Either agree to marry this man or leave my house and never return. We shall see how much you will gain from your belief in Islam."

Sumayah said after a short while, "I have made up my mind."

"Then you will marry the rich man?"

"No. I will never exchange my principles for temporary gains."

Her uncle, greatly vexed, rushed to open the front door of his home. "Then leave. You have no place here, you ungrateful girl. I regret all that I have done for you. Go to your Islam, or to your brother, who has forgotten you. Leave quickly! I cannot stand your presence here any longer."

Sumayah had gathered her few belongings while her uncle was speaking. She only owned a gold bracelet, a Qur'an and some books. She turned to her uncle and said, "Uncle, you may regret this."

"Never. Go find your brother. There is no hope for you."

Sumayah walked out the door, saying, "I am leaving, and I am happy. God has given me strength. Farewell."

She thought that her uncle would change his mind, but he continued to ridicule her until she disappeared around the corner.

As she walked along, Sumayah felt lost. Where could she go now? She detested the corrupt society she lived in, and it, in turn, hated her attempts to reform it. Feelings of despair started to overwhelm her. Suddenly she heard the Qur'anic verse: *Or did you think that you would enter the garden while yet... when will the help of Allah come ? Now surely the help of Allah is near!* (Al-Baqarah: 214)

Sumayah felt as if she was being addressed. The verse renewed her hope and she felt victorious. She calmly thought about where to go. With an uplifted spirit, she recalled her friend Maryam. Maryam's brother was a friend of her brother, and she thought that he could surely help her contact her brother and ask him to return.

She walked to Maryam's house filled with hope. When she knocked on the door, Maryam opened it and welcomed her warmly. Maryam then congratulated Sumayah and said, "God knows how happy I am for you."

Surprised by her words, Sumayah asked, "What on earth are you congratulating me for?"

"Hasn't your brother written to you?" Maryam replied. "He is on his way home, and should be here today or tomorrow."

This unexpected news was too much for Sumayah and she nearly lost her balance." Are you sure he is coming?" she asked.

Maryam took her into the house, where she regained her strength. Sumayah soon began to feel nervous, however, as she imagined how her brother might have changed and that perhaps he was just like her uncle, who had kicked her out of his home only an hour earlier. With a serious expression, she turned to Maryam and said, "How do you know this? What has caused him to return?"

Maryam understood her friend's fears and told her, "He recently wrote a letter to my brother. He said in the letter that he could no longer endure being so far away from you. He experienced western civilization and rejects its values. Here is his letter; read it!"

Sumayah was so overcome with joy that she could not read it. She knew that Allah had answered her prayers. Her religion, as she had always hoped, had strengthened her and brought back her brother to her.

She asked Maryam to read the letter for her. Maryam read, "Oh, dear friend, I have been misled for some time, thinking this loose life is the way to happiness. This western culture has caused me forget my responsibility towards myself and my sister. I confess, my friend, that I forgot myself. Now I have realized the truth. These great buildings where people drink until morning and these night-clubs which are full of indecency are all means to fool and mislead youths and will eventually endanger their future. This generation of women, who are proud of equality with men, is nothing but a mere commodity within the reach of all men for exposure and exploitation.

This boredom and this running after whatever is called civilization and progress, contains hidden sufferings and great problems, which are flooding western society. As a result, I have regained my awareness. Now, I fear for my sister, who is a young girl. I fear she may suffer a similar fate and be caught up in the deviated currents in many Islamic countries under the false names of civilization and progress. I have decided to come home to be with her... We will both find true happiness in the instructions of Islam..."

HAD I BUT KNOWN

Anfal, a rich young girl, sat waiting impatiently at the doctor's clinic to get the results of a medical test. She was in a hurry to attend a party and feared she might be late for her appointment with the hairdresser. She never thought the result would be anything important. It was just a precaution insisted upon by her family. She had never suffered any serious illness, apart from the odd ache in her never suffered any serious illness, apart from the odd ache in her limbs. Then, it was her turn to see the doctor. She hurried inside to get it over with as quickly as possible. She was surprised to see the doctor look sad and concerned as he asked, "Is this yours?"

She answered, "No, it is my daughter's."

She wanted to know the truth and thought that perhaps he would hide the truth, if she told him it was her own. He asked her to have a seat, so she sat feeling somewhat afraid. She looked at him anxiously, as he said,

"Why did not you send a man to get the results?"

Anfal said, "It was on my way so there was no need to send someone else."

The doctor looked sadly at her and said, "You seem to be an educated girl. You understand the nature of life."

He stopped talking, and she began to tremble.

She asked, "What do you mean doctor?"

The doctor said, "The result indicates that there is a blood disease." He looked down at his papers and remained silent. Anfal had to ask him to give her more information. She cried in fear, "Is it cancer?"

He did not look at her, but a cloud of sadness covered his face. It was as if he was sentencing her to death.

She said in a broken voice, "I am finished then." The doctor knew then that she had lied, but it was too late to hide the truth. He looked kindly at her and said, "I am sorry for you. Why did you lie? Anyway life and death are matters within Allah's power. Many sick people live long and many healthy ones die."

Anfal felt as if she were drowning, as if a hard fist was cruelly squeezing her heart. She tried hard to regain her strength and said, "I do apologize. Thank you doctor."

The doctor encouraged her saying, "Be strong and optimistic. Medical science is constantly progressing. Some of today's incurable sicknesses can be cured

215

tomorrow I still have hope. Leave me your telephone number." She repeated the number automatically without knowing what she was saying. Feeling great shock and bitterness, she again thanked the doctor and left.

At home she kept the truth to herself. She did not know how to share it. Anyway, everyone was busy, getting ready for the party. Her mother asked, "Have you been to the doctor? Why did not you go to the hairdresser?" It was just a by-the-way question, needing no answer. She briefly said, "I am not going to the party !"

She went upstairs into her room and locked the door.

She stretched out on her bed fully clothed and listened to her family's voices, as if they were coming from a faraway place. The wind seemed to her to be a funeral sad tune, lamenting her approaching death. The bedroom seemed strange to her as she would be leaving it soon. What about the house? It would not remember her. She was just a guest. Others would take her room and soon forget her. She tried to cry but tears did not help. She looked around her in pain. Those curtains that she had tried so hard to get, would stay after her. It would not have mattered if they had been made of the roughest fabric, she would leave them for others. She wished she had not troubled herself for such things. She wished she had saved her time and money for more useful things, which could have been helpful to her in her difficulty.

She wondered, "What is useful to me?" She was young, beautiful and rich with everything her heart could desire. Could anything help her and save her from death? She had always longed for an official job with a good salary. She had it, but could it save her from death?

An idea struck her. She hurried to the phone while everyone was away. She dialed the doctor's number and asked eagerly, "If I travel abroad can I find a cure?"

He said, "There is nothing new abroad. It is a waste of money."

She put the phone down and sat on a nearby chair.

Her salary would not change matters. She walked through the house's rooms as if saying her farewells. She paced the small garden and looked at the trees. She whispered, "I wish these trees knew I am leaving them, those stones, walls...I wish these doors knew my hands will soon no longer open them. I wish those flowers, that I planted and watered knew. How often the thorns and hard stones tore my hands! How often I watered those dying flowers with my tears when there was no water. I wish they knew the meaning of my departure. These fruiting trees were tiny when I planted them. I did my best to help them flourish until they grew up healthy and fruitful. Will they know I am soon leaving? Will they remember my days in their company? What about these seats, I used to rest on. Will they miss my presence? Will they be ready for someone else to settle on them? My writing desk felt my writing in tears and in smiles, does it know I am leaving? Will it miss my pen and papers in its drawers? I wish they all knew I am leaving. I wish I had known I was leaving, then I would not have cared so much for this life. I would not have felt proud and arrogant…

Had I known I were a guest in this world I would not have been cheated or tempted by its luxuries…

Had I known this I would have been aware that leaving a simple life is easier than leaving a luxurious one…

Had I lived a simple life, I would not have found it difficult to cross from this world to the next. My family is now enjoying the party…how often I longed for such parties, how much I cared for fashion and hairstyles! Can they help me now?"

Anfal threw herself down on the nearest chair as if she had realized a truth previously unknown to her.

She said, "What shall I take with me? Nothing but the coffin and my deeds. What kind of deeds will go with me on my long journey? Nothing! Yes, nothing!" She remembered her friend Sarah, who used to advise her and guide her to the right path of Allah. She used to remind her of the Qur'anic verse: *...and make provision, for the provision is the guarding of oneself.* (Al-Baqarah: 239)

She had never considered the importance of good deeds. Now she was in need of such deeds to present to Allah. She would stand to give her account, but what would she say? How could she expect Allah's mercy when she disobeyed His orders? How could she ask for forgiveness when she never even thought of obeying Him in her life's affairs? She wished she had read the Holy Qur'an instead of all those cheap novels. She wished she had gained some knowledge of her religion instead of reading film-star magazines. She continued wishing she had done few things, and not done other things. She wished she had not angered this person or that, and had never lied or gossiped about anyone. She wished she had not been proud and despised the poor.

She said, "I wish I could start my life all over again to make-up for my errors and to obey Allah's orders. I worshipped my desires and ignored my Creator. I wish I could live for a while to make up for my sins."

She remembered a Qur'anic verse, her grandfather used to recite: *Until when death overtakes one of them he says: Send me back, my Lord. Haply I may do good in that which I have left. By no means! It is a mere word that he speaks, and before them is a barrier until the day they are raised.* (Al-Mu'minun: 99)

Here she said, "Oh God, I do mean it..." Tears burst from her eyes. She cried bitterly in repentance, not pain. She decided to obey Allah in all His orders if she lived a bit longer. The phone rang and she walked towards it lazily. Tears in her eyes she said, "Yes?"

Someone said, "Can I speak to Miss Anfal?" She knew the speaker. It was her doctor. She said, "Yes, speaking."

The doctor said cheerfully, "Congratulations my daughter! There is nothing wrong with you. Thank God!"

She was stunned with surprise. She did not know what to say. "No disease? How? You are joking, doctor!"

The doctor said, "May Allah protect me I am not joking. I have just got an apology from the analyst. He explained that there was a mix-up with the names. Your name was written instead of someone else. I have your medical report here in front of me. You are quite well. Be thankful to Allah my daughter."

Excitedly she said, "Thanks be to Allah, Thank you doctor."

She put the phone down, feeling as if she was new born. She knew she was safe for a while, but death would certainly come one day. She had no time to waste. However long she lived she was a guest. The first thing she did was to perform her prayer, which she had neglected for a long time. She promised Allah to obey His orders to pray, fast, and stick to wearing decent clothes. She would also give up whatever Allah had forbidden. In order not to forget this, she wrote the Qur'anic verse on a placard and hung it on the wall. On the other side she wrote a wise saying:

"Repent the day before you die. Because you do not know when you will die, then always be repentant."

THE DANGEROUS GAME

Asia sat waiting for her friend Baidah who was coming to visit her. She was surprised at her friend's demand for a private meeting. Asia thought Baidah must have a serious problem, so she was anxious to see her friend, when she arrived a few minutes late. Asia waited for her to start talking while Baidah tried to appear composed.

Then she said, "Can I ask you a question!"

"Yes, with pleasure!" said Asia.

Baidah said, "I want you to answer frankly."

"Now you know I am always frank!" Asia assured her.

"Why did you refuse Fuad's proposal of marriage!" burst out Baidah.

Asia was taken aback by the question. She was silent for a while, and said, "Can I also ask you a question!"

"Of course, you can," said Baidah.

"Why do you ask me a question that might upset me? You know he is my relative and I have refused him for certain reasons."

Hesitantly Baidah said, "Well, he has proposed to me. That's why I want to know your reasons for refusing him."

"Oh, I see!" said Asia, and went silent. Then Baidah began to plead with her saying, "I must know. I am your friend, ain't I! Don't you care for me?"

"Yes, you are my friend and I do care for you, so I will tell you the reason. But first of all, what do you know about him?" Asia asked Baidah.

"I know that he is a handsome, gentleman, educated, and well-mannered with a good social position."

"That's right," said Asia. "He is also wealthy. But is that enough?"

Baidah, pale faced, murmured, "He is not a committed Muslim!"

"You know this and yet you still ask me my reason for refusing him?"

"I know that religion is very important, but he might change", said Baidah.

"How?" asked Asia.

"Have you ever thought that he might be guided to the right path?" proffered Baidah.

"Is this what you think?" said Asia.

"I think," began Baidah, "that refusing him is a kind of cowardice. I think we can bring Fuad and the likes of him back to religion, and that we should strive for that."

"O.K., but how are you going to do it?" Asia said.

"I have means" said Baidah. "Anyway why should I refuse him when he has all these good qualifications?

If I leave him, he may marry someone who will increase his disregard for religion. If I accept him, I may bring him back to faith."

"That's your opinion" said Asia. "I won't impose mine on you. However, it is a very dangerous game, or marriage at risk."

"Oh, please do not exaggerate so Asia. Marriage is an adventure. I feel I can tolerate the experience."

"You are quite wrong! Experience does not make a fool wise. There is a great difference between marriage to a committed believer, who is careful of his religious duties which protect him from deviation, and a non-committed Muslim, who cares for nothing but earthly pleasures that change with the times."

"It is a risk" said Baidah, "But if I succeed it would be in the best interests of religion."

"You say: 'If I succeed', this 'if' indicates your doubts. Marriage should start on a firm foundation." Asia told her.

Baidah looked down as if in inner conflict. Then she said, "What is your opinion?"

"I don't know what to say" said Asia. "I am afraid you will suffer as a result of such an experience. It is a dangerous game. A husband does not usually accept his wife's opinion and he may even make her accept his. Then the wife may find herself standing at a crossroad leading either to the failure of her marriage or the loss of her religion. You know both are terribly hard to tolerate."

Asia stopped for a while and waited for Baidah to speak.

When she did it was in a choked voice, "What then?"

"I think you can spare yourself such trouble!" said Asia kindly.

"Suppose I am forced into doing it. What should I do then? "

"That's for you to decide Baidah. No one can impose their will on you, whoever they are!"

Baidah was silent, then said challengingly, "I shall take the risk. I hope that I will be successful."

Asia looked at her and said coldly, "You are free to do what you like. I hope you won't be sorry afterwards." Baidah got up saying, "I apologize for having taking up your time."

Asia, "Nothing to apologize for, I feel sorry for you! "

They shook hands and Baidah left the house. Asia felt she had just lost a friend.

A few weeks later, Baidah sat, waiting anxiously for her husband. It was nearly 11 p.m. and she was very worried. She looked at the clock every other minute, and at half past eleven she heard the door open and close softly. She got up and saw her husband enter. Her face became bright with happiness. She said, "Oh Fuad, you are late!" She was scared when she saw he looked disappointed. He said, "Why haven't you gone to bed yet?"

"How can I sleep when you are still out?" asked Baidah.

While he was taking off his suit and putting on his pajama, he murmured, "That will cause you a lot of worry."

"How?" asked Baidah.

"Because I shall often be late. There is no need for you to stay awake and alone."

She was disturbed at his answer and could not believe her ears. So instead she said, "Your supper is ready." Smiling he said,

"I ate out. Some friends invited me to a club. They held a party in my honour."

"I hope you enjoyed it. But why didn't you tell me about it before?" asked Baidah.

"There was no need to tell you, as you won't go with me to such places," said Fuad.

"Well, at least I wouldn't have got so worried."

Fuad said, "You should have known that I was at a social engagement. I live amongst educated liberals, and cannot be isolated at home with a woman..." he uttered the last words in a sharp tone and then said, "Now, go and have your supper."

With tears in her eyes, she sadly said, "I am not hungry."

Fuad said, "Then let's go to bed."

Baidah said, "I expect you've already done your prayer?"

Coldly, Fuad said, "It is after mid-night. Prayer time is over."

"No", said Baidah, "It is not yet mid-night. Anyway it must be done even if it is late."

"You don't know how tired and sleepy I am!" said Fuad.

"Fatigue doesn't exempt one from one's religious duty."

Mockingly he said, "Allah will accept my excuse."

"No matter-if you love me you must do your prayer." Angrily, Fuad got up saying, "Please do not mix up my love with praying and fasting. Let me love you in my way not yours. Anyway, I will not allow you to call me to account about my prayer every night!"

He threw himself on the bed and fell asleep leaving Baidah shocked at his words. She recalled Asia's words which had apparently come true.

She hurried to the Holy Qur'an to seek comfort and refuge. She opened it at random and read the first verse of the page which said: ...*We did them no injustice, but they were unjust to themselves.* (Nahal: 118)

****

Days and weeks passed. Baidah could find no way of getting Fuad to come to her way of thinking. Whenever she talked about religion, he either mocked her or turned a deaf ear. She tried her best to give him comfort and happiness at home, but she found him more and more interested in spending his time outside. One night she waited long time for him to come home, and when he did he seemed happy, so she thought it would be a good time for her to talk to him.

She said gently, "Don't you see that I am unhappy?"

Fuad surprised said, "You are unhappy? Why? Haven't I provided you with all the means for your comfort?"

"Yes, I must admit you have! Anyway, happiness is what matters; without it, there is no comfort."

"Why aren't you happy then ?" asked Fuad.

Baidah said, "How can I be happy when you are so physically, spiritually and emotionally far away from me?"

"That's partly true," conceded Fuad, "but I love you so I do not completely agree with what you say."

"If you loved me you would please me. You know I am not happy about your behaviour."

"Have I hurt you in any way?" asked Fuad, much surprised.

"You have not hurt me physically, but you have hurt me mentally by your disregard for the belief that you promised to respect. You are not careful enough about religion, to bring us closer to each other."

"Well, I am afraid I cannot change my life style. I cannot give up my friends or my social life. I cannot be cut off from others just to spend my life behind these walls. I cannot perform my prayer in a mosque just to please you. Faith stems from personal satisfaction. It would be nothing but hypocrisy if I worshipped Allah just for you. You know that I am an honest, straightforward person, both in my personal and business dealings. What more do you want? "

Baidah listened, while her heart sank. She said in broken voice, "What about me? Have I no place at all in your life?"

"You are my beloved wife. I love no one but you. Come closer to my heart and you will know real happiness."

"What do you mean?" said Baidah.

"I mean give up ideas that keep you from enjoying life's pleasures. Turn to me whole-heartedly, and I will make you taste a life that you are still unaware of. You are at cross-roads, either you put your hand in mine and I'll take you into a world of happiness, or you stay a prisoner in your house, content with it."

"Isn't there a third choice?" she asked. Fuad was silent for a while and then said, "Yes, there is. We can separate; and though it would be hard for me, it would be less harmful than if you decided to refuse my suggestion."

Baidah was silent. She wanted to scream and run away, but she was helpless. She spent a long sleepless night, feeling as if she was between two fires both of which could burn her. She was about to choose a divorce, but then thought of the tiny creature moving in her womb.

This innocent creature tied her both to the house and her husband. She was soon to be a mother. She felt dizzy with thinking and, throwing her head on to her hand, she went into a dreamless sleep. When she woke up her husband said, "Baidah, why didn't you sleep in your bed?"

She opened her eyes to see him standing near her with a cheerful face as if he was ignorant of the reason why she hadn't gone to bed. She looked at him silently.

Anxiously, he said, "Why are you pale? Are you sick?" He put his hand round her and sat nearby.

She said, "Do you really not know why I am sad?"

He laughed gently saying, "Even if I know, what can I do about it? I have offered you my heart, so is it my fault if you reject it? By the way, today I have some visitors, so be ready for the occasion."

"Who are they?" said Baidah.

"Just some friends with their wives." He was silent waiting for his wife's reaction.

She said, "Will it be a mixed meeting for men and women ?"

"Of course, you do not really expect me to stick to the old tradition of having a separate room for women, do you?"

"What about me then?" asked Baidah.

"You are free to do what you like," said Fuad.

She was silent for a while; then, wishing to compromise and thus show some understanding, she said, "O.K, I shall be present."

Her husband was happy-he kissed her warmly saying, "Do you mean it? How happy I am. I shall be the happiest husband. I shall be so proud of your beauty. You are the sun that will outshine their dim lights."

"What has my beauty to do with anything? To please you, I have decided to be present but I will wear *hijab*."

Fuad drew back in disgust, "In decent *hijab*? No! I do not want you to be mocked. Just prepare dinner and leave the house. That will be better. I can find some excuse to explain your absence."

Baidah could not tolerate such an insult. She got up saying, "It is better if I leave the house at once."

"What about the guests?" asked Fuad.

"You can take them to a club".

"When will you come back?" asked Fuad.

"I may never come back!" retorted Baidah.

"What about my child?" asked Fuad, calmly and deliberately. Those words were strong enough to remind her of the bitter reality, the great dilemma she was in. She despairingly murmured, "Oh, what a fool I was! How right Asia was!"

When he heard Asia's name, he said laughingly, "Oh, that snob! I proposed to her just to crush her pride and religious vanity. Now you remember her; what has she or her advice ever done for you? You are on the verge of destroying your marriage and your family life is about to fail because of this backward Asia!"

Baidah angrily said, "No, I won't allow you to speak ill of her. Had I listened to her advice I would have spared myself such an experience. Anyway, it is my own fault. I must bear the consequences."

****

Two years later, Asia sat thinking of her friend Baidah. She had heard a lot about her that she found difficult to believe. She could not believe that after a bitter struggle Baidah had given in to her husband. She had heard she no longer cared for Islamic *hijab* but accompanied her husband to parties and nightclubs. She had given birth to a boy, Farid and they said she was always sad and hardly ever smiled. Asia heard such rumours and wished she could see Baidah and learn the truth from her.

That morning the doorbell rang and Asia hurried to open it. She was surprised to see Baidah herself standing in front of her. She was pale and unhappy. Asia welcomed her and led her into the living room. Baidah sat silently, not knowing what to say.

Asia said "Oh, Baidah, how I hoped I'd see you; I've heard so much about you, but I was anxious to hear from you yourself."

Baidah cried bitterly saying, "I have no news except of disgrace and shame! I have been the victim of foolishness and self-deceit. Anyway I am not worthy of your friendship. I have fallen to the bottom of the abyss and am hopeless, may Allah forgive me!"

Asia felt great pity for her and kindly said, "You are still my sister and I must help you, to overcome this awful experience. Now, please tell me everything frankly as you did in the past."

Baidah said, "Well, you know that I never listened to your advice. I believed in a dream and ran to get it; I tried hard to get Fuad to come round to my way of thinking but ailed. He never accepted my religious commitment, and treated me cruelly, humiliating me often. Sometimes, he was gentle and kind and sometimes he was frightening. I thought about divorce, but my son caused me to give up that idea, so I gave in, and obeyed him meekly. He exploited my weakness and increased his domination over me, drawing me ever deeper into disgrace. I accepted everything just as a prisoner accepts his sentence. Now, you see me here!"

Asia could not blame her seeing her as she did and asked, "What's the problem now then?"

"He divorced me a week ago, because he blamed me for the death of our son", said Baidah. "Why?" asked Asia incredulously.

"Because I fasted in the month of Ramadhan."

Asia asked, "Did your son die of hunger?"

Baidah replied, "Of course not. He was both breast-fed as well bottle-fed. He died after an illness." Asia was greatly moved and felt sorry for the bereaved mother who had suffered humiliation and disgrace. So you see, I have lost everything," continued Baidah.

Asia hugged her warmly and said, "You have not lost everything. You still have your religion calling you back through repentance, and I am still your loving friend.

You still have the broad road of the future ahead of you. Perhaps this experience will help you to make a new righteous start; a future that is built on firm foundations. Don't despair, *"...surely none despair of Allah's mercy except the unbelieving people." (Yousuf: 87)*

SPIRITUAL SURGERY

Ikhlaas considered her sister-in-faith, Wafa, to be a real help to her in understanding life as being a righteous attempt towards achieving perfection. She could never be out of her company for even a short time, and Wafa was always nearby to support her in times of crisis. She would remind Ikhlaas of her duties, if ever she forgot, and was, to her, like a mirror, gently reflecting any defect or weakness in her character. In fact Ikhlaas felt uneasy and suffered spiritually, whenever Wafa did not call or turn up at meetings. Waiting would cost her a lot; therefore she rushed anxiously to enquire about her friend's absence but could get no news of her. There was nothing for it but to go herself. Wafa, looked rather pale, but welcomed her friend with a smile. Ikhlaas kissed her saying, "Oh dear sister I why haven't you come recently? I hope there is nothing wrong?" Gently Wafa said, "Nothing, but a little surgery." Shocked, Ikhlaas said, "Oh dear, surgery? Where? When? Why? ..." Calmly Wafa said, "Oh sister, you have raised many questions that cannot be answered all at once. Let us answer the first question, 'Where?', the answer is here at home!"

Ikhlaas wondered, "Here? At home? 'Who was the doctor, who performed the operation? Where is the pain? You look, quite well, thank God!"

Wafa said, "You have again raised many questions, I shall therefore, follow your style in my answer. As for the doctor, it has been myself, as for the wound, it is unseen."

Ikhlaas thought Wafa was joking; she said, "When did you become a surgeon? We know you as our spiritual guide." Wafa spoke in a serious calm tone. She said, "Every person should be his own surgeon. A sick man is ready to resort to the doctors to rid him of a tumour or a rotten limb. Why does he do that? Why does he risk his life at the hands of someone else? Of course to be saved from a disease which is eating up his body. As for spiritual diseases, the case is different. When a person feels such diseases keeping him from happiness he should do something to cure himself. Surgery with a difference is necessary, in this case. He himself must be the doctor. By means of faith he can perform the operation, and hence the house replaces the hospital. So I was not joking when I referred to the reason for my absence."

Ikhlaas was excited at this. She was about to cry out of fear for her friend. She anxiously said, "How do you feel now dear sister? Shall I congratulate you on your recovery?" Wafa did not answer, but was silent for a while. Ikhlaas was greatly concerned. It was not easy for her to see her best friend suffer such a dangerous disease and she was relieved when Wafa said, "I think I am quite well again."

Ikhlaas wanted to learn something from her friend, so she asked, "How do you know that you are safe, sister?"

Wafa said, "Life's incidents have helped me to recognize the disease and it's cure. Don't you see that these incidents are the experimental tools which operate upon the human personality?"

Ikhlaas said, "So I see, but still one should not forget the other surgeon's knife." Wafa nodded saying, "That's a fact. Physical treatment is as important as spiritual."

THE GIFT

She spent an uncomfortable day anxiously waiting for, she knew not what. Her beloved husband had left her shortly after their marriage. She was waiting for the gift he had promised her, before he went into death's eternal sleep; into the bright world of heaven. His gift, (whatever it was) would be dear to her. It would be a token, a symbol of the love, emotion and harmony that filled their life together. Yet it was a unique gift; one prepared by the husband to be given to his wife in the wake of his death. It would be one of the most precious presents he had ever given her, and she was anxious to know what it was. She wondered who could tell her something about it. He had mentioned it first during his arms training, whilst preparing to fight for the rights and the dignity of his people, to either achieve victory or enjoy martyrdom. He did not give it her then but left her, waiting for his sake return. But he never returned. How could he come back? Those who rush to fight against the satanic enemy do not come back. They always expect victory or martyrdom. They desire either death, to vex the enemy, or life that pleases the friends. There are many who come and go..., but can a life of compromise and weakness, be considered a real life? It is really only death. Her husband achieved martyrdom in the battle of Al-Karamah (a village in the occupied Palestine). He fell whilst defending his homeland that had been seized by the Zionists. They did not even celebrate one wedding anniversary as he left during the early days of their married life. Her beloved husband knew that someone's precious life, was worth sacrificing for a noble cause. He left her and joined the combatants in the battlefield, promising her his gift. He was away often and for long periods of time, but she got news of his struggle. She prayed to Allah to give him strength, patience and fortitude with which to face the brutal enemy...then, she was awaiting his return. But now she no longer waited. He had enjoyed martyrdom in the battle of dignity and justice and she would never forget his promised gift. His bright figure was etched deep into her heart and his martyrdom had increased that brightness. He was her love whether dead or alive, and she lived with him and for him. She was proud of, and happy with, him. She had a right to anxiously await his gift. At last, after waiting for what seemed ages, but was really only a few days, the gift was brought to her.

She looked at it as if she were looking at his angelic luminous shadow. She remembered him when he was her hope in life, the man of her dreams. He went for the sake of her and every oppressed wife, every unhappy child, every lost young man... He went in order to liberate his country, for her and for all the people. He sacrificed himself for the sake of the country that was invaded by imperialists and strangers. He was worthy of her love and high respect. She got the gift. She was both happy and sad. She looked at it. It was balm for her wounded heart.

What could it be? It was a green board on which was fixed in big letters, the following Qur'anic verse: *"...who when a misfortune befalls them say: surely we are Allah's and to Him we shall return..."* (*Al-Baqarah: 156*)

She hung it on the wall where she could see it every morning, when she opened her eyes and every evening when she went to sleep. She looked at it and promised Allah the Almighty, and her martyred husband that she would tread the road of struggle till the banner of justice could be raised in Palestine. Whenever she longed for her husband she read the Qur'anic verse and a feeling of calm crept through her.

A BAD BARGAIN

Early on in their engagement, he sat near his fiancée saying, "Oh, how I love you...in fact I adore you, you are my life..." He uttered words of love that she vainly enjoyed listening to. He told her that he could hardly wait for their wedding day, as life away from her was meaningless to him. He wondered how he had managed to live before knowing her. He assured her that she was the source of happiness in his life. He was sure to rent a great house that would match his feelings. They would spend their honeymoon abroad, in one of the western capitals.

He carried on talking, repeating words of love, while his girl was lost in her daydreams, which had at last come true. Suddenly she was aware of her hair dropping across her forehead. She raised her hand to put it in place and said flirtatiously, "You were in such a hurry that you did not even give me time to have my hair done."

He said, "Your hair is lovely anyway, and you are quite beautiful."

She smiled, proudly encouraging him to praise her still more. She said, "You did not even wait for me to get my new dress from the tailor."

He said, "Have not I said that this does not matter. I never worry about such things as my real aim has been reached."

She eagerly said, "Are you quite sure?" He said,

"Yes. I swear by my love, that I mean every word."

She said, "I am very happy. I have always hoped to get a husband who does not care for material things..."

He said, "I am just like that, you can be sure."

She went on, "You know that money is something that comes and goes. I don't care much for it. In fact, I give all of my salary to my father who suffers financial difficulties."

At first he did not answer, then he said: "It is nice that you help your father. Financial problems cannot be tolerated. Then I suppose we can't rent a big house!"

She said, "Whether big or small, it does not matter .It should at least be comfortable."

He said, "Yes, there should be all the necessary amenities: a refrigerator, a cooler, a washing machine..."

She interrupted him saying, "Such items can be bought one by one. At first we can start a simple life. You know that at present my father cannot help us."

He was silent again. He looked at his watch and then said, "Simplicity is nice. I think we should not go abroad! "

She answered, "Yes, that is much better. You know I must pay back my debts!"

No longer could he conceal his disappointment, so he said sharply, "Then, your salary is already spent in advance!"

She said, "Nearly!"

He moved in discomfort saying, "I, myself am in debt, so, I'd better not marry at present."

Standing up he said, "We may not meet again. I wish you good luck!"

He left quickly as if running away from a monster! Only few minutes before he had spoken words of love and claimed that he could not live without her. The waiter came to her with the bill that the young man had not paid.

Amused she said to herself, "I guessed right! I was right to lie about my wealth. How stupid he is! He never thought I was testing him. My bank balance is good and I am not in debt to anyone! Anyway, it was a good experience for me, even if it was a bad bargain."

THE LAST DAYS

In despair Sarah wept saying, "Oh! I didn't know that those were her last days or that that was to be our last meeting with her! Had I only known...", her tears choked her. Saliha, the friend who had brought her the sad news, was brave enough to have carried the message. She offered condolences to her friend and stretched her cold and shaking hand in comfort, to Sara. She said, "It would not have made any difference. She kept it to herself and suffered in silence, patiently awaiting her end. She tolerated the horrors of waiting death. What could you have done, had you known?"

Sarah said, "I would have learnt much from her, I would have learned lessons that would have helped me to find my way in life. I would have said farewell to her, and have assured her of my undying love and respect. Oh! I am lost since her departure..."

Saliha said, "She knew how much you appreciated her friendship that is why she left you her writing."

Sarah dried her tears and said wonderingly, "Her writing? "

Saliha said, "It seems to be her diary ...I've come to give you this precious trust."

She opened her handbag and got out the diary. Sarah took it and noticed on the cover the Holy Qur'anic verse: *We are Allah s and to Him we shall return. (Al-Baqarah, 156)*

On the first page she read:

...So, my life will come to an end soon. It is a matter of just a few days. Only yesterday was I informed of this fact. Anyway, it is the end, but I am not thinking of the end so much, as I am thinking of the beginning, and the incidents that have filled the space between the beginning and the end. Those incidents will strongly affect the end.

They indicate the end, as it says in the Qur'anic verse:

Allah is the Guardian of those who believe. He brings them out of the darkness into the light...(Al-Baqarah: 257)

Thus, I must review my past deeds and call myself to account, in order to know what is awaiting me. Light or Darkness, joy or sadness, chains or freedom...

In fact, I am seriously thinking of the beginning. What was the beginning? When and where should I start? Should I start at my childhood? Oh, no. I don't want to write my life story that takes the time of whoever reads it. I shall express the feelings of one who stands at the crossroads of this life and the hereafter. My childhood has nothing to do with that. It has nothing to do with what is waiting for me now! Childhood is a break in man's life, before he is required to perform his responsibilities. Yet, childhood signifies many meanings. I have heard and read about childhood. They say it is the happy joyful world of hopes and wishes. They say it is the time when a child gains the necessities for a life that will give him satisfaction. They say this and more. Though I have read about childhood, I have never realized the meaning of my childhood as defined by others. My childhood was a stage in life; I crossed it with no weapons of knowledge or faith. Hence I suffered a lot and was bewildered at the conflict between my inner self and the tiny body, between my great responsibility, which was ahead of me, and the limited range of my thinking. Childhood means nothing to me but a fruitless expanse of frozen time. So I won't put those days of childhood on trial. I will start with the early days of youth and girlhood. What is youth to me? It is a film full of images; some are dull and heavy, some are light and bright. It is a theatre where one's story is told; the story of someone searching for perfection; one who looked all around for the thread that would lead to it. I tried to understand life. I was never satisfied with its outward face. I dived deeper to reach my aim. I came to understand, through this universe, that there is a mighty Power with firm laws that regulates its movements. That is why it is so wonderful, so magnificent. I strived to understand people, but faced amazement, hesitation and disappointment most of the time. How often I returned home crying and broken-hearted; but, it was not always like that. Thank God! Through experience I gained more knowledge and more understanding of human nature and personal habits. I persisted in the pursuit of knowledge and understanding. Where did I find it? It was in Islam, in my Qur'an that is the message from Heaven. I felt so thirsty that I hurried to this spring. This was my early youth which I intend to record in this diary...' shall write down its hours whether of happiness or sadness, satisfaction or disappointment. I will consider my life's course and whether or not it was on the right path. I must tell the truth, whatever that may be. I am now standing at the doors of other world. What was my reaction to incidents and events in those past days? What was my reaction to faith and belief in Allah the Almighty? Hiding, or running away from the truth won't help. I am on my way to stand in front of a Just Judge. There is no room for denial or lying. The Qur'anic verse says:

On the day when their tongues and their hands and their feet shall bear witness against them as to what they did... (Al-Nur: 24)

I need to be frank and put myself on trial. I must be serious in calling myself to account, for haven't I known that death is the certain end of every human being? It is written on every person clearly as a necklace on a young girl's neck. Did I not hear that Imam Ali (as) said, *"Oh people! you are chased by death...!?"* Then it is not only I who should call myself frankly to account. Everyone should know that he is created to achieve perfection through the worship of Allah the Almighty. When one dies, one will reap what one has sown. Oh, you who think you are safe, be careful! You will not be spared.

HARD TIMES

I must admit that I suffered poverty in my early youth. There was nothing to eat or drink, no home no clothing! Poverty is a cruel situation. It brings all kinds of misery and pain. How did it affect my life? Did it destroy me? Was I strong enough to pass the experience successfully? In fact, it was an experience that caused me to learn the importance of faith in the human life. It made me understand the great Prophet's (swas) saying: *"Whoever does not comprehend the Qur'an is not among my followers."*

Anyone can undergo the experience of poverty and financial difficulty and if one lacks tolerance and self-control, one may suffer an unimaginable situation. Tolerance and self-control stem from faith that can help man to successfully overcome difficulties. It teaches him to be master of himself and of others. Whatever earthly pleasures a man gets, will soon come to an end. It is no wonder that I was content with the little I had. I never thought poverty meant disappointment or failure. On the contrary, I tried to benefit from my spiritual strength and make use of it in fruitful deeds. I lacked the material necessities to help me carry on in life. Hence it was necessary for me to stand on the firm ground of constructive and creative values and ethics which help one to form a character completely aware of the dimensions of one's existence. I came to understand the real meaning of poverty and richness. I came to know that a poor person is one whose social worth depends on his wealth. It is high when one's bank balance is high, and low, when it is low. He needs money to prove his social existence, property to make people point at him, and luxuries to make others gather around him. He considers money as being the pivot of his existence and his dignity. He is careful to keep it because its disappearance means his own non-existence. I never let such thoughts about poverty poison my life with weakness and gullibility. I never allowed it to make me look at life with feelings of deprivation. I was happy despite my poverty. I was carefree, busy gaining religious knowledge that could shape my personality. The very little knowledge that I gained gave me so much pleasure and self-contentment that it gave success it's real meaning. I was, thank God, happy with the little I had. It is a Divine Blessing in a believer's life.

IDLENESS

This was a period of inactivity. Thank God, it did not last long. Now that I see my end approaching, before the fulfillment of my aim, which is to worship for the sake of Allah, I feel sad about that period of idleness. Man's life is worthless, unless it is devoted to work for the sake of Allah, the Almighty. How despicable idleness is! How strange that man is careless of his religious duties and neglects religious rituals! Now, I feel those past days blame me for neglecting them. They are sorry for having passed by without the performance of anything but the ordinary duties. Nothing more has been recorded in the pages of good deeds. Those days are ashamed to demand Allah's pleasure, on the Day of Judgment. What can I do? Whatever passed away won't come back. I should have made up for those days later. I know that one's days are counted. I wonder if I did my best. Only Allah the Almighty knows that.

A NEW START

However, because of Allah's mercy, my idleness did not last long. Something happened to shock me and inject new life into me. It caused me to understand my responsibilities more fully. Usually one gains experience through hardships and difficulties. Thank God, such hardships caused me to understand the importance of faith in my life.

Thus, I thank God, for His trying man with troubles and hardships that must be considered as some of His bounties. Such hardships and difficulties must not be considered in terms of their cruel appearance alone, but rather through whatever good lessons are gained from them. We should consider them spiritual benefits and face such situations with strength and determination.

I recall such an experience and how deeply it affected me. Its effect was so great that I was on the verge of hopelessness. All that time I dragged myself from the house and strolled the streets, as if to escape the barbs of that experience. I found that I was wrong. The house had nothing to do with that difficulty. Leaving the house did not make any difference. I was defeated and at a loss as to where to go or what to do. Then suddenly I listened to the Qur'anic words that came from a distance, as if I was hearing them for the first time:

Until when the apostles despaired and the people became I sure that they were indeed told a lie, Our help came to them and whom We pleased was delivered and Our punishment is not averted from the guilty people. (Yousuf: 110)

On hearing those words I was made aware again, I woke up as if from a sleep that could make me despair. I remembered that Allah, the Almighty never leaves His faithful believers in trouble. Those troubles are nothing but a means or a method towards perfection. To a human being they are the same as a laboratory where the real nature of man is analyzed so that he can learn things about himself that he ignores and discover his weaknesses and defects. After that experience I continued my life amid hopes and pains, flowers and thorns. Thorns are only found near flowers. Hope comes from pain. Hence I found myself in harmony with various roles and incidents. Good things did not tempt me, neither did bad things lead me into despair. I waited for the relief after hardships and expected darker times after happy days, as if those happy days warned of what might follow. The years passed on and I enjoyed Allah's mercy in full. I felt I was too unworthy to receive such mercy and compassion. I belittled whatever I did for the sake of Allah. My pains increased due to my shortcomings in serving Him. Such shortcomings seemed the result of weakness or laziness. I felt uneasy in my surroundings as if I were an intruder. I tried to keep away. How hard it is for one to feel handicapped in the performance of one's duties. I was overwhelmed with sorrow and pain that tarnished my spiritual pleasure in serving Allah the Almighty...it was Allah's mercy that engulfed my inner self and helped me to overcome the obstacles in life. Thanks are due to Him Who keeps the doors open for His worshippers.

THE LAST HOURS

Now I must write about the last hours, which have been imposed, on me. There is no way out; death spares no one. The Holy Qur'an says,

Wherever you are, death will overtake you though you be in lofty towers... (Al-Nisa: 78)

Is there any escape from Allah's order? The Divine narration says, *Whoever rejects My rule, should leave My Earth and Heaven.* Every believer should accept death willingly; with whatever pleases Allah, the Almighty. Am I sorry to be leaving this world? The answer is: Yes and No. I am sorry at leaving it because it is the way that leads to Allah's pleasure and mercy. Its days are trials offered to man in which to make his choice. Had I to live longer I might achieve a better level in the worship of Allah. There is another reason for my sorrow. My friends and relatives will feel sad and miss me; but this is the nature of life. I am not sorry, because it is not worth a feather, as a poet says, ...One should be careful of its plots. Divorce is thrice (three times in the Islamic Religion) yet I divorced it a thousand times...Its changes are fearful, its promises are false and its hopes are worn out. I wonder how some hold onto such a hope Don't they know, good deeds are the best provisions and that the final settlement is in graves? ... Oh, how sorry one feels when the last hours draw near. How regretful one is for past errors! How one wishes for a new chance to make-up for them! One is ready to give whatever one has, to make-up for those sins. How wonderful it is for one to call oneself to account. How wise it is for one to consider the result of each step one takes in life, so that one may not feel sorry at the last hours. The Holy Qur'an says,... *most surely (one's) self is wont to command evil except such as my Lord had mercy on, surely my Lord is Forgiving, Merciful. (Yousuf: 53)*

Oh God, I do love Thee, the same as I fear Thee... Oh God, grant me Your mercy and forgiveness, deprive me not of Your pleasure...Oh Mighty God, how happy I am to be released of the chains and concerns of this world. I am happy to becoming free of its evils and sins. Oh God, grant those who loved me patience and double their reward. Oh God, keep them on the right path, so that they can continue their good deeds through which I may survive...*Oh God, grant me mercy... surely Thou art the most liberal Giver....(Aale-Imran: 8)*

FRIENDLY LETTERS

PART ONE

Wafa and Raja are two sisters in religion. They exchange letters, which indicates that one of them has been a religious guide to the other.

Dear sister Wafa,

Assalamu Alaikum,

I must confess that you have been a real guiding light to me in my life...I am writing to you, while darkness has engulfed the Universe. Night has gently put out its fingers to wipe away the troubles of the day and give rest to the exhausted. Everything around me is silent; a hidden tune is being played, giving the soul the pleasure that it seeks. One wonders how darkness can be changed into brightness, illuminating the features of a new road. Rough words are changed into gentle ones that heal the wounds of the hearts.

Faith can do miracles. Belief in Allah makes one seek His mercy. Such a call to Faith is as pleasant as a spring breeze, as clear as the blue sky, and as beautiful as a flower. It is a clear voice that dominates the soul. One surrenders to it as a prisoner to his watchman and a child to his mother. The soul heeds it to drop anchor at its shore. I hearken to it and hear the story of a new birth. It is the echo of a Qur'anic verse that says, ***Our Lord, surely we have heard a preacher calling to the Faith saying: Believe in your Lord, so we did believe, Our Lord forgive us therefore our faults and cover our evil deeds and make us die with the righteous.*** *(Aale-Imran: 193)*

Hence I come to understand that I am newly born to lead a new life. After utter darkness, firmly knitted by torturing days, keeping the soul chained to bitter weakness, I started feeling my new life. The mind has been the arena where severe conflict randomly took place. Nothing was clear in the vast desert where everything could be lost. Darkness, throughout those years, colored my life black. All things seemed to me utter blackness. I looked at life through dark-glasses. I suffered the rough winds and the dangerous sea waves against which my life's boat was about to crush. Allah the Merciful watched that tiny boat struggling against the fearful waves of destiny. Then kind hands stretched to save the drowning soul. Those were your kind hands dear Wafa. Allah sent you to save this tired heart and disturbed soul. I was kindly led towards the safe harbour of comfort and rest; radiant awareness defeated the disputes of the inner enemy ...I prayed to Allah the Almighty for His bounties. I uttered words which no one but He is worthy of receiving. I promised Him to tread His road to the end.

I am anxious to give you this good news of my new birth...with your help and Allah's, Mercy I came to understand the meaning of happiness or misery in life.

I pray to Allah to keep you safe, dear sister.

Raja

****

Dear sister Raja,

Your letter has been a source of pleasure to me. Its lines and words were in a new bright frame, telling the story of a new birth. I rejoiced, just as a player rejoices over winning the first round of a game. What a game Life is! It shapes the feelings, and colours its own toys through various incidents. Hence you see when I win a round, I make a step forward to save one deviated soul, one victim of a misleading society.

I am sure your wonderful letter was motivated by Faith ...yet I wished you would not have used words such as "prisoner" and "watchman"...A different expression would indicate satisfaction...I hope you go ahead, increasing your faith...you should perform righteous deeds for the sake of Allah, love the good and hate the evil. Be angry for His sake and rejoice at what pleases Him. Depend on Him and you won't face failure.

I pray to Allah to guide you well.

Wafa

****

Dear sister Wafa,

Assalamu Alaikum,

Still, I cannot explain the confusion that overtakes me sometimes. I do not say that happiness and comfort within my soul has come to an end. This has never been temporary joy of Faith. I still feel the ecstasy of the new birth, but I still feel some pain from an unknown source.

Perhaps I still live the life I led prior to Faith. Please help me pass this crucial phase. Many have tried to help me change my view of life, but I could never respond to them. I have to confess that you are the only person who managed to make me change that black vision I had. Now, I seek your help in overcoming this pain, the source of my discomfort...So please talk, since I find the comfort and security that I seek in your words. Your talks are of Faith and its creative power. Your words fill my soul with bright righteous guidance.

May Allah keep you safe.

Raja

****

Dear sister Raja,

Assalamu Alaikum,

Pain for no special reason is a mere illusion. Everyone can destroy pain in his life, if he searches for its source in reality. Unreasonable sufferings may bring more sufferings. One should not give way to such pains, which bite the weak with sharp teeth.

You should be ready to resist such feelings. Those things of the world make you forget your religious duties and-take the worship of Allah with a pinch of salt. It is a pity for one to find the source of light and then be pushed away before reaching it. I pray to Allah to give you more strength to fight against your desires. At this stage you need to stand firm, and have a strong will.

Wafa

****

Dear sister Wafa,

I wish I never had the word "pain ", in my vocabulary...How wonderful it is for one to have a nice dream that comes true and brings a real not a forced smile to one's lips. You may wonder what kind of dream it is! Well, it is to enjoy happiness in the shadow of Faith and to reject the suffering of an aimless life...I wish, I could forget this word "pain" with all its reflections.

At the order of Allah, your helpful hand has broken the chains of pain and released my soul. Your kind heart has destroyed the shadows of torture. You have outlined the righteous road and scattered along it the flowers of hope whose scent touches the soul and removes dark shadows. Such hope in Allah's pleasure is most wonderful. It is a stage of transfer, not only from deviation to righteousness, or from doubt to certainty, but also from misery to happiness and from despair to hope and from darkness to light... to Allah and Religion which I am ready to sacrifice myself for.

I pray to Allah for your strength and fortitude.

Raja

****

Dear sister Raja,

I am sorry to say that I missed optimistic words in your letter; words that foretell a promising new birth. I missed in your letter words that indicate achievement in destroying pains and sufferings. I frankly say that your letter disappointed me. How hard it is to see a long awaited hope vanish in front of one's eyes!

You still talk about pain. What pain is it that can stay, despite a Faith that overwhelms the soul with its light? You should rather talk about happiness, which is at the threshold of your door, though you ignore it. How happy one is to rid oneself of pain and purify one's soul that will soon enjoy the eternal sublime world! How wonderful it is to set up the fortress of Faith on the ruins of pain; such a fortress cannot be destroyed with the passage of time.

Oh sister, how dear you are to me. I feel that your soul, that has suffered this world's pains, has been released, rejecting this world, turning towards a great aim of all souls. It is to gain the pleasure of Allah and to get His Paradise. You should therefore pray to Allah always, for more piety and faith. Pray to Him for mercy and help, since He is ready to answer those seeking His help; He is most thanked and praised for that. Recite, whenever you can, the Holy Qur'an, which gives comfort to the troubled soul and purifies the self of its sins. Fear the Creator and seek refuge in Him. Pray to Allah, as the Qur'anic verse says: *And glorify the name of your Lord morning and evening.* (Al-Insan:25)

Go ahead and rid yourself of all that which causes you pain...Be happy with your belief in Allah...I am waiting for good news from you, to remove my disappointment.

Wafa

****

Dear sister Wafa,

I do apologize for causing you disappointment. What can I write? Well, the one who wished to die, is now interested in life. This is not for the sake of enjoying life, but for the sake of a sublime aim that one strives to attain through the worship of Allah. Hence, you see I am no longer disturbed by life's troubles. This life with all its hardship and suffering is of no more concern to me. This world is nothing but a tiny portion of the great universe. I feel satisfied wherever I go. Despite the unpleasant reality, the feeling of spiritual security gives me ease. I came to understand that life will go on whether one is sad or happy. The past days won't come back; time does not bother with one's tears or one's smiles. Why should one, then, demand what time cannot offer?

Now, I don't build castles in the air. I have made a new start on the firm foundation of Faith. Life's troubles won't be allowed to keep me under the domination of pain. I want to achieve a life of Faith and piety. I'll make use of this life for the sake of the other one.

Pray for me dear sister.

Raja

****

Dear sister Raja,

Thanks be to Allah, your letter has been a source of joy to me. How happy I am to know one desires life after being in the pursuit of death. 'This is just what I expected of you. Now you are quite sure that life is precious despite its troubles, which are sometimes too cruel to be tolerated. This is a facet of its nature; hence we should adjust ourselves to its reality with firmness.

Those lines in your letter will be your witness in the Hereafter. The Holy Qur'an says: *Our Lord, surely we have heard a preacher calling to Faith, saying: Believe in your Lord, so we did believe...(Aale-Imran: 193)*

How happy I am that you are now on the right-path. You have set out with new determinations and awareness. You have left behind the deceptive materialistic pleasures. With all my heart, I pray for you, that Allah may keep you safe.

Wafa

****

Dear sister Wafa,

You have been a source of light and a means of guidance to me. I shall be strong enough to destroy pain... I'll forget all my sufferings. With the weapon of faith, I shall break down many pains that spoiled my life. My awareness is back after a long absence. I am fully awake, making my way towards the Divine light and forgiveness.

"Oh my Lord, how great is Your mercy. How easy difficulties are, for Your sake! How wonderful is struggle, for Your pleasure! How sweet bitterness is to get near You. No aim is worthy of struggle, but Yours. Oh God, despite troubles, I find happiness in my striving towards You. However narrow this room is, I enjoy the horizons of Faith, praying to You. Oh my Lord, how wonderful it is to get free of these earthly chains, setting out towards You...! Oh God! I seek nothing but Your pleasure, I need nothing but Your forgiveness. I tread only towards Your orchard. Oh my Lord, this life is nothing but efforts for your sake. My soul, Oh God, is full of hope in Your forgiveness. It longs for Your bounties and waits for Your pleasure...Oh God, this hardship is only a means of bringing me nearer to You...Oh God, my tears are for Your sake, Oh God, how great my need of Your pleasure is...!"

Finally, dear sister, I confess my gratitude to you for all your help.

Raja

****

Dear sister Raja,

How wonderful for one to place one's hopes in Allah the Almighty. Such hopes make one smile amid tears and laugh despite suffering. Hope of Allah's pleasure and forgiveness changes darkness within oneself into a bright light reflected on one's face. Such hopes help the believers to tolerate the hardships without despair or retreat. They make the bitter taste of life, sweet, and heal wounds...Imam Ali (A.S.) refers to this when he describes the believers. He says, *"...their bodies are on earth, but their souls are attached to the sublime world..."* How difficult life is, for one who does not seek the source of hope! How hard it is for one to tread difficult roads without the help of Divine Guidance! Faith is, dear sister, a paradise full of shady trees for one seeking refuge from poisonous life. Faith is a spring of water that can never dry up. It is man's provision in this life and the Hereafter. Keep on seeking Allah's mercy.

May Allah keep you safe.

Wafa

****

Dear sister Wafa,

I have not written to you for some time...not because of feelings of disappointment or negligence...I am, thanks are due to Allah, still happy with my faith. Yet I need to be assured of Allah's forgiveness. I am afraid He may chase me out of His presence...How concerned I am for such feelings! Please write to me, give me some comfort.

Raja

****

Dear sister Raja,

Allah, the Almighty never drives away those who seek His door. He never turns away hearts treading towards Him with pure love and absolute worship. He never disappoints those who ask for His mercy and forgiveness. The prophetic narration says: *"Whoever takes one step towards Allah, Allah will take ten steps towards him."*

The Qur'anic verse says: ***Whoever brings a good deed, he shall have ten like it...*** *(Al-Anam: 160)*

Hence you see, Allah never rejects the sincere words of Faith...I pray to Him to guide you well in this life.

Wafa

****

PART TWO

While Zahra (with her husband Barrir) are abroad she exchanges letters with Asma. Through them, Asma becomes a real sister in religion to Zahra. Zahra's husband Barrir is a committed Muslim believer.

Dear Asma,

Assalamu Alaikum

I am sure that you spend a good deal of your time engaged in the worship of Allah the Almighty. As for me, I have grown a bit fat, due to the nice weather and good food. Yesterday we (I and Barrir) took a long walk but we, didn't get a bit tired. We came across an orchard full of scented flowers and I picked a beautiful one. Barrir said to me, "I wonder if you heard the conversation between your flower and its neighbor. "I was surprised at his words and said, "No I have heard nothing." Barrir said, "When you put out your hand to pick it, it laughed proudly and said to its neighbors, "Oh, stay in this spot forever. As for me, I shall be taken to have a rest in a magnificent vase on a wooden or marble table...perhaps I'll decorate the blouse of a beautiful lady or crown her blond hair! I'll get rid of these roots that tie me to the earth and get free of these branches, which are supposed to provide me with water and sunlight. I no longer need wait for the gardener to water me, or look for shade to protect me from the sun's heat. Oh poor sister, now I pity you..."

I listened to him while he said, "Of course neither did you hear the answer. The flower's neighbour sadly murmured: "Oh I feel sad for you dear sister you are quite wrong. Those roots that tie you to the earth are a symbol of your life. These branches are to provide you with security and survival. You are quite misled by your supposed freedom. It will cause you to fade and die. Your petals will fall dry and be carried away by the wind. This will be the result of your supposed freedom. As for me I shall stay alive and fresh since I am still tied by my roots, which give me life." Barrir then stopped talking, though I was very interested in his dialogue. I was very happy to have comprehended the significance of the two flowers...I feel happy whenever I learn more and increase my knowledge. I am sure you can also comprehend the significance of the two flowers.

My best wishes to you.

Zahra

****

Dear sister Zahra,

Assalamu Alaikum,

How I miss you dear sister. Your letters are a source of pleasure to me. They help me tolerate this boring time. I enjoyed reading your letter and your "flower's dialogue". Of course I understood the significance of the two flowers; they symbolize two girls. The first one is fooled by false propaganda and supposed freedom, and is the victim of ideologies that exploit her identity, the same as the flower carried from here to there as from vase to vase until it dies.

As for me, dear sister, I am often alone...I have recently been hurt by my nearest and dearest. A stone has been thrown at me, which has caused me to seek isolation...I am now busy reading a book about living creatures and their habits. The book is very interesting and useful, and it stirred, in me a great sense of awe for the greatness of the Creator. It deals with: light-giving creatures and fire worms that live in the sea and fireflies that live in the farms and the bat and its strong sense of hearing. This creature can hear ultra-vocal waves, with a vibration rate of 500,000 per second, and other such scientific facts, which are all created by Allah the Almighty. So you see I do benefit from this isolation and have enough time for reading and writing.

I hope to hear from you soon.

Asma

****

Dear sister Asma,

Assalamu Alaikum,

I got your dear letter yesterday and was eager to read it...I sensed some feelings of distress in your words... what do you mean by this isolation? You should have a social life that will benefit you as well as others. What is this stone thrown by your nearest and dearest? Anyway, haven't you ever seen the fruiting coffee tree, called a "Beauty Tree"? Its roots go deep into the earth; its branches grow high and green to provide a source of hope for the spectator. It bears white flowers in clusters, to decorate its branches. Such a tree is a source of pleasure to others. When someone throws a stone at it, it trembles gently and rains countless white flowers upon him.

A believer can resemble this worthy tree. He devotes his life to Allah. When he suffers injustice, he responds with good advice and gentle words, with prayers for the guidance of others. When a brother believer throws a stone at him, he wishes he could put in that hand a torch of light in place of the stone, and he is kind and loving. He wishes he could replace the stones with olive branches in order to spare the believers the difficulty of carrying stones.

A believer is all good and kind and loving. Hence you should tolerate the wrongs of your nearest and dearest. You should not isolate yourself from society. Isolation is nothing but a kind of cowardice. You must surely remember our talk about the impossibility of finding a perfect person who never gets angry at others who hurt him. Now can you try to be such a person?

With best wishes and heartfelt prayers.

Zahra

****

Dear sister Zahra,

Assalamu Alaikum,

I got your letter for which I was in real need, as it was a source of guiding light for me. Certainly women believers are expected to heal the wounds of each other and help each other. The Holy Qur'an says, ***Muhammad is the Apostle of Allah and those with him are firm of heart against the unbelievers, compassionate among themselves...*** *(Al-Fath:29)*

Your letter has caused me to reconsider my decision of isolating myself... I confess that isolation is not a solution...I should keep on guiding others to Islamic instructions. Our religion is in need of illustration and Qur'anic explanations and prophetic Sunnah.

Have you enjoyed reading during your travel? You haven't mentioned anything about such in your letters. Can I ask: why? Nice weather and beautiful quiet surroundings encourage one to read and write a lot. I have recently had such an experience when we went for a picnic on the riverbank. I was motivated to perform my duty, though it was a mere picnic with some relatives and friends. I sat under the olive and rose trees, and watched the flowing river carrying dead leaves and petals along, with its fish and other water creatures useful for people. It seemed to me that it told the story of life with all its hopes and sufferings and its hardships and pleasures.

I felt in need of my pen and paper...I got them from my handbag and started writing. I was very satisfied with that occasion.

My prayers for you, dear sister.

Zahra

****

Dear sister Asma,

Assalamu Alaikum,

However beautiful nature is, it cannot make one forget one's dear friends...Hence I long to see you and the other sisters...In fact, I am counting the days till my return... You may notice a delay in my reply to your letter. This is because we made a short trip to a nearby place. We hired a small car to go, and the driver drove as if he were sailing! Barrir asked him to slow down a bit, but he didn't. Barrir then said to him, "If you don't care for our lives, at least you should care for your own car!"

The driver answered indifferently, "Why should I? It has been insured since the day I got it." Barrir turned towards me saying, "Did you hear him?

He is not concerned for his car because the insurance company will pay for any damage or loss. That's why he drives at such a high speed. Otherwise, he would not risk it. Can you take a lesson from this?" I said, "I think it is similar to the life of a human being and the Divine insurance that is expected for any loss as in the Qur'anic verse:

...this is because, there afflicts them not thirst or fatigue or hunger in Allah s way, nor do they tread a path which enrages the unbelievers, nor do they attain from the enemy what they attain, but a good work is written down to them on account of it, surely Allah does not waste the reward of the doers of good. (Al-Tawba: 120)

254

Barrir said, "But there is a big difference between the two. The Insurance company won't make up for a loss except through efforts that take a long time and much money, while the Divine insurance is offered several fold and without an appeal. The Qur'anic verse says, *Whoever brings a good deed, he shall have tell like it...* (Al-Anam: 60)

Hence despite the losses that a believer suffers he is still the winner."

Barrir continued talking about the conditions of the Divine contract, which are genuinely good intention and straight forwardness. Then he explained the two requirements necessary to benefit from Allah's mercy. I was very interested and forgot all about the dangerous roads and the dreadful high speed. The place was not comfortable so our stay was short. We returned and I was happy to see your letter waiting for me. How nice of you to ask me about my reading. You may rejoice to know that I am reading an interpretation of the Holy Qur'an. I am quite fascinated by the deep meaning of the holy verses. I am taking notes in a special notebook, which you will see when I return home, God willing.

Till then, may Allah keep you safe.

Zahra

****

Dear sister Zahra,

Assalamu Alaikum,

In fact, reading has to some extent spared me from boredom. Yesterday I visited our friend Dunia. There I met a host of guests for the first time. I felt uneasy and regretted being there doing nothing useful for our religion.

Then one of the guests asked about the meaning of the word Dunia (this world). Some showed interest in the name others rejected it. One said, "This word reminds me of a prison." I wondered why when the world is quite wide. She said challengingly, "It is a prison for the believers and a paradise for the disbelievers. Therefore, if we are believers we are in a prison. If we are infidels, we won't get the eternal paradise." I said to her, "Listen to me sister. This narration refers relatively to prison and paradise. If all pleasure were within the reach of a believer's hand, what he enjoys in the other world is still greater. Hence this world to him is a prison. As for the infidel, whatever disasters he suffers in this world will be nothing compared to the horrible suffering in the other world, hence it is his paradise here, while what is awaiting him is unimaginable."

So you see I could benefit from that visit by explaining the prophetic narration to the guests. As for your letter, I was happy to get it after that delay. I enjoyed your conversation about the Divine insurance and Divine rewards. Such rewards make one smile despite tears. They cause the hopeless to catch sight of a ray of light in the utter darkness. The Divine promise of rewards helps the believers to tolerate sufferings and hardships with patience. Hence life's bitterness is changed into sweetness; its hardships into mercy and compassion. Such Divine rewards should be the aim of every believer, otherwise life is quite hard and its passages are quite dark for one to tread. 'Oh God how narrow the roads are for one who does not seek your guidance.'

Our sisters, Zainab, Saliha and Inam, send their best wishes. Inam has rejected an official job. She prefers to take care of her family and perform her religious responsibilities.

Asma

****

Dear sister Asma,

Assalamu Alaikum,

I am always eager to get your letters... I feel quite happy on reading them...Yesterday we went for a walk. Our destination was a spring whose waterfall comes down a high mountain. We walked across the green fields and it was a bright day; the sky was a clear blue. We walked down the valley quite slowly; between the big rocks springs of clear water flowed musically along. We stopped to drink some water and splash it on our faces. The naked rocks of the high mountains had deep lines cut across their surfaces. I tried to understand something about these high rocks and I said to Barrir, "Do you think these deep lines are quite ancient." He said, "Yes, they are quite old." I said, "How old are they? It must be quite difficult for the wind to cut such deep lines on the solid surfaces." Barrir said, "It is a long process, otherwise such lines would not have existed. One can easily put one's hand in this stream and find a space for it. But as soon as one draws back one's hand, no trace is left behind. The water will go on flowing filling the empty area on its way. This easy action is nothing significant. But if one tries to cut across a solid stone, certainly one will need great efforts and a substantial length of time. One may fill the cuts with sweat or stain the stone with bleeding fingers. With firmness and determination, it may take days and nights to achieve one's aim. Then the result will be wonderful. Troubles and hardships are soon forgotten. Such an achievement produces great happiness and survives for a long time. The traces will stay to relate to future generations the story of a hard struggle. Hence, there is a big difference between an easy achievement without the least effort and the difficult one which survives the ages."

Barrir ceased talking and I thought of the effort and hard work that produce good results, I recalled the Qur'anic verse: *...then as for the scum, it passes away as a worthless thing, and as for that which profits the people it tarries in the earth... (Al-Ra'ad :17)*

Certainly, we are in need of making efforts to achieve good deeds that can survive for the benefit of people.

My best wishes.

Zahra

****

Dear sister Zahra,

Assalamu Alaikum,

I got your letter just in time. I was in real need of something that could give me rest and ease since I suffered a crucial stage of confused thoughts and sad feelings. I suffered days of pain, despair and bitterness and often wondered: How can one laugh, when others cry nearby! How can one smile in this miserable world! How can one seem happy while one hears the wailing of despair day and night!

Some will surely collapse...yet some may fight back and refuse to surrender. Such people, of course, need a weapon with which to confront the fatal attacks in life. They are ready to fight, but they lack the weapon, hence they may give in. While I was thinking of this matter I listened to a person reciting the Holy Qur'anic verse, *...no soul knows what is hidden for them of that which will refresh the eyes... (Al-Sajdah:17)*

I thought of this verse and found in it a source of light that removed all amazement and loss. I knew it was faith. Faith is the weapon of fortitude and the assurance of Allah's mercy in this world and the Hereafter. Faith can amend personal behavior; can change despair into hope, difficulty into ease and fear into security. All this can happen if one knows it is for the sake of Allah and within His sight. Then I came to the conclusion that a believer should be optimistic as long as he is sure of Allah's help and content with what he gets or faces. I felt better and hopeful of relief...Your letter had a wonderful effect on me, the first sign of my optimistic theory. I hope you won't be disturbed by this letter. With faith I could overcome this kind of unease.

My prayers to Allah to keep you safe.

Asma

****

Dear sister Asma,

I hope you feel much better now since you have managed to rid yourself of all bitterness and pain and have tasted the sweetness of Faith and Patience. A believer should know that whatever he suffers is for the sake of Allah and within His watch. Such knowledge will strengthen his firm stance and open new roads of hope for him. However difficult the path is, and he can keep on treading it. Allah the Almighty ordered the prophets: Moses and Haroun, to go to Pharaoh.

The Qur'anic verses relate: *Go both to Pharaoh, surely he has become inordinate, then speak to him a gentle word, haply he may mind or fear. Both said: Our Lord, surely we fear that he may hasten to do evil to us as he may become inordinate. He said: Fear not, surely I am with you both. I do hear and see.* (Taha: 43-46)

With these Divine words Allah sent two of His worshippers to Pharaoh. These words indicate a serious situation with certain results. Pharaoh might hasten to do evil and increase his oppression, and the two Apostles feared this possibility. They were two of the oppressed masses to face the mightiest tyrant of that time. A tyrant who claimed without the least right to be himself a god, and dared to ask the people to worship him. The two prophets were to face him and tell him to bear witness that: There is no Lord but

Allah the One, with no other partners. The two prophets were in need of a mighty power though they were strong enough to perform the mission. Hence they said, *...our Lord, surely we fear that he....* That mighty power was felt with the awareness that Allah was with them, hearing and seeing. Allah did not fight for them, but just informed them that He was near them, hence they were ready to take all risks and rush into a difficult situation.

When the believer thinks he is striving along the road marked by Allah the Almighty, Who knows everything about that road and observes the performance of His creatures it becomes easy for him to carry on his way, despite the rough terrain. Allah does not provide man with an easy passage along a paved scented road. It is enough for a believer to know that Allah is with him, for him to feel happy and strong. He then tastes happiness despite hardships. Every believer may face a lot of obstacles throughout his life's course, struggling for the sake of Allah. Sometimes he gives in and wonders: 'Why is all this, Oh my Lord? I am striving for Your sake, treading Your path...but...?'

Such a person should know that, it is not an easy task at all to get to the happy end. One, therefore, needs great spiritual determination and has to pass many stages.

Throughout his drive to achieve his aim, a person needs certainty (in Allah's help), persistence, fortitude and sincerity. He must be aware of such qualifications manifested in his life, and should prove himself worthy, of such qualifications with satisfaction. One cannot achieve the apex of happiness without going through difficulties. However great the troubles are, one should consider them nothing compared to the sublime aim and worthy reward...those troubles indicate the expected good rewards. Finally, I am happy to tell you that we are coming home within a few days, Allah willing.

Zahra

****

THE END